1994

University of St. Francis
GEN 361.0068 B599o
Billis, David.
Organising public and voluntar

3 0301 00067524 5

W9-ANH-142

Organising public and voluntary agencies

One of the legacies of the Thatcher years to the social services has been the restructuring of both public and voluntary organisations through legislation, privatisation and changes in funding. Consequently, voluntary organisations have been forced to take on more and more responsibility originally belonging to the public sector so that now the voluntary sector plays a substantial part in the provision of social care in Britain. As a result, academics, students and policy makers must understand the similarities and differences between the two sectors.

Organising Public and Voluntary Agencies presents essays drawn from many years of research in the organisation and management of governmental and voluntary welfare agencies. It offers theories which are crucial for an understanding of many key problems which continue to plague governmental welfare agencies. Why are there chronic problems of accountability and standards of care? What is really meant by prevention? Can social service departments survive into the next century? David Billis also presents a major new theory of voluntary organisation based on a pioneering long term research programme which demonstrates how the fundamental structures of voluntary organisations differ from those of government, and examines the implications for social policy into the next century.

Organising Public and Voluntary Agencies is invaluable to social workers, policy makers, lecturers and students of public and social administration, as well as senior organisers and staff in the public and voluntary sectors.

David Billis is Reader in Social Services Organisation at the London School of Economics and founder and Director of the LSE Centre for Voluntary Organisation. He has more than twenty years' experience as a researcher and consultant in the public, private and voluntary sectors in the UK and overseas.

Organising public and voluntary agencies

David Billis

London and New York

First published in 1993
by Routledge
11 New Fetter Lane, London EC4P 4EE

Simultaneously published in the USA and Canada
by Routledge
a division of Routledge, Chapman and Hall Inc.
29 West 35th Street, New York, NY 10001

© 1993 David Billis

Typeset by LaserScript Limited, Mitcham, Surrey
Printed and bound in Great Britain by
Biddles Ltd, Guildford and King's Lynn

All rights reserved. No part of this book may be reprinted or
reproduced or utilized in any form or by any electronic,
mechanical, or other means, now known or hereafter
invented, including photocopying and recording, or in any
information storage or retrieval system, without permission in
writing from the publishers.

British Library Cataloguing in Publication Data
A catalogue record for this book is available from the British Library.

Library of Congress Cataloging in Publication Data
Billis, David
    Organising public and voluntary agencies / David Billis.
    p. cm.
    1. Human services–Great Britain–Management. 2. Voluntarism–
Great Britain. 3. Corporations, Nonprofit–Great Britain–Management.
4. Charity organisation–Great Britain. I. Title.
HV245.B55   1993
361'.0068–dc20   92–13100

ISBN 0–415–07439–8

361.0068
B599o

To Jacquie

,50, 129 College of St. Francis Library
Joliet, Illinois

Contents

Illustrations

FIGURES

TABLES

Acknowledgements

The writer of any book accumulates debts of many kinds. When that book draws together the products of research undertaken over more than twenty years, the list of those who deserve acknowledgement becomes huge. When, in addition, the research is of the sort that involves collaborating with actors in the field, acknowledging the indebtedness warrants a research project of its own. In these few words, I can do no more than note some of my main debts.

Several thousand people from the public and voluntary sectors have played a part in the writing of this book. They include paid staff, committee members, volunteers and members. Many participated in research projects and workshops. Yet others were students on a variety of postgraduate courses. All of these were both a constant source of ideas and sympathetic critics of my wilder propositions.

Much of the research reported in Part I of this book was undertaken whilst I was a member of Brunel University's Institute of Organisation and Social Studies (BIOSS) where Elliott Jaques was the director. He was an inspiration to all those who worked with him, and I trust that my early intellectual debt is clearly signalled in the text. Ralph Rowbottom is another colleague from that early period with whom I worked closely and fruitfully for many years.

With the addition of the voluntary sector as a major research interest during the 1980s, I started to accrue yet more debts. I began to encounter the world of charitable foundations and was fortunate to meet a handful of people who shared a belief in examining the management of the voluntary sector. David Gerrard, Tessa Murray and Dudley Coates from BP, Calton Younger and Peter Kilgarriff from the Lankelly Foundation, Morton Creeger from the Heron Foundation, John Shelley from the Save and Prosper Educational Trust, Joel Joffe and Des Palmer from Allied Dunbar – all have been firm supporters of the research and postgraduate teaching programme.

My debt to my colleague, Margaret Harris, is a large one. She has been with me almost from the start of my work in the voluntary sector, and has played a key role in the development of what is now the Centre for Voluntary Organisation at the LSE. Many of the chapters in Part II have benefited from her numerous helpful contributions. My thanks are also due to Joy MacKeith, who has recently joined the staff of the Centre. She has made useful comments on several chapters, and has helped to steer the manuscript into the hands of the publishers. The Centre has been fortunate in having administrative and secretarial help from Louise Dunkley, whose calm efficiency has ensured that the research could indeed take place. Susan Hackney has been responsible for the typing of much of the manuscript, which benefited from a final scrutiny from Colin Rochester, the Centre's Research Development Officer.

I would like to express my gratitude to the following publishers for permission to reproduce, in part or in whole, several essays in this book: Chapter 2, 'The Stratification of Work and Organisational Design' (with R.W. Rowbottom), *Human Relations*, 30, 1, 1977; Chapter 4, 'Managing to Care', *Social Work Today*, 6, 2, 1975; Chapter 6, '"Development" in Social Services – the Birth of Administrative Obscurity', *Public Administration*, Summer 1977; Chapter 7, 'At Risk of Prevention', *Journal of Social Policy*, 10, 3, 1981; Chapter 8, 'Reforming Welfare Bureaucracies: The Seebohm Report Outcome', *Policy Studies Journal*, 9, 9, 1981; Chapter 12, 'The Roots of Voluntary Agencies: A Question of Choice', *Nonprofit and Voluntary Sector Quarterly*, 20, 1, Spring 1991.

Finally, earlier versions of some chapters have been presented to conferences or published as research documents: Chapter 3, Organisational Responses to Social Problems, paper presented to a seminar of the United Nations Centre for Social Welfare, Austria, 1977; Chapter 5, Delegation and Control: The Experience of SSD Directors and their Deputies. SSORU. Brunel University. Mimeo. Document 2879. March 1981; Chapter 9, Voluntary Sector Management: Research and Practice. Working Paper No 1. (PORTVAC) Centre for Voluntary Organisation, LSE, 1979; Chapter 10, Self-help and Service. Working Paper No 2. (PORTVAC) Centre for Voluntary Organisation, LSE, 1984; Chapter 11, A Theory of the Voluntary Sector: Implications for Policy and Practice. Working Paper No 5. Centre for Voluntary Organisation, LSE, 1989; Chapter 13, Government–Voluntary Sector Partnership: A Policy in Search of Implementation. Paper presented at the Annual Conference of AVAS, Washington, 1988; Chapter 14, Unravelling the Metaphors: Government and the Voluntary Sector in the UK. Paper presented to an international conference in Israel on 'Voluntarism, Nongovernmental Organisation and Public Policy', 22–24 May 1989; Chapter 15, Planned Change in Voluntary and Government Social Service Agencies. Paper presented at the Annual Conference of AVAS, London 1990.

Introduction

This book comprises essays drawn from my research in the organisation and management of governmental and voluntary welfare agencies over the past two decades. In the early period I was primarily engaged in research with social services departments (SSDs) and, to a lesser extent, with health, housing and education departments. In the second decade my main interest moved to the voluntary sector. In all, several thousand staff from hundreds of agencies in both sectors have participated in workshops and collaborative research projects. Overwhelmingly, those participants shared a common interest in understanding how organisations that are concerned with 'welfare' and 'social problems' function, and can, if necessary, be changed. That common interest is the focus for this book.

OBJECTIVES

The book has four objectives. The first, and most important, is to present ideas that will be of use to those who are concerned with the organisation of welfare agencies. This objective arises from the evidence of continuing confusion and anxiety in many public and voluntary agencies. In the light of current social policy complexity, it is perhaps not surprising that the professional press is full of articles written by bewildered practitioners and managers. In the governmental sector many of the problems appear to have a long history, a view shared by other observers. For example, Challis (1990: 64) has argued persuasively for a return to 'basics' and asks: What are social services departments (SSDs) for? A host of other essential questions, also with a lengthy history, still await resolution. These include, for example, issues of accountability, delegation, the management of residential care, co-ordination, quality of care, and staff training and satisfaction. I have chosen therefore to include essays from my early research which still appear relevant and have something to say to today's dilemmas.

Voluntary organisations – for reasons that will become clear in Part II – have to cope not only with many of the problems of governmental agencies; they also possess their own distinctive agenda of questions. I suggest that stumbling into change is the main hazard facing the voluntary sector, and this is a central theme of Part II.

However, identifying the problems and raising key questions is only a first, albeit essential, step. What is needed is 'usable theory' (Billis 1984), ideas that make sense and can be utilised by those whose business it is to cope with the complexity and chaos. That is why the first objective of the book is to provide such ideas so that we may understand how governmental and voluntary agencies function and can be *changed*.

The second objective is linked to the first. It is to contribute to a better understanding of the similarities and differences in the fundamental structures of the sectors. My intention is to uncover underlying organisational features of the two sectors, rather than attempt a comparative study. This objective flows from recent social policy developments, particularly the slow but steady movement away from the provision of welfare services by large governmental agencies. These agencies may still dominate the scene, but the voluntary and private sectors now have a higher profile. Further erosion of the state service delivery system seems to be under way with what, on the face of it, appear to be new forms of organisation. These new forms have in some sense 'opted out' of the governmental system, or have become 'self-governing'. The organisation of social welfare has become more complex and chaotic, and the public–voluntary sector divide has become more permeable. It has now become essential for policy makers, practitioners, funders, managers and all those involved with social policy to understand the workings of both sectors. (Indeed, there is a strong case to be made for a better understanding of private sector provision, but that is not the subject matter of this particular book.)

My third objective is to contribute to an understanding of the organisational dimension, and to demonstrate the links with social policy. This objective stems from a continuing belief that social policy and organisational form and structure are inextricably intertwined. Social policy, it has been suggested, 'is essentially concerned with the question: what is the scope for social, as distinct from individual, action?' (Glennerster 1989). I suggest that social action, and social policy, must consequently be concerned with systematic, rather than individual and isolated response to social problems. Whether it is in a large department of State, a hospital, a prison, a 'patch' team, or a national or local voluntary organisation, 'policy' requires 'organisation'. The precise form of organisation may vary, and it may be under different auspices (public, for-profit, or voluntary). The extent of what is defined as appropriate for 'social' action, as distinct from individual and family response, may also change as political, social and professional ideas change. And it is highly likely that many, perhaps most, of the issues will be resolved in an 'unorganised' way, in a personal and discreet fashion with the aid of neighbours, friends and carers of many sorts. Nevertheless, the organised territory is vast, and has remained so during the twenty years covered by this book.

The fourth objective sounds rather quixotic. It is to fight against 'administrative obscurity': the tendency to create administrative 'concepts' that cannot stand up to serious analysis. In this book I discuss 'development', 'prevention' and 'partnership'. Many others might have joined the list, and some have been subjected to critical review elsewhere, for example, 'community care' (Goodwin 1989) and 'quality' (Pfeffer and Coote 1991). Occasionally, a particular term appears to disappear, at least for a while, but the underlying disease may remain, and the introduction of a new obscure term remains a constant threat.

These four objectives are interconnected. My argument is that in order to understand, and possibly change, welfare agencies in the public and voluntary sectors it is necessary to develop usable theory (objective one) which appreciates the distinctive organisational features of the two sectors (objective two). Such theory must form an essential part of any social policies which are to move beyond mere pious hopes (objective three). And, part and parcel of the same desire to move beyond unrealistic policy expectations, is the analysis of confused administrative concepts (objective four).

PLAN OF THE BOOK

The book is not a collection of essays on disparate topics, but is a record of a long search for theory. Because individual chapters form 'building-blocks' with several of them dependent on what went before, there are some technical problems of presentation. The original essays were written to be read as freestanding pieces; yet to have left them precisely in their original format would have resulted in tedious repetition. Part I, for example, makes considerable use of the 'levels of work' ideas, and several of the original papers had substantial definitions of the theory which have therefore been omitted or edited. Part II presents more difficulties since it makes heavy use of a theoretical framework, and also recounts the development of that theory. Again, wherever possible, repetition has been weeded out of the original papers. However, sometimes I have felt that it would be impossible to cut passages that would make the result too telegraphic for the reader whose interest was confined to individual chapters. On the other hand, I naturally hope that most readers will find the material of sufficient interest to follow the whole story of Part II. So I have compromised in the hope of meeting the needs of both types of reader.

Chapter 1 places my research and the accompanying theoretical developments since 1970 into a brief historical perspective. Chapters 2 and 3 present the levels of work theory and its further development into a typology of organisations. In Chapter 4 the levels of work ideas are combined with the concept of managerial accountability to examine the organisation of residential care. Chapter 5 takes the preceding analysis one stage further. It explores the nature of 'delegation' and 'control' and presents a more detailed structural organisational model. Chapters 6 and 7 attempt to unravel the meaning of 'development' and 'prevention'. Part I concludes with an essay (Chapter 8) which reflects on the experiences of SSDs in the 1970s and looks forward to the following decade.

The opening four essays in Part II trace the development of a new theory of voluntary organisation. Chapter 9 presents an early analysis of the voluntary sector and argues the case for an alternative to previous approaches to bureaucratic organisation. This is followed by a case study (Chapter 10) of an action-research project which illustrates the tension between 'self-help' and 'service'. Chapters 11 and 12 represent the core of the alternative theoretical approach. The following three chapters bring the governmental sector more fully into the picture. 'Partnership' with government is explored in theory and in practice in a case study in Chapter 13; some implications of the new theory for the nature of governmental intervention are examined in Chapter 14; and organisational change in the two sectors is discussed in Chapter 15.

Finally, in Chapter 16, I have permitted myself the luxury of some selective crystal ball gazing.

Part I
Public welfare agencies

1   Overview: beyond bureaucracy in welfare

INTRODUCTION

The purpose of this chapter is to provide a brief 'companion' to the book. It sets the theoretical developments recorded in the individual chapters against the background of a twenty-year search for a better understanding of organisations. During the latter part of that period I discovered that, whilst many of the ideas developed in the public sector continued to serve a useful purpose, they were less helpful for voluntary organisations. I concluded that it was time to move beyond traditional ideas about bureaucratic organisation. The two parts of this chapter outline the search for new ideas; a search which took place in very dissimilar decades. We might first however recall the flavour of the different periods.

The complexity and lack of certainty with respect to social policy and the provision of welfare which characterised much of the 1980s can be compared to the confidence of the 1970s. The optimism of that earlier period was typified by the Seebohm Report (1968). This led to the establishment of large governmental agencies – social services departments (SSDs) – which were intended to resolve most social welfare problems. As one observer, looking back to that time, commented, those were the 'halcyon days when social services were young, glamorous and exciting' (Dossett-Davies 1989).

Economic decline and a change in the political map are among the familiar reasons given for the fall from grace of the public welfare system in the following decade. In social services, a stream of scandals were seized upon as proof that social workers, the core professional group, could not deliver what they promised. The decline in public confidence coincided with renewed interest in the voluntary sector after a long period, during which it had kept a low profile and carried on without much public attention.

For many public sector agencies, the new decade (the 1990s) has brought with it, yet again, major changes, 'scandals' and low morale. For voluntary organisations the decade promises to be no less turbulent. Whilst some see the prospect of the 'contract culture' as a challenge and opportunity, many others are wondering whether so much public attention might damage their health (Billis and Harris 1991).

PART I: GOVERNMENTAL WELFARE BUREAUCRACIES IN THE 1970s

In 1970 I joined one of several research teams at the Brunel Institute of Organisation and Social Studies (BIOSS) under the directorship of Elliott Jaques. The teams were attempting to help health departments and SSDs devise and implement viable organisational structures. The other, no less ambitious, objective of the research units was to develop theoretical insights and models to help resolve organisational problems. As a member of a team trying to meet these objectives, I was able to draw upon an inherited body of knowledge which included (a) a methodological approach to the study of organisations, and (b) many ideas regarding the structure and operation of those organisations.

The *methodology* which was employed to study organisations was known as 'social analysis', an approach that had been extensively used for about forty years by specialists in organisational development.[1] Rowbottom described social analysis as:

An activity devoted to (1) gaining scientific understanding of, and thereby (2) facilitating enacted change in (3) social institutions, through (4) collaborative exploration by those actors immediately concerned in their working, and an independent analyst.

(Rowbottom 1977: 21)

My own approach to the social analytic methodology was to place it within the context of the work of Karl Popper. I contended (Billis 1984) that models and theories for understanding the nature of organisations could be generated from the problems posed by those organisations. These theories are, in Popper's terms, 'tentative' and, after a process of critical discussion or tests, present further problems. A new cycle of problems, tentative theories and critical evaluation is then set in motion (Popper 1974a, 1974b). For me, this cycle appeared not only to serve as a methodological approach to the development of usable theory; it also seemed to reflect my own personal search.

But it was not only a methodology that I had inherited in 1970. There was also a body of knowledge which could be traced back to the immediate post-Second World War period. At that time Wilfred Brown was the chairman and managing director of the Glacier Metal Company and invited the Tavistock Institute of Human Relations to collaborate in a research project. Jaques, a psychoanalyst, led the Tavistock research team, and the results appeared in his classic *Changing Culture of a Factory* (Jaques 1951).

The Glacier approach, despite many unique features which had been developed during its long history, shared many of the common assumptions of the literature on bureaucratic organisations. It remained firmly in the Weberian tradition, an intellectual heritage that Jaques made more explicit in his later works. Thus his *A General Theory of Bureaucracy* (1976) abounds with references to Weber, a name notable for its absence in earlier writings such as *Equitable Payment* (1961) where the psychoanalytic debt to Sigmund Freud and Melanie Klein is more clearly acknowledged.

One of the strengths of Jaques's analysis of bureaucracy was its clear definition of 'bureaucracy' as:

a hierarchically stratified employment system in which people are employed to work for a wage or salary . . .

(Jacques 1976: 49)

Bureaucracies were regarded as secondary institutions, dependent on the employing body which decided to establish the bureaucracy in the first place, and whose existence was essential to the continued existence of the bureaucracy. These bureaucracies were distinguished from *associations* which established the bureaucracies in order to get work done. In taking this approach Jaques adopted what he regarded as the more limited sense of bureaucracy 'in which Weber was himself driven to use the term in practice' (p.49).

That view of bureaucracy may be seen as resting on what I shall now call *the ABC division*. The Association (A) appoints the Bureaucracy (B), the paid staff who deliver services or produce goods for Clients and Customers (C). Each category is clearly separate. This was in fact the traditional view of organisations in general held by many management writers. For example, Bertram Gross's major work, *Organizations and their Managing* (1968 edition), shared the traditional ABC division. The view that all organisations should follow the ABC division remains influential.

The purpose of the chapters in Part I of this book is to understand the structure of governmental agencies as a basis for planned change. These chapters accept the basic ABC division and focus on the core management task of making the system of roles of paid staff – the bureaucracy (B) – work.

Underlying these chapters is what I suggest is a 'four-dimensional' view of organisations: three dimensions (authority, level of work and activities) comprise the structural boundaries of organisations.[2] The fourth dimension (capacity or ability) centres on the role of individuals in organisations and complements the structural dimensions. Individual capacity has been considered in considerable detail elsewhere (see for example Jaques 1976) and is not discussed in this book.[3] Summarised very crudely, the Jaquesian theory held that people develop at different rates in their ability to handle work. The graphs that were used to demonstrate growth in capacity depicted an optimistic yet realistic picture. The 'individual capacity' curves moved upwards, demonstrating the ability to handle more complex tasks as the years passed. Yet at the same time some people developed faster than others – not everyone could do everything.

It is the three structural boundaries which are my concern in Part I of the book and, of these, the theory of 'levels of work' has pride of place. This was developed with my colleague Ralph Rowbottom and has been adopted and used in many and varied organisations.[4]

The levels of work ideas (presented in Chapter 2) were generated in response to a gap in the inherited theoretical armoury after many years' testing in a large number of different settings. The Glacier–BIOSS tradition had built up a solid body of tools and concepts, it addressed live organisational problems and it could be implemented in real organisations. Foremost amongst the ideas was what became known as the 'tool kit' of role relationships with its centrepiece – the 'managerial' role. These role relationships were definitions of some dozen organisational relationships (manager, supervisor, co-ordinator, monitor, prescribing, service-giving, etc) that had been identified in organisations, and were expressed in terms of the authority (our first dimension) that attached to each role. They went a long way along the path of resolving many of the boundary problems (for example: who was accountable for what?) which bugged life in large organisations. The manager was the pivotal role in the organisation as is illustrated in the case of residential care explored in Chapter 4. What we later called 'the main management spine' was posited as the key to understanding organisational structure (Rowbottom and Billis 1987). Not everyone who appeared on the charts as a manager turned out to be a 'real' manager as defined. Some could be better regarded as one of the other, less powerful, roles (see Chapter 5). At the very least, forcing organisations to face up to the reality of the managerial definition shortened the apparent hierarchical line of command. It 'stripped down' the bureaucracy. Often, the 'tool kit' enabled the usually incoherent organisational charts found in agencies to be transformed into agreed patterns of interaction.

However, we were still left with a major problem and gap in theory. The analysis of authority and accountability relationships lowered the height of the organisational building. For example, the 'deputy', as can be seen from the discussion in Chapter 5, could often be taken out of the main management spine. The high-rise departmental blocks of government were redesigned as more civilised low-storey organisations. But we had no theory which explained the distinctive work that was to be done on each floor. For example, what work was the higher-level manager doing, other than managing more people? What was the distinctive difference in work of the 'higher'-level professional? Was there any real distinction?

The levels of work theory provided a tough instrument against which to examine these questions. It proposed that all organised work – managerial or non-managerial – fell into a hierarchy of discrete levels or strata. In each level the range of the objectives to be achieved, on the one hand, and the range of environmental circumstances to be taken into account, on the other, broadened and changed in quality at successive steps. Definitions were provided for five levels. Later, I developed the theory into a typology of organisations by introducing the concepts of 'basic expected work' and 'highest expected work', or 'client' and 'societal impact'. This typology, presented in Chapter 3, helps to explain past changes and also continues to serve as one way of exploring possible future developments in welfare organisation.

By the beginning of the 1980s the levels of work theory had become more central than the other dimensions for my own research. As noted earlier we produced it in response to a felt gap in the theoretical armoury. Prior to its development, the ideas of role relationships (analysed in terms of authority and accountability) and capacity had dominated the Glacier–BIOSS tradition. For Jaques, work and capacity came first:

> . . . . the nature of work is examined in greater depth as it appears from within the person, in order to understand the way *bureaucracies are formed and shaped in relation to the work process in human beings*.
>
> (my italics, Jaques 1976: 12)

The levels of work ideas, by focusing on the work that the *organisation expected* the individual to undertake (rather than starting with the individual), stood the entire way of examining agencies on its head. It became possible to discuss both the 'business' that agencies were expected to be in, and the level of response to the environment that they expected to make.

To sum up so far. The theoretical equipment of the 1970s included ideas about authority and levels of decision making. The notion of 'activity' – the third dimension – was introduced in order to describe the 'business' the organisation or role was engaged in. What bundle of activities made a coherent whole? At the grass roots of the organisation it could involve a study of the work undertaken by field social workers, residential workers or day care staff. Thus, in Chapter 4, ideas about authority, levels and activities were combined to examine the management of residential care. The main problems and themes discussed in this chapter continued to remain particularly, and depressingly, familiar.[5]

The issues raised in Chapter 4 (delegation, control, and accountability) were not confined just to the organisation of residential services. They were central problems for most SSDs.[6] For example, I was struck by the way the word 'development' was employed as a cosmetic to cover up organisational problems, and as a way of avoiding genuine analysis about standards of service and accountability (see Chapter 6).

I was not satisfied with the prevailing 'top-down' and 'bottom-up' approaches to these organisational problems and produced a critique which combined notions of levels of work, and 'client' and 'societal impact', together with additional ideas of 'control' and 'assistance' roles (see Chapter 5). The analysis of the top roles, such as directors, or deputy directors which formed part of that critique, inevitably involved discussions about the position of the department as a whole. In the governmental sector, where it was possible to examine the position in many similar departments, it led me to doubt the basis of social policy in that area.

Thus, by the end of the decade, I began to question whether our previous analysis (Rowbottom *et al.* 1974) of the activities of SSDs – 'the prevention or relief of social distress' – was still tenable. Having dissected 'prevention', I suggested (see Chapters 7 and 8) that the concept of *social breakdown* would lead to a more useful boundary definition. A state of breakdown meant either that institutionalisation was an immediate response or, if no action was taken, then some form of institutionalisation would result within a specified period of time. I saw 'breakdown', with its explicit time boundary, as a defence against just about any intervention in human situations which could be claimed to be 'preventing' eventual social distress.

I concluded that the Seebohm vision of comprehensive welfare agencies dealing with all the community's social problems, together with one of its essential props – the notion of 'prevention' – was misguided and of dubious benefit to those it was intended to serve. Of particular concern to me was the plight of groups such as the elderly in residential care, and the severely handicapped in the community, who appeared to get a raw deal compared to the more professionally attractive 'preventive' work. I argued that such groups were genuinely 'at risk of prevention'.

Rather hesitantly I introduced the term 'welfare bureaucracy' (Billis 1984) both to describe those agencies that employed staff to deliver personal social services and, more broadly, to cover organisations that were responding to social problems. Now, when the term appears to have found fairly wide currency,[7] hesitation will only be appreciated by those who can recall the particular state of theory and practice of the Seebohm period. Then, there appeared to be two main choices for students of social policy and administration. The dominant academic tradition in Europe and the United States had been described as the 'social conscience' thesis (Baker 1979). This was an optimistic view (see Chapter 8) which seemed to imply large-scale governmental intervention, often driven forward under the banner of 'prevention'. The other choice was what I called 'community administration'. This strand of thought was strongly against 'bureaucracy' (Hadley and Hatch 1981), and implied small-scale organisation. I claimed (Chapter 8) that both approaches failed sufficiently to take into account the reality of organisations, and the term 'welfare bureaucracy' was introduced in an attempt to capture the tensions between the two approaches.

In the years that followed I began to look again at the nature of welfare and bureaucracy, and spent much of the following decade attempting to understand the nature of voluntary organisations and how they differed from governmental agencies.

PART II: VOLUNTARY AGENCIES IN THE 1980s

In 1978 I founded the first university-based initiative in the organisation and management of voluntary organisations.[8] Others in the UK eventually joined in the concern about voluntary sector management and, from a rather lonely and idiosyncratic pursuit, the study of voluntary sector management eventually became a topic of interest to governmental policy makers and academics. Isolated scholars from around the world began to find each other, and the international growth in public policy interest in the 'voluntary', 'nongovernmental' or 'nonprofit' sector has been matched by the growth of a thriving specialist academic community interested in the management of 'nonprofits'.

However, the establishment of a small programme of work with voluntary organisations was rather tentative. It was a tentativeness that reflected the lack of interest in the topic by funding bodies. Naturally, I employed in the work with voluntary organisations the concepts and theories that had previously given such good service in the governmental sector, and I included in my 1984 definition of welfare bureaucracies those voluntary organisations that employed paid staff. My theoretical kitbag at that time contained ideas about the four dimensions of organisations which rested on the traditional ABC division discussed earlier.

The work with voluntary organisations followed the same methodological approach of earlier research. But the workshops and collaborative research rapidly revealed that the agenda of problems was significantly different to that presented by governmental agencies. The theories based on the ABC division were usable, but did not address many of the most critical problems (see Chapter 9). One major example of the inadequacy of prevailing theory was the vexed problem of the tension between the board or management committee, and paid director. It was not an unknown problem in the private and governmental sectors, but was evidently far more widespread and disturbing in the voluntary sector. If this was the starting practical problem, we then had at our disposal a number of tentative theories, including the traditional theory of bureaucracy with its suggested distinctive roles for owners and management. This was helpful in drawing attention to the core role of trustees, but there were numerous unresolved issues. For example, a bald statement of trustee duties did not get to grips with agencies whose trustees and/or paid staff were highly committed and were also recipients in some way of the service. Again, the existing theory did not get to grips with the position of voluntary sector trustees who often appeared to occupy a very different role to their counterparts in the other sectors, for example in their fundraising and even operational service activities.

The ABC division just could not handle the complexity of voluntary organisation. A search through the limited organisational literature revealed most authors had resorted to a 'typology' or a 'continuum' in their efforts to analyse the sector. Furthermore, almost every researcher in the field identified the voluntary sector as 'messy', 'blurred' and 'ambiguous'. The typologies cut up and allocated the voluntary sector and its component parts according to variables such as key functions. Although they had the virtue of establishing clear boundaries they were unable to cope with the 'messiness' of the sector. The continuum, on the other hand, dealt with blurring but lost the distinctive and core characteristics of the sector. Neither approach appeared to offer the policy maker and practitioner models which responded to the particular dynamic tensions within voluntary organisations.

Dissatisfaction with the existing approaches to voluntary sector complexity sparked off a search for alternative approaches, and a closer look at the word 'ambiguity' which surfaced with regularity throughout the literature. Although it appeared often, it served primarily as a description of a muddled or unclear state rather than as a tool of analysis. The concept of the 'ambiguous zone' described by Leach (1976), on the other hand, seemed to offer the possibility of resolving the dichotomy between the standard form of typology and the continuum. Although it was not intended to be used to examine organisations, the notion of an area of (voluntary) institutions that could have the attributes of two adjacent 'unambiguous' sectors appeared to lead to a better tentative theory. In the early work using ambiguity, described in Chapter 9, I envisaged the voluntary sector as merely falling between the unambiguous bureaucratic and personal 'worlds', being pulled in both directions and subject to constant tension. This explanation was taken up with enthusiasm by UK practitioners who immediately identified with the strain, for example, between paid staff and lay leaders, or between democratic and bureaucratic rules of the game. Chapter 10 presents an early case study of these tensions, and the way in which models helped organisational exploration and change.

However, my model failed to take into account the private welfare sector, perhaps a not unreasonable assumption in the UK at that time. It was received with more scepticism in the United States, with its substantial private sector welfare provision. A second stage in the model followed with the introduction of a division between the for-profit and governmental sector bureaucracies. At the time this seemed to produce an unduly complicated new model, but with the changes in UK social policy it became more and more relevant to current developments. In the following years yet another problem appeared, and I began to differentiate the genuine 'association' of members from the 'personal world' of family and friends. The introduction of the world of associations, again with its own border territories, brought the model to the form in which it appears in this book (see Chapter 11).

This model of three organised worlds (governmental bureaucracies, private sector bureaucracies and associations) appeared to make sense to those working in the voluntary sector. In particular it provided an explanation for the dilemmas facing those voluntary organisations that employ paid staff to undertake significant work, or those that are contemplating taking such a step. However one additional theoretical contribution was needed if the ideas were to be more fully employed in discussions about organisational change and indeed about the role of the sector in welfare policy. The question that concerned me was: what were the levers of change that lay behind the models?

Most explanations of change in voluntary agencies were, and continue to be, 'deterministic'. Typical examples are the 'life cycle' and resource dependency literature which leaves little scope for individual behaviour and ideas, and agency policies, in its account of organisational development. This did not fit the reality of my own research, or the experiences of those working inside agencies. Many participants in workshops and projects felt that they had choices and could control change. They also talked about the way in which the 'roots' of their organisations were important in considering organisational change.

My early response to the question of roots and organisational change was to regard roots as a mixture of resources and 'philosophy' (Chapter 11). The introduction of a 'philosophical' component was a first step towards bringing agency 'policies' into the study of change. More recently the notion of roots has been developed (Chapter 12) into a fuller exposition. This offers an alternative to the deterministic school since it gives due recognition to what I call 'implicit policies of welfare accountability', human and financial resources and the system of governance. It begins also to offer some explanations of the possible levers of change, the forces that affect agencies and the delicate balances that together comprise the voluntary agency.

It was difficult to be concerned about organisational change in voluntary organisations in the 1980s without considering their relationship with governmental agencies. It was not surprising, therefore, that I found myself engaged in a collaborative project between a local authority and a voluntary agency which explored the way in which the concept of partnership was being implemented (Chapter 13). I was struck both by the difficulties of achieving change at the local agency level, and by the confusion which surrounded 'partnership' when it was treated as a policy concept which was intended to be capable of implementation. It seemed to me that, as with 'development' and 'prevention', this was yet another example of 'administrative obscurity'.

Can the model of the voluntary sector, developed by the end of the decade and described in Part II of this book, be of wider use than its employment as a tool by individual agencies facing choices about change? I believe that it can, and that it provides a new way of looking at the voluntary 'sector' and the relationship with government. Chapter 14 utilises the model to explore the way in which government intervenes in the sector, and the relevance of several metaphors used to describe state–voluntary sector relationships.

I have argued throughout the book that models of organisation can help to shed light on public policy and, conversely, that public policy must take account of the fundamental structural characteristics of different organisations. In other words, changing public policy requires a deeper understanding of organisations that are the bearers and implementors of those changes. This central theme, and in particular the nature of planned change in the governmental and voluntary sectors, is explored in Chapter 15.

What will be the fate of welfare agencies in the public and voluntary 'sectors' in the 1990s? And to what extent does the concept of distinctive 'sectors' (public, private and voluntary) have relevance for the study and practice of management? With respect to the first question, the final speculations in Chapter 16 lead me to question the continued viability of SSDs. I also question the wisdom of social policies which are built on what I call an 'instrumental' approach by government towards the voluntary sector.

As far as the 'sector' as a concept for management is concerned (the second question), the theoretical path charted in these essays illustrates a growing emphasis on the significance of a 'sectoral' view of management. I believe that the 1990s may well see the public and voluntary sectors throwing off the shackles of domination by private sector management approaches. But for that to happen, academics and practitioners will need to work together in what can – on this occasion – quite appropriately be termed a 'partnership'.

NOTES

1   One of the earliest reports appeared in Jaques (1951) and some of the main literature can be traced in Brown and Jaques (1965).
2   For a detailed discussion of organisational structure see Billis (1984).
3   For a further discussion of the ideas of capacity in the kibbutz situation see Billis (1977).
4   In the years since its formulation the 'levels of work' theory continues to be employed well beyond its origins in SSDs. For example, Kinston (1987), and Owens and Glennerster (1990), have used the theory to examine nursing and, in a rather different business, Unilever are currently implementing the ideas in several continents.
5   Pindown (A. Levy and B. Kahan, *Community Care*, 13 June 1991) is just the latest in a long line of tragedies. The central questions raised in Chapter 4 still stand as major challenges for welfare administration. For example, following the pindown inquiry report: '...the ensuing debate....has suggested that residential child care everywhere has a case to answer....remarkably little is known about the standards of care in homes....and the kind of regimes operated by individual officers in charge' (M. Ivory, *Community Care*, 13 June 1991).
6   Much has been written about these issues since the research reported here was first undertaken. For example, more recent literature can be traced in Day and Klein (1987), yet the question clearly continues to perplex policy makers and practitioners.
7   The term seems to have been picked up fairly rapidly; see, for example, Howe (1986) *Social Workers and their Practice in Welfare Bureaucracies*, Gower, Aldershot.
8   This initiative was called the Programme of Research and Training into Voluntary Action (PORTVAC) and was based at Brunel University. In 1988 the programme was incorporated into the new Centre for Voluntary Organisation at the London School of Economics.

2   Levels of work

INTRODUCTION

What is the hierarchy of management levels in organisations *about*? In keeping with the spirit of their age, the earliest writers on management, the so-called 'classical' school – the Fayols, Taylors, and Urwicks – simply took them for granted. These people were not so much concerned with why management levels were there, as how to strengthen them and improve their efficiency. In a different way the subsequent human relations writers also took them for granted, in their case by largely ignoring the 'formal' system in the pursuit of supportive, participatory processes. It was not until the advent of the later, more sociology-minded and systems-minded researchers, that managerial systems as such came under stern and critical review. Generalising very broadly, two models were identified. The first was a conventional or traditional model variously described as 'hierarchical', 'bureaucratic', 'mechanistic', and 'authoritarian'. The second was a new, emerging model, by implication more suited to the turbulent social environment of the twentieth century, and variously described as 'non-hierarchical', 'antibureaucratic', 'organic', 'responsive', and 'democratic'. (We might take as key works here those of McGregor 1960, Burns and Stalker 1961, and Emery and Trist 1965.) But a whole host of other names could be added to the founders of, and subscribers to, this now-dominant ideology – Argyris, Bennis, Blake and Mouton, Katz and Kahn, Lawrence and Lorsch, etc.

However, in spite of the general enthusiastic espousal of the second vision, not only by the academics and commentators but by many of the more lively and forward-looking of managers themselves, strong elements of hierarchical structure still manifestly and stubbornly abound in most real-life organisations, public as well as private. The men or women at the top (or more modishly, the 'centre') still seem to carry significant extra increments of power and authority, not to speak of pay and status.

In this paper we shall be examining a detailed thesis which serves to explain this persistence of hierarchical structure on the general grounds that there are different kinds of work to be carried out in organisations which can quite reasonably be described as 'higher' and 'lower'. Although we shall not be concerned with how these different kinds of work might justify difference in pay or status, we shall be very much concerned with what they imply in terms of authority. We shall also be concerned with the question of how the existence of work at a variety of levels is related to differing capacities amongst organisation members and, more especially, to the way in which the capacity of any one individual member may develop through time. Here we may note the considerable influence on the ideas expressed in this paper of the theories and findings of Elliott Jaques on these same subjects.[1] We may also note, without further pursuing, the links at this point with more general issues of 'social stratification'.[2]

ORIGIN OF THE WORK-STRATUM MODEL

The ideas to be described arose from an action-research programme which has been in progress since 1969 in the new social departments (SSDs) in local authorities (Rowbottom *et al.* 1974). In the course of work with a number of these departments one of the recurrent problems noted was that of the precise role within the hierarchy of certain particular groups of senior staff. Time and again in field or seminar discussions members of departments would spontaneously refer to the difficult organisational position of social work 'team leaders' or 'seniors', in relation to the members of their teams; or of 'homes advisers' in relation to the heads of the various residential homes for children that they were expected to supervise; or of 'specialist advisers', 'principal officers' and the like at headquarters in relation to teams of social workers at area offices; or of 'deputy directors' in relation to 'assistant directors'.

Although each of these groups of staff were shown 'higher' on the charts than their counterparts, and were often, indeed, in more highly graded posts, analysis often revealed considerable uncertainties or disagreements about the extent of their managerial authority. There would be doubt as to how far they had the right to set policies or general authoritative guides for work which were binding on their counterparts, or to make authoritative appraisals of their performance, their suitability for promotion, etc. There would be doubt as to how far it would be right to describe them as accountable for the work of their counterparts.

By contrast, none of these same doubts would usually exist to any significant extent for certain other posts in the hierarchy – 'area officers' in relation to 'team leaders'; 'heads of homes' in relation to the staff of the home; 'assistant directors' in relation to 'principal officers'; or indeed directors of departments in relation to any or all other staff.

The attempt to probe further into why these distinctions should arise (and the answer was obviously more general than that of the personal strength or weaknesses of particular individuals) led to a general consideration of the *kinds* of work carried out in these various positions, and whether any significant stratification in the work itself might be observable. Clearly these 'kinds' of work would be perceived as not just different but, themselves, as 'higher' or 'lower' in responsibility. However, there would be no need to deny as well the presence of some continuing scale of responsibility within each discrete kind or category. Hence, what we should be seeking to identify would be a series of discrete, qualitatively different *strata* of work, superimposed on a continuous scale of work of increasing responsibility from bottom to top of the organisation.

In the attempt to identify these various work-strata some immediate observations appeared relevant. Ignoring the manifest hierarchy of authority and grades, it was noteworthy:

1 that certain social workers talked of 'their' caseload, and apparently carried a full measure of responsibility for each case within it;
2 that others – students, trainees, and assistants, for example – did not talk in quite the same way and apparently did not carry full case responsibility, but carried out work under the close supervision and direction of some of the first group of staff; and
3 that there were others again – more senior workers, area officers, and specialist advisers, for example – who often spoke with regret about being unable at this stage of their careers to carry a personal caseload, and who seemed to be more concerned with general systems of provision and general procedures for work, training, administration, etc. than getting involved in particular cases.

Gradually, from these beginnings a general thesis grew; and as it grew it seemed that it might be applicable not only to social services departments but to a much wider range of organisations. In essence the thesis was this:

1 that the work to be done in organisations falls into a hierarchy of discrete strata in which the range of the ends or objectives to be achieved and the range of environmental circumstances to be taken into account both broadens and changes in quality at successive steps;
2 that the work at successively higher strata is judged to be more responsible, but that significant differences of responsibility are also felt to arise *within* strata; i.e., that these qualitative strata form stages within a continuous scale of increasing levels of work or responsibility;

3 that at least five such possible strata can be precisely identified in qualitative terms; in successive order and starting from the lowest: *prescribed output, situational response, systematic service provision, comprehensive service provision*, and *comprehensive field coverage*;

4 that these strata form a natural chain for delegating work and hence provide the basis for constructing an effective chain of successive managerial levels within the organisation; and

5 that the understanding of these strata can also provide a practical guide to designing new organisations (or part-organisations) according to the kind and level of organisational response required in relation to the social and physical environment in which the organisation is to operate.

One important proviso needs to be added to the fourth point just made. It is assumed there (and for the rest of this paper) that managerial relationships are not for any reason inappropriate in principle. It should be noted that there are some situations in which the development of full managerial relationships (in the precise sense in which 'managerial' is defined later in the paper) appears for good reasons to be specifically excluded – as, for example, in the organisation of medical consultants (Rowbottom 1973). However, even in these situations the questions of the various levels or kinds of work to be done still remain, as well as the question of who is expected to carry them out.

This descriptive model of the natural hierarchy of work in organisations outlined above has been tested and developed over the year or so since its first formulation in a series of seminar discussions with groups of senior staff from social services throughout the country. More specifically it has been employed in a series of exploratory projects during this period (some of which are described below) undertaken within specific social services departments, and has already been absorbed into executive action in several of these projects.

The main features of each stratum of work in the model are summarised in Table 2.1 and elaborated one by one below. Illustrative examples are taken from the project work described in social services but, since the thesis is in such general terms, tentative illustrations have been offered as well, drawing upon recent work in the field of health services (Rowbottom *et al.* 1973) and certain other material from the authors' combined experience. In addition precise definitions of the boundary between strata are given in clear-cut terms of the kinds of decisions which the worker at any level is or is not expected to make in the course of their work. (These boundary definitions provide the ultimate test in practice in classifying the kind of work required in specific given jobs.)

Table 2.1 Summary of work-strata

Stratum	Description of work	Upper boundary
1	*Prescribed output* – working towards objectives which can be completely specified (as far as is significant) beforehand, according to defined circumstances which may present themselves.	Not expected to make any significant judgments on what output to aim for or under what circumstances to aim for it.
2	*Situational response* – carrying out work where the precise objectives to be pursued have to be judged according to the needs of each specific concrete situation which presents itself.	Not expected to make any decisions, i.e., commitments on how future possible situations are to be dealt with.
3	*Systematic service provision* – making systematic provision of services of some given kinds shaped to the needs of a continuous sequence of concrete situations which present themselves.	Not expected to make any decisions on the reallocation of resources to meet as yet unmanifested needs (for the given kinds of services) within some given territorial or organisational society.
4	*Comprehensive service provision* – making comprehensive provision of services of some given kinds according to the total and continuing needs for them throughout some given territorial or organisational society.	Not expected to make any decisions on the reallocation of resources to meet needs for services of different or new kinds.
5	*Comprehensive field coverage* – making comprehensive provision of services within some general field of need throughout some given territorial or organisational society.	Not expected to make any decisions on the reallocation of resources to provide services outside the given field of need.

Stratum 1 – Prescribed output

At the lowest stratum of work the output required of the worker is completely prescribed or prescribable, as are the specific circumstances in which this or that task should be pursued. If they are in doubt as to which task to pursue, it is prescribed that they take the matter up with their immediate superior. Work consists of such things as rendering given services, collecting given information, making prescribed checks or tests, producing predetermined products. What is to be done, in terms of the kind or form of results to be achieved, does not have to be decided. This will (either) have been specifically prescribed for the occasion or (frequently) have been communicated during the process of induction to the job as the sorts of response required when certain stimuli are experienced. If there is any doubt about the result required it can be dispelled by further description or demonstration to the point where more detailed discrimination becomes irrelevant to the quality of result required. What does need to be decided – and this may not necessarily be at all straightforward – is just how to produce the results required, that is, by what method and also with what priority. Thus, greater or lesser exercise of discretion is necessary – the work is far from being prescribed in totality.

The personal qualities called for within this stratum include possession of knowledge of the range of demands to be expected in daily work, knowledge of the proper responses called for, skills in carrying out these various responses and, not least, appropriate attitudes to the work in question and the people to be dealt with.

And so within this stratum we have the typical work of those in social services departments described as social work assistants, care assistants, cleaners, cooks, drivers, and clerks. More generally, it may be assumed that most artisans and craftsmen work within this stratum, and also those professional trainees and apprentices destined for work at higher levels who are as yet in some early and preparatory stages of their career.

Stratum 2 – Situational response

Within the second stratum the ends to be pursued are again in the form of results required in specific situations, but here the output required can be partially, and only partially, specified beforehand. The appropriate results or output must now depend to a significant degree on assessments of the social or physical nature of the situation which presents itself and in which the task is to be carried out. The work is such that it is impossible in principle to demonstrate fully beforehand just what the final outcome should look like – this could only be established by actually going through the task concerned. However, by way of limit, no decisions, that is no commitments to future action, are called for in respect to possible future situations which may arise. The work is still concerned with the concrete and the particular.

Rather than collecting given information, or making prescribed tests or checks as in Stratum 1, the task would now be redefined in Stratum 2 in the more general form of producing an appraisal or making an assessment.

Rather than rendering a prescribed service or making a prescribed product, the task would now be redefined as producing a service or product of a certain kind but shaped according to the judged needs of the particular situation. The 'judged needs' might, for example, be those of a person in distress (social services), or a child at school (education), or a customer (commerce). Within this stratum 'demands' can never be taken at their face value: there is always an implicit requirement to explore and assess what the 'real' needs of the situation are.

Thus, in addition to the technical skills of the Stratum 1 worker, the worker in Stratum 2 must have the ability to penetrate to the underlying nature of the specific situations with which they find themselves in contact. Indeed it is this latter ability, based on some body of explicitly theoretical knowledge, which perhaps distinguishes the true 'professional' in his or her particular field from the 'craftsperson' or 'technician' who is only equipped to work within the first stratum described above.[3] However, this is not to imply that only members of the acknowledged professions may work at this stratum or higher ones. The ability itself is the thing in question, not any body of explicit theory.

Within this stratum the sort of managerial roles can be expected to emerge which carry full accountability for the work of Stratum 1 workers and the duties of assessing their needs and capabilities in allocating work and promoting their personal development. (In contrast, what might be called 'supervisory' roles may exist in the upper reaches of Stratum 1, but those in them will not be expected to make rounded appraisals of the ability and need of subordinate staff, but rather to carry out such prescribed tasks as instructing staff in their work, allocating specific jobs and dealing with specific queries.) However, it is not at all necessary to assume that all roles within this stratum have a managerial content, and indeed the kind of definitions proposed here and below surmount the problem of being forced to describe higher-than-basic strata of work in a way which automatically links them to the carrying of managerial or supervisory responsibility. The example of the experienced social worker who takes full responsibility for cases but works without subordinates has already been cited.

Stratum 3 – Systematic service provision

At Stratum 3 it is required to go beyond responding to specific situations case by case, however adequately. It is required to envisage the needs of a continuing sequence of situations, some as yet in the future and unmaterialised, in terms of the patterns of response which may be established. Relationships of one situation to another and the characteristics of the sequence as a whole are crucial. In order to design appropriate responses some general specifications of the *kinds* of services which are required must be available.

Thus, in social services departments an example of Stratum 3 work would be the development of intake and assessment procedures for all those clients who apply to, or are referred to, a particular area office; or the development of standard assessment procedures for the range of children being referred by existing fieldwork services for residential care. In health services an example might be the development of systematic accident and emergency services in a particular hospital. In education, it might be the development of a general curriculum for all the infants who present themselves at a particular school for primary education. In manufacturing, it might be developing a system for handling orders for a particular kind of product.

Within this stratum, however, work is confined to dealing with some particular flow or sequence of situations which naturally arises from the given organisational provision. The work does not extend to considering and dealing with various situations of need that do not, without further investments of resource, yet manifest themselves in any particular organisational or territorial society – for example, needs for social work that might be manifested were additional local offices to be opened in new districts. Although staff working within Stratum 3 may draw attention to the possibilities of such new investments, they will not be expected to make any *decisions* about them.

Stratum 3 work is essentially concerned with developing systems and procedures which prescribe the way future situational-response work is to be carried out. There is seemingly similar work in Stratum 2 which consists of laying down general rules, methods or standards. However, this, if it is indeed within Stratum 2, will be pitched in terms of the totally prescribed responses required in completely specifiable circumstances. Thus at Stratum 3 the first genuine policy-making type work emerges: that is, the laying down of general prescriptions which guide, without precisely specifying. In using the word 'system' here we are referring to prescriptions of this general type. Characteristically, the work involves initial discussions and negotiations with a number of fellow workers and co-ordinating with them the introduction of new schemes. Necessarily, it involves some use of conceptualisation, both of types of situations likely to be faced and of appropriate kinds of response.

Within SSDs it has become clear that many 'specialist advisers' and 'development officers' work at this level; and also the 'area officers' in charge of large local offices containing several teams of social workers and ancillary staff. 150, 129

College of St. Francis Library
Joliet, Illinois

Stratum 4 – Comprehensive service provision

At Stratum 4 the definition of the aims of work and the environmental situation to be encompassed takes a decisive jump again. No longer is it sufficient to stay passively within the bounds of the succession of situations with which contact arises in the normal course of things. Now further initiative is required. It is required to take account systematically of the need for service as it exists and wherever it exists in some given society, territorially or organisationally defined. However, within this stratum the identification of the need to be met is still limited by a particular conception of the kinds of service which the organisation is understood to be legitimately providing. Let us elaborate this last point.

At Stratum 2 the identification of need which can be met is limited both by the existence of certain given systems and procedures and the existence (or non-existence) of substantive organisational resources with which to carry out work at a given point in the broader society concerned. At Stratum 3 the former constraint disappears but the latter remains. But at Stratum 4 both these constraints disappear. The only constraint on developing new services or proposals for new services is the constraint of given policy, explicit or understood, on the particular kind of services which will be regarded as well-established, sanctioned, and legitimated.

The starting question at Stratum 4 is: what is the extent of the need for services of these kinds throughout the given territorial or organisational society? New information about the various ranges of past situations encountered is not enough. More information must be fed in, of the kind that can often only be discovered by systematic survey or deliberate 'intelligence' work.

Thus, in social services the starting point may be all those in a given county or borough, known or unknown, needing advice or material aid or other specific services because of their physical disabilities; or all those who could benefit, for one reason or another, from, say, meals on wheels or home-help services. In commerce, it might be all those in some given regional, national, or international territory who would be potential customers for certain established ranges of product or service. Within any given organisational society, it might be the internal needs for facilities to carry out various kind of personnel, administrative or financial work.

At Stratum 4 then, the essence of the work is concerned with developing comprehensive provision of services or products of a specified kind throughout some defined society. Financial investment in plant and buildings and, in general, recruitment and training programmes are a natural concomitant. Since new capital investment of any significant size is always a sensitive matter, the final sanction for it may often rest at higher organisation levels, or indeed within governing bodies of various kinds. Organisation members within Stratum 4 may not themselves have authority to make the final decision on investment therefore, but at least they will need some degree of authority to reallocate existing resources so as to cope with emerging or as yet untapped areas of need within the society concerned.

Within this stratum in SSDs are to be found various 'assistant directors' and 'divisional directors'. In health services it is presumed that most of the new community physicians, the chief nurses, and the administrators at area and district level are also working within this stratum. It appears unlikely that any people within this fourth stratum can carry out their work without assistance; all appear to need access to subordinate or ancillary staff.

Stratum 5 – Comprehensive field coverage

At Stratum 5 need has to be considered again in its complete incidence throughout some given territorial or organisational society, but the scope is broadened by moving from a framework of accepted, specified, and sanctioned kinds of service on offer to a framework which simply defines some general field of need. The work consists essentially of developing whatever comprehensive provision may be required within this given general field. Thus, in social services departments, in moving from Stratum 4 to Stratum 5, the focus changes from things like needs for homes for the elderly, casework with problem families, provision of home help, to the general question 'how can social distress in this district, in all its forms, best be prevented or alleviated?' In health services the question changes from 'what sorts of hospital, general practice, and public health services are needed throughout this district?' (with the meanings that these terms already attract) to 'what are the basic health needs of this district, group by group, and how may they best be met in any combination of old or new services?' Other general fields of need in the public sector whose nature would imply potential Stratum 5 work would include education, leisure, housing, physical environment, transportation, etc., where similar questions might be posed. In industry, needs in Stratum 4 terms for things like 'overcoats', 'telephones', or 'calculators' would presumably become redefined as needs for 'clothing', 'communication systems', and 'data processing', respectively, in Stratum 5 terms.

Thus there is an important distinction to be observed here between what we have called *particular kinds of services* and *general fields of need*. As we are using it, the phrase 'particular kinds of service' is one which at a given point of cultural development would conjure up a precise picture of what the services comprised and what kinds of physical facilities and staff were needed to provide them. On the other hand, a field-of-need description would convey no such precise image. (Presumably, in the normal course of social development, many terms which initially imply little more than fields of possible need later acquire much more concrete connotations. Think, for example, of the now-specific connotations of such phrases as 'general medical practice' or 'social casework' or 'television services' or 'life insurance' compared with their imprecise significance at earlier points of social history.)

Work within this stratum involves much interaction with directing and sponsoring bodies of various kinds – boards of directors or other governing bodies, financial bodies, trusts, public authorities, and the like. Inevitably, staff within this stratum spend much time 'outside' the immediate operational zone of the organisation.

Within this stratum, then, we should expect to find the chief officers of at least the major departments in local authorities, some senior executive posts (as yet not altogether clear) in the new health authorities, and the chief executives of many large commercial operating organisations, freestanding or part of larger financial groupings.

Possible higher strata

So far we have described five discrete strata of work but there seems no necessary reason to stop here. Jaques (1965a) for example, has assumed on the basis of his own observations of viable managerial structures in a number of varied organisational settings that at least seven distinct levels can be identified. There is evidently further work above the fifth stratum concerned with the interaction of many fields of need at local, regional, national, or even international levels. There is the need within local authorities to produce plans which intermesh the whole range of public services – education, social services, planning, leisure, etc. – provided at local level. The same intermeshing of various broad fields of public service, together with nationalised industries, arises at national level. In the private sector there is the increasing growth of national or multinational conglomerates bringing together operating divisions or subsidiaries in many broad fields. For the moment the existence of such higher level work is noted, but no definite classification can be advanced.

'ZOOMING' AND 'TRANSITIONAL PHASES'

Before passing on, however, two important elaborations of the thesis which have been developed in discussions of its applicability to social services departments must be mentioned. The first is the idea of 'zooming', the second what might be called the 'transitional phase'.

It is evident that staff at Stratum 3 and upward are not able to spend, and do not spend, all their time simply considering extended ranges of work and needs, as it were, in abstraction. Stratum 5 staff will frequently get involved in discussions of the comprehensive provision of existing kinds of services, the establishment of specific systems, or the correct handling of the specific and perhaps quite crucial cases; Stratum 4 staff will quite frequently get involved with particular systems or they too with particular cases; and so on. Such phenomena may be described as 'zooming' (Evans 1970). There may be a variety of causes: direct externally given requirements, such as insistence by the governing body that the head or director of a public agency looks into a particular case; or the need to help some subordinate in difficulty; or a laudable aim to get the 'feel' of lower-level and more concrete realities, from time to time; or even perhaps the occasional attempted flight from higher demands!

Does this mean that more senior people commonly act at several different levels of work, concurrently or in rapid succession? To assume this would in fact be to assume that they experienced rapid expansion and contraction of personal capacity, one moment capable of seeing aims and situations only in a narrow context, and at the next far more broadly – which seems implausible. On the contrary, it is readily observable that when people capable of operating at high levels get involved in work which is at apparently lower levels they tackle it in crucially different ways, ways that constantly exhibit the characteristics of the higher-level approach. Where people with Stratum 3 capacity become involved in concrete situations needing their attention, these specific situations are rapidly seized on as illustrative instances of a general problem demanding a more systematic response. Where Stratum 4 people become involved with particular ailing systems or procedures, their interventions inevitably lead to considerations of how the benefits might be extended comprehensively throughout the organisation concerned.

An actual illustration of this process which has come to our notice is that of the industrial chief executive who asked his secretary to prepare and maintain in an up-to-date state an organisation chart of his company for the wall of his office. Given the written, highly explicit accounts of jobs and organisation which were current in this particular company, this task would appear to have been straightforward enough, but nevertheless the chief executive found himself dissatisfied in this instance with the results of his secretary's work. As anyone knows who has tried to draw charts of the detailed and complex relationships, however well-established, in large organisations, the sheer job of charting itself is not so simple as it might seem. The chief executive grappled with it for several hours – indeed all evening. What he began to devise was not simply an answer to his immediate problem (Stratum 2) but the outlines of a general system of organisational charting (Stratum 3). Moreover, having devised such a system he proceeded to think about, and later to act upon, the possibility of its useful employment throughout the company (Stratum 4). (Whether he proceeded to any further action which indicated a Stratum 5 or higher outlook is not known; however, the point is made.)

What this suggests then is that 'zooming' is a normal or proper part of executive work, and must be thought of as not simply a 'zoom down' into a lower stratum of work (leaving apart, that is, the case where the person concerned is not in fact capable of operating at the higher stratum) but also properly a subsequent 'zoom up', or return, the total sweep in fact providing valuable concrete experience for the more abstract work to be carried out.

The second phenomenon which must be taken into account is that of the *transitional phase*, which is to do with the observable development in people's abilities as they approach the points in their careers where they are ready to take on work at the next higher stratum. Now it is possible, as described above, to define a completely sharp boundary between strata in terms of certain kinds of decisions which may or may not be made, but it is not easy to believe that human capacity develops in the same completely discontinuous way. One does not go to bed one night unable to think beyond the case in hand and wake up next morning unable to do other than see cases as illustrative of whole ranges of work to be tackled accordingly. There is evidence that personal capacity to do work at various levels develops in a continuous pattern over time, though at different rates for different people – as A, B, and C in Figure 2.1 (Jaques 1967). Moreover, for those like A who are on their way to achieving not merely a higher ability within a given stratum, but ability of a different and higher kind (and only for those people), observation now suggests that they begin to show evidences of this higher ability in a nascent form well before it has reached its fully realised state. The one- or two-year practical post-qualification experience in 'responsible positions', required by many professional bodies before full professional registration is awarded, is no doubt a particular recognition of this phenomenon at the Stratum 1–2 boundary.

The organisational consequences of this phenomenon are as follows. Whereas the manager within the next higher stratum, say, for example, the *systematic service provision* stratum, Stratum 3, may involve A, B, and C, who are all at this moment of their careers in Stratum 2, in discussion about new policies (say, the introduction of new systems or procedures), they are likely, it seems, to get contributions of a different quality from A than from

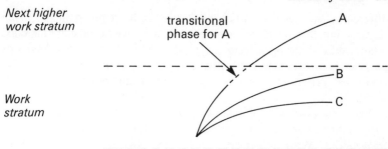

Figure 2.1 Differing patterns of development of personal capacity

B or C. Such discussion may help to train people A for their forthcoming leap. Indeed, they may be asked to do such things as chairing working parties to produce ideas for new policies, though at this stage of their career they will not be judged quite ready to take full responsibility for the final formulation of such policies or responsibility for their implementation following approval.

APPLICATIONS OF THE MODEL

Having now laid out the model, at least in its present stage of development, the remainder of the paper is devoted to the uses to which it can be put. We shall consider:

1 how the ideas can be used to clarify roles and organisational structure within existing organisations; and
2 how ideas may help to design new organisations considered as total systems from which a particular quality of response is required in relation to their environment.

Illustrations of both applications will be given from actual developmental project work that has been carried out in particular social services departments.

The clarification of existing organisational roles and structure

As has been noted, the theory under discussion grew out of observations of the equivocal position of certain apparently managerial posts in many SSDs. Such posts seemed regularly to attract conflicts about their status and authority in a way not true of other posts within the hierarchy. Earlier studies in manufacturing and nursing organisations had revealed similar phenomena (Brown 1960, Rowbottom *et al.* 1973). Generalising, it seems that if a hierarchy is set up in any organisation on the basis of all the various different grades of post which may exist or be required in the given organisation, then not all of them will turn out in practice to carry the same relationship to those beneath them. Moreover, to the extent that this phenomenon is denied officially, or by those in the particular posts concerned, certain inevitable and quite painful stresses and conflicts will result.

Let us start with a definition. Let us describe the strongest, most secure, most authoritative posts in the hierarchy as 'fully managerial' or simply 'managerial'. We shall associate these with unquestioned rights to set or sanction general aims and guides for subordinates, and with rights to appraise their performance and capacity in practice and to assign or reassign work to them accordingly. Then we may pose a simple proposition: that no more than one of these managerial posts can be sustained in any one stratum of work (as here defined) within the hierarchy. Thus, knowing the range or strata of work to be carried out within any organisation, we can readily compute the maximum number of viable managerial posts in the hierarchy. In the case of social services departments, for example, assuming the desire to carry out work at all five of the strata identified above, there would be room for only four such managerial posts in any strand of the hierarchy.

However, as it happens, there are something of the order of 10 or 12 main *grades* of post in SSDs, and indeed it seems quite usual for organisations to generate many more steps in their grading hierarchies than can be justified in terms of the basic managerial hierarchy required. What is the position of the people in all these other posts? Judging from project work in various fields that has been quoted, the answer, it appears, is that they will in reality tend to carry roles which are less than, and crucially different from, full managerial roles as they have just been described. At least four possible alternative roles have been identified in these various fields of project work – 'co-ordinating roles', 'monitoring roles', 'staff-officer roles', and 'supervisory roles' (Brown 1960, Rowbottom *et al.* 1973, Rowbottom *et al.* 1974). Each has its distinct qualities but, in general, none of these types of role carries authority to set general aims and guides for those in posts of lower grade, or to appraise their performance and capacity, or to assign or reassign work accordingly.

In other words, these other people will not naturally and readily be identified as the 'boss'. It will be more natural and satisfactory to have a 'boss' who is (and is capable of) working at the next higher stratum of work, and one who is therefore able to make a radical adjustment to the whole *setting* within which work is carried out when major problems loom. What is unsatisfactory and a constant source of tension is a supposed boss who goes through some motions of appraising performance and setting general aims and guides, even though in reality they are only carrying out work of essentially the same kind themselves, and therefore need to refer any major difficulties requiring radical readjustments in work or circumstance to some further point still in the hierarchy. This is indeed 'bureaucracy' with a vengeance!

Some examples from social services

Let us briefly illustrate how this idea of linking managerial roles with different strata of work has been applied in actual projects in SSDs.

One project is concerned with the managerial structure of an area social work office and in particular with the role of the team leader, which has been felt in this department as elsewhere to raise considerable problems. There are four teams in this particular Office and each team leader is 'in charge' of a team of up to a dozen or so people. Manifestly, the hierarchy is as shown in Figure 2.2a. On the surface it appears that all members of the team are managed, directly or indirectly, by the team leader. Collaborative analyses, using these ideas of discrete strata of work and managerial and other roles, have revealed a very different situation, one much closer to the model of Figure 2.2b, which, now it has been made explicit, seems to command considerable approval. In reality it appears that team leaders, senior social workers, and certain of the more experienced basic-grade workers are all working within the same 'situational response' stratum – they are all carrying full 'professional' responsibility for their cases, drawing only on voluntary consultation with colleagues as and when they require it.

Moreover, when large issues appear on the scene, they all tend to look directly to the area officer for guidance rather than the team leader. In respect of the other workers at this second stratum, then, the team leader has essentially a co-ordinative role – co-ordinating the daily flow of work, co-ordinating duty arrangements, chairing team meetings, etc. – though in addition he provides advice to his colleagues, when asked. In contrast, the social work assistants, the trainees and students, and other of the basic-grade social workers, both unqualified and newly qualified, are still working in Stratum 1, although many of them, particularly the students and newly qualified social workers, may be expected to be within the 'transitional phase' leading to Stratum 2. This latter group clearly requires special treatment. However, since none of these people have actually realised a Stratum 2 capability, they can all be expected to find it acceptable to see the team leader (or perhaps one of the other Stratum 2 workers to whom they may be attached for training purposes in the case of students) in

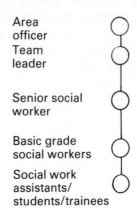

Area
officer
Team
leader

Senior social
worker

Basic grade
social workers

Social work
assistants/
students/trainees

a. *Manifest organistion*

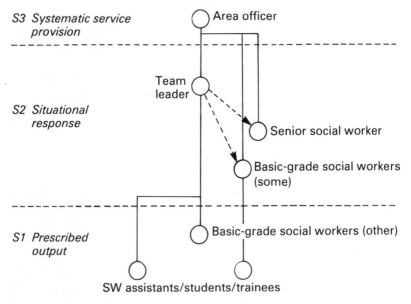

S3 *Systematic service
provision*

Area officer

Team
leader

S2 *Situational
response*

Senior social worker

Basic-grade social workers
(some)

S1 *Prescribed
output*

Basic-grade social workers (other)

SW assistants/students/trainees

b. *Requisite organisation explicated in work-strata and roles*

managerial   co-ordinating

Figure 2.2 Organisation of an area social work team

a managerial role – in conventional social work terminology as a realistic and accepted 'supervisor'.[4] Thus, what could easily be seen and interpreted (or misinterpreted) as a long, complex hierarchy within the area office can now be seen in a much clearer, simpler, and more functional form, with only one intermediate management level, and that not applying to all staff within the office.

Another project has been concerned with helping the top management group of an SSD to redefine and clarify their own roles and relationships. One issue concerned the role of the deputy director. His position was publicly portrayed as in Figure 2.3a. His role was generally described in terms like 'doubling for the director' and 'dealing with day-to-day matters', but carried some specific areas of responsibility as well. Although on examination the roles of the assistant directors revealed clear Stratum 4 work, examination of the deputy's role failed to reveal the same. The new organisation (Figure 2.3b) which was introduced made specific use of the idea of work-strata and, failing to find room for any intermediate managerial level between the work of the director (Stratum 5) and his assistant directors (Stratum 4), the deputy was assigned a senior Stratum 4 post, with responsibility in this case for the comprehensive provision of all 'fieldwork' services. Although a significant co-ordinative role was also recognised in relation to his other Stratum 4 colleagues, it was clearly established that all these people were to regard the director and not the deputy as their immediate manager.

A third project (supported by seminar work of the kind described above) has been concerned with the nationally important question of the future role and organisation of the Education Welfare Service, at present usually attached to education departments but with strong links to SSDs. The distinction between Stratum 1 and Stratum 2 definitions of the role of the education welfare officers turns out to be of central significance. In a Stratum 1 conception, their work is describable in terms like enforcing school attendance, providing specific information to parents, and providing or arranging specific material aids. In a Stratum 2 conception their work becomes redefinable in terms such as dealing in a flexible, responsive way with problems of non-attendance and their social causes, with a view to promoting a situation in which the child can best benefit from the educational facilities available. The indications are that the strong preference will be for the second definition of the role – a decision with profound implications for the training and deployment of staff – with perhaps recognition of the need for the provision of ancillary staff at Stratum 1 as well.

Other projects have applied similar analyses to the kind of work required of heads of homes in residential social work – whether it should be at

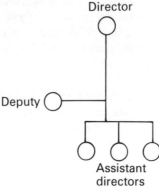

a. *Manifest organisation*

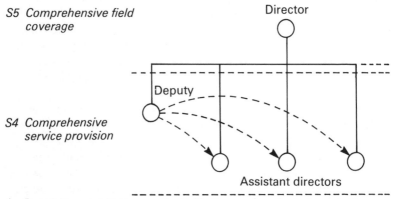

b. *Requisite organisation explicated in terms of work-strata and roles*

Figure 2.3 Top management structure of a social services department

Stratum 1 or 2 (Chapter 4); to the kind of work required of so-called 'training officers' – whether it should be at Stratum 2 or 3; and to the kind of work required of those developing new types of social work with disturbed adolescents known as 'intermediate treatment' – again, whether at Stratum 2 or 3.

Designing new organisational structure

The examples quoted so far have all been of situations where staff and organisation already exist and the problem is to clarify the levels of work to be done, and the consequent managerial and other role structure called for. In a more fundamental application, the theory can also be applied to the design and establishment of new organisations by posing the question: what strata of work is the organisation as a whole required to encompass?

A current example from our own project work is that of the setting up, or rather re-establishment, of hospital social work organisation following the recent transfer of hospital social workers *en bloc* from health authorities to social services departments. We have become involved in helping in this task of integration in three departments. Nationally, the difficulties of integration have been much exacerbated by uncertainties about relative gradings. Although the same sort of grade-titles have traditionally been used in both hospital social work and local authority services – 'principal', 'senior', and 'basic' grade – the actual associated salary scales have been lower for workers in hospitals. There has been considerable argument as to whether this in fact betokens less responsibility, grade-title for grade-title; or whether it simply reflects the continuous history of comparative underpayment of hospital workers.

Here, the work-stratum theory has provided a useful cutting edge in project work. Separating and leaving aside for the moment any questions of grade and pay, it has been possible to expose the basic issue: what kind of work is required to be carried out in hospital settings of various types? The answer from the field has been unanimous on the need in all hospital settings for work of at least Stratum 2 – the total 'situational response' of the fully responsible caseworker. The remaining issue is then seen to be whether to provide on site, in any hospital or group of hospitals, an organisation capable of carrying out systematic provision of social work services (that is, Stratum 3 work), or to leave the on-site organisation as one merely capable of co-ordinated Stratum 2 work, the necessary higher-level work being done by others not specifically associated with the particular hospitals concerned.

Given this analysis, the three project departments concerned are now in processes of making explicit choices, and seem in fact to be opting for full Stratum 3 organisations in the larger hospitals or hospital groups, and Stratum 2 individual posts or teams in the smaller hospitals. Questions of appropriate grading can properly follow, starting with the question of whether there could be any justification for lower grades for the same stratum of work in one setting or the other.

Thus, the work-stratum theory appears to offer a new way, not only of deciding the design of extensions to existing organisations, but of designing organisations from new. It is a way which starts from the question of the *kind* of impact required on some given social and physical environment. At the same time it is a way which does not seek to deny the fundamental reality of the stratification of authority in many situations. Such stratification is justified in defensible terms of higher and lower kinds of work to be performed, rather than in such crude arguments as the inevitability of having those who direct and those who obey.

It may be stressed that the quality of organisational impact on, or response to, its environment can be a matter of *choice*. As Silverman (1970) and Child (1972) separately observe, organisations are the creation of conscious decision-taking actors, not simply a product of a 'causal' environment. Much has been written about the correlations between various kinds of organisational structure and organisational environment, but not a lot has been said about the precise mechanisms by which managers might create so-called 'organic' or 'mechanistic' organisations. Apart from some of the Tavistock work on detailed systems design, using ideas of 'primary tasks' and 'sentient groups' (see for example Miller and Rice 1967), the literature is content for the most part to rest at broad descriptive or ideological levels; or to observe empirical correlation in certain organisational and environmental characteristics. But the levers of change are rarely revealed.

The work-stratum model, as described here, offers one very concrete way in which organisations may be designed to react in various ways, or various degrees of depth, to their environment. Thus, a Stratum 3 system will respond in quite a different and perhaps more 'organic' way than a Stratum 2 system. Conversely, the model also offers a precise way of categorising the various possible stages of evolution of any given organisation from the Stratum 2 'solitary-jobber' type of organisation, capable only of a prescribed response to its environment, right through to the fully mature Stratum 5 type of organisation. (This may be compared with other published descriptions of organisational evolution such as those of Chandler 1963, Jaques 1965a, Greiner 1972).

From this viewpoint the Stratum 5 organisation with its fully realised capability for self-development emerges as the system of special interest. It appears to offer one concrete answer to the general problem posed by Schon (1971) of how society is to produce organisations, both public and private, capable of coping with the demands of an increasingly unstable world. The increasing establishment of Stratum 5 organisations at the 'periphery' (in Schon's term) seems to offer a means of getting away from a society dominated by the exclusive development of new ideas at the 'centre', and their diffusion on a 'centre periphery' model, with all the attendant problems he so ably identifies. It offers a means of retaining coherent organisational structure. At the same time it does not exclude the possibility of basic political and legal control from the centre. Thus, to stick to the examples quoted extensively in this paper, the current establishment in Britain of new organisations at local level in the fields of both social services and health services, capable of working to the most general, i.e. Stratum 5, terms of reference, while still subject to the overall legal–political control of central government, seems a development to be welcomed.

At this point the thesis leaves us with some large questions: Are there other public services which could benefit from establishment in Stratum 5 organisations, either by extension or reduction of their present structure? What is the justification for the many large national public services which presumably require more than four-level executive structures, but with a brief which suggests only a Stratum 4 definition of need, such as providing comprehensive national rail services or a national supply of coal? What is the social justification for the existence of larger-than-Stratum-5 industrial and commercial organisations? How far might we see the proliferation of these as symptomatic of a society over-obsessed with the advantages of economy of size and scale, and neglectful of the needs for more convivial institutions in which people can live and work?

NOTES

1   See Jaques, 1965a, 1965b, 1967, 1976. His own initial conception of the stratification of work was based on empirical observations of a natural spacing of managerial tiers in terms of 'time-span' measures of levels of work (Jaques 1965a). If the two approaches, his and the one described here, are consistent (as it is assumed they are) then his critical time-span boundaries between strata – 3 months, 1 year, 2 years, 5 years, and 10 years – will correspond to the boundaries between successive strata of work identified in the qualitative terms used below. In the various descriptions of work-strata offered below the links may also be noted with the idea of the 'perceptual–concrete' nature of the lowest stratum of human capacity; the 'imaginal–concrete' nature of the second stratum, and the 'conceptual–concrete' nature of the third stratum (Jaques 1965b).

2   For the general terms of the social-stratification discussion see the Davis and Moore versus Tumin debate (Bendix and Lipset 1953) and also Dahrendorf (1968). Specifically, the issue may be noted of how far, in general, differences in power, status, and wealth in society may be explained or justified either in terms of the need to have a variety of different social functions carried out (which bears an obvious relation to the present discussion of 'work-strata'), or in terms of the existence of a given 'natural' distribution of human abilities (which bears an obvious relation to Jaques's notion of 'capacity').

3   The introduction of ideas of discrete work-strata into theories of occupation and profession presents intriguing prospects. Apart from the possible distinction of 'craftsmen' and 'technicians' from 'professionals', just described, it also draws attention to the likely presence of many different strata or levels within any one occupational group – or, putting it another way, of finding social workers,

teachers, doctors, etc. within any one of Strata 2, 3, 4, etc. This stratification *within* occupational groups is usually obscured by a sociological habit of treating each group as if its members had one unique status or prestige level – treating the house-surgeon as identical with the president of the Royal College of Surgeons, for example.

4   It may be noted that the term 'supervisor' as used in social work practice implies in fact a range of authority and accountability commensurate with a 'managerial' role, as defined above. However, the term 'supervisor' in the Glacier Project (Brown 1960) and later work was used, in keeping with industrial and certain other practice, to define a role with precisely *less* than full managerial characteristics.

3   Models of organisations

INTRODUCTION

The purpose of this paper is to present a new typology of organisations and to explore briefly the way in which these emerging ideas about the design of social institutions might illuminate three issues: (a) central–local relationships, (b) inter-agency planning, and (c) centralisation and de-centralisation. The first part presents the typology, building on the levels of work theory. The concepts of 'highest expected work' and 'basic expected work' are introduced. The second part of the paper contains a few brief comments on the relevance of the typology and the theory for the three issues.

The paper draws on six years' action-research in English social services departments (SSDs), and to a lesser extent in housing and education departments, on numerous research conferences with hundreds of senior social welfare staff from central and local government, and discussions with practitioners at all levels.

'ADMINISTRATORS' NEED RELEVANT THEORY

We are meeting to discuss training in management for social welfare administrators. If the English experience is at all relevant for other countries, it may be necessary to explain what this term 'administrator' really means. Briefly, we have in English departments met two different interpretations of the word. In the first place, there are those whose prime concern is with providing support or services to others engaged in the operational work. Their activities centre around:

- *finance* (collection and disbursement of cash, accounting, budgeting and budgetary control);
- *logistics* (provision of premises, equipment, materials and other

supporting services to enable operational and other work to be performed);
- *personnel* (recruitment, general training, and welfare);
- *secretarial* (recording and communication of others' decisions, actions and events).

Secondly, there are 'administrators' who are managerially accountable for the work of staff providing services in the clients' homes, at agency offices, at day centres, or in residential settings. These are *not* usually called administrators but area officers, team leaders, assistant and divisional directors, directors, homes and day care advisers and so on. In SSDs the term 'administration' is primarily used when referring to the first group of activities outlined above. This is the reality at the present moment. (The position in central government is more complex and I prefer to leave explanations to those more conversant than myself with the precise details.)

This state of affairs in the local government agencies raises many, as yet, unresolved questions. For example, must the director of social services necessarily be a qualified social worker, as is the current general national policy? Is the existing split (as outlined) tenable in the long run? Is it in the best interest of social welfare provision? What new alignments may emerge? And, of course, what are the implications for training of the different interpretations of the role of welfare administrators? It would seem that the general field of activity of administrative work – like many others – is in a state of flux.

However, these are questions peripheral to the main theme. Here I wish to register my own plea for the development of relevant theories to help welfare administrators (of whatever kind) design their responses to social welfare problems. It is crucial but insufficient just to train administrators in the utilisation of new techniques and skills. The institutional base from which services are provided must surely be the subject of an equally intensive scrutiny. To achieve this we require theories of organisational design and response. But such theories may be most realistic and efficacious if they are problem-based and bound to issues confronting workers at all levels of decision making. The work levels theory and the additional models and concepts represent an effort to widen the choices and increase the alternatives available for policy decisions. They provide the possibility of translating the general descriptive terms 'centralisation' and 'decentralisation' into more precise language.

MODELS

The stratification of work

A full exposition of this theory is contained in Chapter 2. It has been found useful to colleagues working in an ever-increasing range of social welfare problem areas. In essence, what we are saying is that work in response to social needs and problems can be performed in a number of qualitatively different ways. These are at increasing levels, or strata, of complexity delineated by the broadening and changing of the range of objectives and environmental factors which are taken into account as we move from stratum to stratum. We have, so far, identified five such levels. They are described and illustrated in Figure 3.1.

We must emphasise that this is a theory of stratification of work. Whether it is translated into a hierarchical employment bureaucracy, or whether alternative forms of organisation are designed, is another issue. Using the work levels language, it is quite possible to discuss the level of work in social welfare or elsewhere, irrespective of the question of the political control of the agency.

Rather than repeat the detailed argument I propose to move to the next stage on the assumption that the basic notion may have some worth – a not unreasonable assumption given the intensive testing of the last two to three years. The next section will provide an opportunity for minimal exploration of the levels.

Basic and highest expected work

From the notion of stratification in work I intend to build a model of responses which could be used in tracing the historical development of welfare provision and as a tool in organisational design. This typology can also be utilised to analyse not only the broad sweep of the main response, but also the response of various parts of the total organisation. (There are models which are more realistic than others, but this will not be discussed.) However, for present purposes, I need to introduce two complementary concepts – *basic expected work* and *highest expected work*. They are not elegant phrases, but will suffice to provide the main gist of the argument.

'Basic expected work' is, as it suggests, that minimum level of work of the organisation, occupation, or professional groups. It is their 'public face'. It is often what is meant when we talk of the 'grass roots', 'coal-face', 'front line', 'shop-floor' and so on. But basic expected work is not necessarily the lowest level of work. A Level 2, or higher, professional social worker or doctor may have assistants and trainees at a lower level, but we expect case accountability to rest with the designated 'professional'.

Stratum	Description of work	
5	*Comprehensive field coverage —* making comprehensive provision of services within some general field of need throughout some given territorial or organisational society.	social territory general field of need
4	*Comprehensive service provision —* making comprehensive provision of services of some given kinds according to the total and continuing needs for them throughout some given territorial or organisational society.	social territory specific services Unmet need
3	*Systematic service provision —* making systematic provision of services of some given kinds shaped to the needs of a continuous sequence of concrete situations.	Range flow
2	*Situational response —* carrying out work where the precise objectives to be pursued have to be judged according to the needs of each specific concrete situation.	Partially presented outputs
1	*Prescribed output —* working towards objectives which can be completely specified (as far as is significant) beforehand.	Prescribed outputs

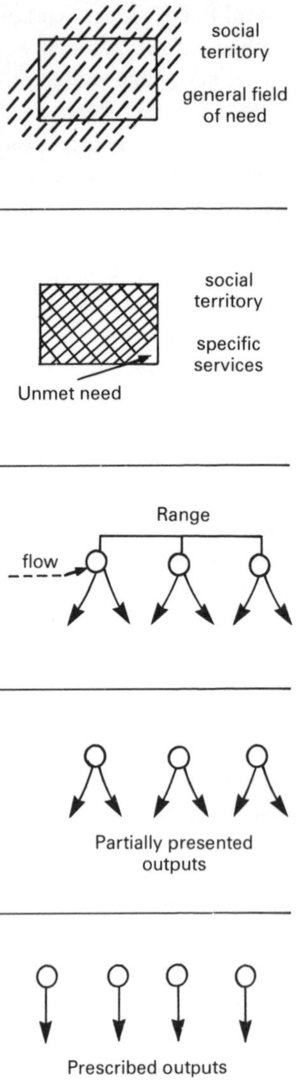

Figure 3.1 The stratification of work

It is that basic level of production or service for which the organisation was set up in the first place. It is of crucial importance.

We may note that many areas of social welfare provision in England hover uneasily between alternatives. What, for example, is the basic expected work in the various parts of residential care? I am not asking what it actually is; but at what level do we wish to plan for, strive, and train? There would be general agreement that in many instances too much emphasis is placed on bricks and mortar, on the fabric of residential institutions. Work with residents is often performed in a routine, straightforward fashion (Level 1) rather than responding to the judged needs of individual clients (Level 2). Another example is the social welfare provision in schools, where much of the current controversies can be seen as an attempt to move the basic expected work of the occupational group concerned from that of the 'policeman-type' activities to a professional (Level 2) response.

In these and other examples tens of thousands of clients and vast sums of money are involved. It is not an exaggeration to state that, together with the staff, national training programmes hover between these alternatives. The significance for the recipients of the services – the clients – is, we may presume, enormous.

'Highest expected work', or 'societal impact', represents the other end of the decentralisation–centralisation ladder. Thus, in a stratified system of the sort that exists in English SSDs, the highest expected work is represented by the role of the director. (We are of course discussing here *models* for the provision of welfare services: the real performance of the director, or any other person, may be higher or lower; the point is that without a model of expected response it is difficult to plan anything!) Thus, the 1968 Seebohm Report, upon which was based the creation of the new departments, speaks of the qualities of the 'principal officer of the proposed new department capable of looking outwards well beyond the limits of his [sic] own department and authority, and well into the future'.

He will face problems different from those facing heads of existing established departments . . . . He will have to survey the needs of the area and the deployment of workers to meet them . . . . He must be able to command the confidence of members, to persuade them to provide more resources for the services, to maintain a reasonable balance between the demands made on behalf of different groups in the population . . . . [He must] consider further adaptation and the introduction of new methods to meet developing needs in a society which is undergoing rapid, economic and social change.

(Seebohm 1968: 618–19)

I apologise for the lengthy quotation but it comes from sources far from our own research, yet corresponds very well to what we have referred to as the need for Level 5 work.

So, highest expected work may be seen as representing the total impact which those who established the organisation have in mind. Thus:

– Do we desire an agency which can deal systematically with the flow of problems as they appear (Level 3)? or
– Do we expect our agency to embrace a defined social territory, to seek out unmet need, to provide a comprehensive service of an accepted, precisely recognised kind (Level 4)? or
– Are we attempting to respond to a general and vaguer 'field' of need (Level 5)?

Recent developments

The theory can be utilised in describing changes in English social welfare provision. To do this we refer to Figure 3.2. The developments may be represented by a rather unusual mathematical equation: $1 + 1 + 1$ does not equal 3. That is to say, the amalgamation of the three smaller departments – children, welfare and mental health – has not resulted in one (larger) department. There has been, if you like, a dialectical level leap from one form to another. Discussions with staff who worked in the earlier agencies indicate a wide variety of organisational responses. Some of the highly professionalised children's and mental health departments were, as far as could be judged, operating models $^4/_2$ or $^3/_2$ – at the top comprehensively covering social territories or flows of cases – with an objective that the basic expected work would entail a Level 2 response. Welfare departments, many of them concerned with more tangible, prescribed outputs, appeared to fit model $^3/_1$, although there may well have been both more comprehensive responses ($^4/_1$), or smaller sections fitting the $^2/_1$ model.

Whilst it might now be generally accepted that SSDs are expected to provide their top response at Level 5, other agencies in the broad social welfare field are struggling to define their objectives. I refer, for example, to housing. In a recent research project, utilisation of the typology enabled the dilemma of the housing department in one London borough to be described in succinct fashion. The core activities of the department, its prime emphasis, was in 1974 as indicated in Figure 3.3. The basic expected work was concerned with defined, tangible outputs – with the technical maintenance of housing estates and the compilation of waiting lists for council housing according to prescribed criteria. Its

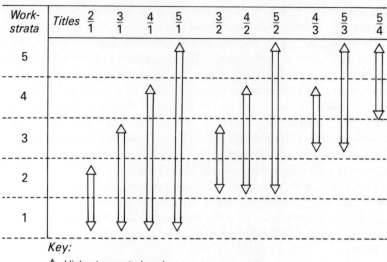

Figure 3.2 Typology of organisational responses

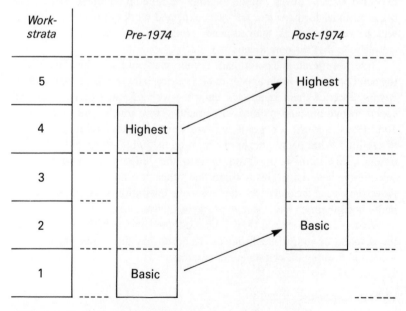

Figure 3.3 Changing structure of a housing department

top work revolved around the precise notion of 'houses' – with a housing manager at the head of the department.

A change in policy and the arrival of a new director has led to a qualitative shift at both ends of the organisation. Housing becomes transformed into the desire for a 'comprehensive housing service', concerned not just with houses but encompassing a much wider range of social variables. The boundaries at the top of the agency become more hazy. There is the inevitable increase in interaction and overlap between the restructured department and other Level 5 agencies. Joint planning becomes an issue. At the bottom there is pressure for an equally radical move away from the tight constraint of the points system of local authority housing and towards more flexibility and greater discretion for staff when assessing the problems of people in housing distress. There is now a housing advisory service with the expectation that staff will be judging needs and not just answering enquiries and giving standard instructions and advice.

Demand and judged-need models

To simplify discussion of the typology, the four models where the basic expected work is Level 1 might together be called a 'demand' model. The organisational forms where the basic expected work is Level 2 and above will be referred to as 'judged-need' models. (I am once again grossly simplifying the true complications.)

Thus, to reiterate the point made earlier, many organisational responses to social problems would appear to be swaying between these two models. Behind each of them stands the complex web of value judgements and social, economic and political arguments. How much, and under what conditions, should we grant welfare administrators wide powers of discretion? What paradigms are being used to 'judge' the needs? To what extent are clients being brought into the judgement? Universality, selectivity, benefits, rights – these and other concepts enter the debate. Nevertheless, at the end of the day, we make institutional responses, and we badly need theories which can express the alternatives.

Which of the models in Figure 3.2 is adopted and, in particular, whether the demand or judged-need model is chosen has direct relevance to the work and training of welfare administrators.

Hybrid responses

The exposition, so far, suffers from at least one omission obvious to all who work in, or study, welfare agencies. I have, in the typology, portrayed one main response. But even in the examples already provided and certainly in the field as a whole, there are what we might call 'hybrid' models. Thus, an area office of an SSD might have two main operational responses. There would be the fieldwork staff where the general expectation would be that the judged-need model would be implemented; other staff, providing basic services such as meals on wheels and home helps, might be operating a demand model. In addition, Level 2 fieldwork staff would probably have assistants of one form or another. So we could well envisage a hybrid model as depicted in Figure 3.4.

It cannot be denied that models of this sort are widely found. I confess, however, that much remains to be understood regarding the workings of organisations and part-organisations (such as area offices), where two different basic expected work levels are to be found. Are there significant implications for the management of work and the delivery of services? What about career development, training and future prospects for the two different groups of operational workers? Perhaps these are irrelevant questions – I merely note my unease. An understanding of the structure of the distinct and different work to be done is a basis for some of the main themes of this workshop, such as mutual appreciation and constructive interaction between welfare administrators *within* and *between* agencies and between local and central government. This, and inter-agency collaboration, decentralisation and centralisation, will be the subject of brief comments in the second part of this paper, below.

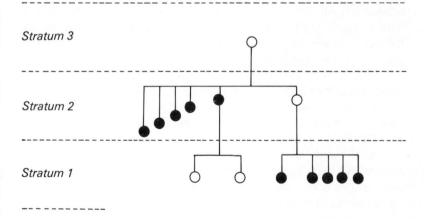

Key: ● Basic expected work

Figure 3.4 A hybrid operational response (partially illustrated)

RESPONSES

Central–local relationships

The changing SSD equation, described earlier, has major repercussions. Many directors are now influential figures moving amongst the political structures in a manner previously unknown or rare. The balance of power has changed, both at the local level and in central–local relationships. SSDs are in most cases more powerful and interact with other agencies on a more equal, and more than equal, basis.

Central government advisers can no longer always obtain the same quick access that they may have been accustomed to with the directors' (less harassed) predecessors in the 'old days'. The imbalance between central and local government may develop in an unexpected fashion. Directors and their senior staff may be thinking in broader, more theoretical and innovatory terms than the central department advisers. Unless central government changes its own approach, the impact of its 'advisers' is likely to be treated with less and less significance. The real experts might be found in the locality. What are the implications for the level of work of central government staff? What is the present position and how can new structures be achieved if desired? These remain intriguing questions. It may be argued that the present dominant expenditure and control paradigm does not call for a complex, high-powered model, which, for some, may perhaps be one of its attractions.

Planning and control systems may be dependent on the organisational model in operation. For example, the output of the demand model, if not actually tangible, can usually be counted or measured, or visualised in near concrete terms. Whilst grass-roots staff have discretion it does not include the possibility of changing the nature of the output itself. Level 1 staff carry, as it were, the boundaries to their discretion in their briefcases. The rule-book provides the tangible boundary of the demand model in service organisation. We may note in passing the extraordinary difficulties that the Supplementary Benefits Commission in England has encountered and the consequent rule-books of incomprehensible complexity (Donnison 1976: 337–359).

Central control of the demand model is a different proposition and requires different approaches, techniques and abilities. For example, redistribution of resources in the National Health Service – as proposed by the Resource Allocation Working Party (HMSO 1976) – does not necessarily correlate with a redistribution of standards of treatment. Take an area with two hospitals. One is modern, luxurious, with small wards and splendid equipment. The other is housed in an ancient, musty building, with old-fashioned, large wards – it does however possess one 'minor' benefit –

its consultants are generally thought to be the finest in the profession. Which hospital would we choose? Care cannot be measured by capital expenditure alone.

Inter-agency collaboration and planning

I can do no more in this paper than indicate the utility of a theory of levels of work for analysis of the problems of inter-agency collaboration. The complexities, particularly between health and social services, are in general well known and documented. I would just draw attention to a major working paper which deals specifically with health–social services interaction (BIOSS 1976).

At the same time we ought not to underestimate the significance of interaction between personal social services and other agencies such as education. My own research experience over several years, attempting to assist in the clarification of the role of part of the educational welfare service, reinforces the utility of a theory to guide us through the maze.

One of the virtues of the theory is that it establishes realistic points of reference for the collaborating agencies. Thus, we can build natural bridges between the participating agencies based on partnership between people with parallel levels of complexity of work. Efforts that have been made to create 'unbalanced' long-term working groups of, say, Level 1 or 2 operational workers from one agency, and Level 4 or 5 senior managers from another, do not appear to be successful. Each group has a different view of the world. It is more productive to consider establishing 'equal-level' groups. (I am making the assumption that everyone is doing the job he or she is capable of – unrealistic, I know, but once again the theory does permit the construction of clearer job specifications.) In broad terms we may distinguish between:

- planning at the *individual case level* (Levels 1 and 2);
- planning the *systematic development of services* – that is to say, the systematic development of the way in which individual cases are dealt with within given capital facilities, staff, establishment (Level 3);
- planning for *comprehensive services* – meeting social needs throughout the whole of some defined geographical area (Levels 4 and 5).

So we can begin to pinpoint specific areas of confusing overlap both within massive services such as the National Health Service and also between various levels of central, regional and local provisions. If we are to do this fully, however, we require not only a theory of decision making but an analysis of the activities in order to establish workable boundaries between allied agencies such as social services, social security, housing, education and health.

Centralisation and decentralisation – some comments

As they stand, 'decentralisation' and 'centralisation' represent useful declarations of intent. But it is difficult to undertake a rational discussion without further elaboration. Thus, in SSDs, the statement 'we have a decentralised pattern of organisation' can mean any of the following statements:

1 that a divisional, geographical structure has been established in the local authority – the divisional director will be asking the question: what is the extent of the need for services of these kinds throughout my division (i.e. Level 4);
2 that an area office has been opened which will deal with the flow of cases, but the area officer, unlike the divisional director, cannot make decisions on questions concerned with unmet needs and the reallocation of resources (i.e. Level 3);
3 that a small neighbourhood 'sub-office' was being established to deal with existing caseloads (i.e. Level 2).

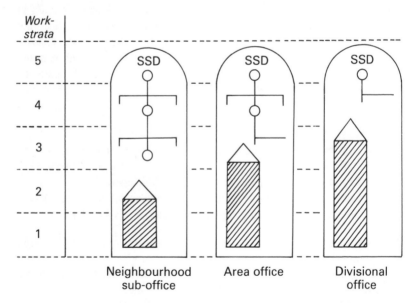

Figure 3.5 Levels of decentralisation in an SSD

Figure 3.5 illustrates these three interpretations of local government 'decentralisation'. We can see how it becomes possible to discuss the various levels of decentralisation in terms of the work that is expected from each level.

CONCLUSION: PEOPLE AND STRUCTURES

I would submit that welfare administrators have a continuous and urgent need for relevant theories of organisational analysis and design. What problems are we trying to solve? What institutions and part-institutions must we construct to tackle this problem in an organised fashion? What work needs to be done? What staff do we require? What training consequently follows?

It will not be enough to have at our disposal theories of human behaviour. These will need to be matched with theories about the more enduring institutional structures which play such a critical part in the functioning of welfare agencies. Frequently we have, in our research, encountered recurring patterns of problems. At first, many have been interpreted as 'personality differences'. But when the same difficulties recur up and down the country, we must begin to be suspicious. The causes, it is suggested, are often structural.

4   Managing to care

BACKGROUND

This chapter examines the organisation and management of state residential care for the elderly in the first years of the Seebohm period. This had previously been the responsibility of welfare departments which had been widely criticised for being too concerned with 'bricks and mortar', and for a lack of professional social work support. Their absorption into the new SSDs with their (mainly) social work qualified directors and social work focus would bring them – it was hoped – into the mainstream of professional practice.

The research upon which this chapter is based revealed several major problems. Numerous heads of home remained isolated in the new structures. In some cases they were almost a law unto themselves, brooking no interference in 'their' homes. Others were well trained and committed, but they often suffered from a lack of positive guidance and support from an effective middle manager. And, at the senior management level, there were still staff who had risen rapidly to their new statuses and responsibilities often without the necessary training or indeed ability. In general, residential care remained a Cinderella service.

Many writers and practitioners felt that the problems of residential care could be resolved by creating a suitable 'milieu' or environment. Others saw the solution in a search for 'non-hierarchical' organisation. In some quarters there was a strong belief that 'management' was unnecessary and even dangerous. None of this added up to a policy capable of translation into practice. Neither did the answer seem to lie just in the provision of additional resources, since it was difficult for the outsider not to be struck by the great differences in care in residential homes in the same department, or in different departments with similar resources.

I was concerned that the search for solutions to the problems of residential care did not pay sufficient attention to the immediate and dire needs of the residents. The analysis in this chapter draws on the ideas of authority-backed roles and the emerging levels of work theory in order to approach the problem of improving the quality of residential care.

INTRODUCTION

What impact, if any, have the new large social services departments made upon residential work – previously described as being 'in the backwaters of the social services' (Beedell 1970)?

The particular area chosen for analysis is that 'messy' middle ground where grand theories have to be translated into purposeful action. At one extreme are 'the ends', which can be, in Righton's telling phrase, 'immensely respectable and dumbfoundingly vague'; at the other extreme, the blow-by-blow accounts of the daily minutiae of residential life (Righton 1971). More specifically our concern will be to examine the nature of the links between work, care, policy and organisation.

The proposed examination is dangerous. In some eyes the mention of the word 'organisation' is to identify the writer willy-nilly with the camp of social conservatism. It is a process of instant classification pursued strangely enough by those who in other contexts are most sensitive to the nature of 'stigma'. There is no contradiction between care and organisation *per se*. What we might discover is that it is precisely *lack* of analysis, thought and interest in organisational design that contributes to unsuitable standards of care.

The analysis will utilise three sets of concepts: (a) functions or activities; (b) roles; (c) levels of work.

TWO APPROACHES TO RESIDENTIAL CARE

Two contrasting approaches to residential care can be identified. They might more accurately be thought of as opposite poles of a continuum which has been split to aid clarity of exposition. One view places its main emphasis on the milieu, the environment. Everything that happens in and around the home is potentially therapeutic. Accordingly, there is not thought to be much point in attempting to disentangle the multifarious activities of the centre. Life is seen as a continuous and bewildering interchange of work and roles. As one housemother put it, her general duty was to establish a milieu and 'once having established the milieu the unit is itself therapeutic'.

The pioneering Williams (1967: 28) Report, while noting the importance of special skills and knowledge required in residential care, sees the chief work as the creation of a 'harmonious group'. Other writers also noted that the report contained no analysis of the actual work undertaken by staff. We may all concur with enthusiasm about the need to establish harmonious groups, stable environments, a helpful atmosphere – at the same time these phrases, left at this level of generality, do indeed seem 'dumbfoundingly vague'. The 'environment', the prime therapeutic factor, is so flimsy a concept that 'care' trails in its wake as a matter of chance and individual idiosyncrasy. How can we talk of overall policies in this situation? Flair, however brilliant, is a shaky foundation upon which to build a caring system for half a million people.

An alternative approach attempts to disentangle the strands of residential work and examines the prime forces which lie beneath the concept of therapeutic environment.

In order to begin this investigation some knowledge is needed of what actually happens in and around a residential home. This knowledge must be of a particular kind. It cannot be so general and vague as to have little practical significance, similarly it should not be so detailed as to overwhelm us with its unwieldiness. We require, therefore, 'middle range' of functions or activities which can be used as a tool for the discussion of environment, standards of care and departmental structures. An attempt to provide such a list, abstracted from our recent book (Rowbottom *et al.* 1974), is provided in Table 4.1.

The distinction between 'output' and 'supporting' functions is crucial to the argument since it enables us to delineate and discuss the prime orientation of residential care. The client becoming a resident may expect that his or her 'state of social functioning' will be maintained and developed (Bartlett 1970). At the very least residents may expect that their social functioning will not deteriorate at a rate faster than it would were they not to have entered the residential establishment. The positive change or prevention of deterioration in social functioning is the output of the residential establishment.

Output activities can be distinguished from 'supporting' activities which have no *raison d'être* by themselves and, however vital, are means for assisting the achievement of the department's or establishment's prime function. Let us not diminish the importance of supporting functions such as finance and logistics, but at the same time we must not lose sight of the differences in one porridge of therapeutic environment. The basic premise is to draw some line between these two distinct sorts of activities, not to present an inflexible list. The division between output and supporting activities may vary somewhat between types of homes, between different authorities, and over given periods of time. The contention, tested with many social services staff, is that this delineation leads to important conclusions.

Table 4.1 Analysis of functions to be carried out in the residential setting

Output functions	*Supporting functions*
Basic social work (all residential establishments) – making or contributing to assessments of need and of appropriate response – providing information and advice – monitoring and supervision of residents – helping individual residents to maintain and develop personal capacity for adequate social functioning – arranging provision of other appropriate services for residents	Staffing and training work – recruitment of domestic and other staff – student training – dealing with welfare problems of all staff
Basic services (all residential establishments) – providing clothing, other goods, and money – providing meals – providing accommodation – providing help in daily living (including help with personal hygiene, dressing, moving, looking after personal property. etc.) – providing recreation, social and cultural life (including the fostering of links with the local community)	Managerial and co-ordinative work – selection or sharing in selection of domestic staff and care staff – induction of new staff and prescription of work – personal appraisal and development of staff – dealing with problems of staff, and of staff interaction – (in some cases) co-ordination of work of non-residential staff in relation to needs of particular residents
Supplementary services (provided as needed, and varying from establishment to establishment) – providing aids for the physically handicapped – providing medical or paramedical treatment – providing formal education, etc.	Logistics, finance and secretarial work – ordering of supplies, replacements, and repairs – collection and banking of incoming money – control of petty cash – local fundraising – maintenance of various records and preparation of various reports – care and security of stock and premises

STANDARDS OF CARE

The concept of output and supporting functions may be considered to be the first of a number of interlocking strands. For the moment, we shall leave this first strand on one side and consider the familiar phrase 'standards of care'.

How can we define standards? Of course the tangible indicators are important. Calories, financial expenditure, living space, staff ratios – all these and other hard statistical data provide essential minimum facts. But a moment's thought is sufficient to indicate the dangers in relying solely on such apparently reliable indicators. Indeed, they can be positively misleading. High expenditure on food (or on anything else for that matter) may not reflect a luxurious standard of living, but might primarily be the result of waste and inefficiency. Perhaps it could all be summed up by saying that what is missing from the data is the 'human element'. We need to know *how* people are being cared for and this of necessity demands human evaluation. Two establishments may produce almost identical indicators but to the informed and expert eye standards may be seen to vary widely. The Curtis (1946) Report commented on the same phenomenon. 'The differences between the results achieved in what would appear to be precisely parallel conditions are often striking.' The report emphasises that 'on the personality and skill of these workers (Matrons, Superintendents) depends primarily the happiness of the children in their care'.

The second key point – the head's accountability for standards of care – needs to be pursued beyond mere statements of idealistic intent. This pursuit is, I believe, in the interest of all concerned parties. It is a search, where the prize is not a rigid, mechanistic definition of role, but a system which enables the optimum realisation of community goals. We shall not, however, be able to proceed further along this path without the introduction of two additional concepts – role and level of work.

ROLE AND HIERARCHY IN THE SOCIAL SERVICES

Since the establishment of social services departments we have made strenuous efforts to identify some department, somewhere, that has succeeded in abolishing its hierarchical structure. We have now discussed the issue, in conferences and project work, with many hundreds of staff from departments throughout the country. In this quest we must frankly admit total failure. The quarry is as elusive as the Loch Ness monster. On closer inspection our new discovery turns out to be merely another variation of that persistent organisational animal – the hierarchy. The search goes on but, given the present state of the social work profession and the

Managerial role

A managerial role arises where A is accountable for certain work and is assigned a subordinate B to assist him/her in this work. A is accountable for the work that B does for him/her.

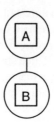

A is accountable:

– for helping to select B
– for inducting B into his/her role
– for assigning work to B and allocating resources
– for keeping himself/herself informed about B's work, and helping B to deal with work problems
– for appraising B's general performance and ability and, in consequence, keeping B informed of his/her assessments, arranging or providing training or modifying role.

A has authority:

– to veto the selection of B for the role
– to make an official appraisal of B's performance and ability
– to decide if B is unsuitable for performing any of the work for which A is accountable.

Figure 4.1 Definition of a managerial role

departments' statutory obligations, we might expect no dramatic changes in the near future. If this indeed is the immediate prospect, then the radical critique might sound rather hollow to the half million residents under the care of hierarchical organisations! Simultaneously with our dreams we might ponder on the more prosaic question – what do we really mean by hierarchy? Perhaps if we define it we may understand and conquer undesirable manifestations. The need for a precise definition is paramount. Without it we remain babes in the organisational jungle.

Following previous work we shall define hierarchy 'as meaning nothing more nor less than a structure of successive managerial roles' (Rowbottom 1973). In turn, a managerial role is defined as shown in Figure 4.1.

At a stroke, this definition has flattened what, in many instances, passes for 'the hierarchy'. The chart on the director's wall may portray eight or more 'links' in the managerial chain but our research indicates that four is the maximum number of *real* managerial levels found in SSDs. (Level or rank is the distance between A and B in Figure 4.1). To general relief, not everyone, even near the top, is a manager. Within each rank there will probably be a number of grades, primarily indicating differences of pay. The assumption that differences in grades (for example, senior social workers and basic-grade social workers) implies some particular relationship of organisational authority is a common cause of confusion.

We must emphasise that the managerial role is only one of a range of roles that have been identified in SSDs (Rowbottom *et al.* 1974). For brevity and simplicity we shall concentrate only on this role which, together with an emerging theory on levels of work, will enable us to return to the pursuit of the main theme.

LEVELS OF WORK

Current research (reported in Chapter 2) leads us to the tentative proposition that each of the five levels involves distinct kinds of work. Once again, the test of the theory is not whether it is ideologically palatable but whether it can help us to understand reality. Will it help us to design organisations that aid, rather than hinder, the realisation of community objectives? A condensed outline of the theory is presented below.

Prescribed output – working towards objectives which can be completely specified (as far as is significant) beforehand according to defined circumstances which may present themselves: for example, social work aides and assistants, students, trainees, clerks, typists, etc.

Situational response – carrying out work where the precise objectives to be pursued have to be judged according to the needs of each specific concrete situation which presents itself: for example, experienced social worker, residential head, section manager, etc.

Systematic service provision – making systematic provision of services of some given kinds shaped to the needs of a continuous sequence of (concrete) situations which present themselves: for example, area officers, principal officers in specialist fields, residential group managers.

Comprehensive service provision – making comprehensive provision of services of some given kinds according to the total and continuing needs for them throughout some given territorial or organisational society: for example, assistant directors.

Comprehensive field coverage – making comprehensive provision of services within some general field of need throughout some given territorial or organisational society: for example, directors.

ROLE OF THE HEAD

The concepts of function, role and levels enable us to reconsider the role of the head of home with added insight. A whole range of conditions and problems begin to unfold. We are forced to consider, and perhaps more importantly reconsider, the following problems:

- What functions do we expect heads to be primarily performing?
- At what level of work should they be operating? What are the implications for the work of other members of the department concerned with residential care?
- What are the personal characteristics, abilities, capacity, that would be sought for in the various levels of residential staff?
- What are the appropriate links between the head and other members of the department?

To claim that complete 'answers' to all these questions are readily available, and even if they were, could be covered in a brief paper, would be presumptuous. The most that can be done is to outline possibilities, hint at avenues of further exploration and concentrate on a major theme.

If the earlier output–supporting classification is tenable, heads can be expected to be 'output-orientated'. It is in the area of basic social work and basic services that we should expect to find the prime focus of the head's attention. We shall be looking for people capable of understanding and assessing the real needs of residents and staff, heads who are capable of responding to various situations not merely in a routine, prescribed fashion characteristic of Level 1 work. It is not enough conscientiously to apply the rule-book, to present the budgets on time, to worry that the building and equipment are in an adequate state – in short, to ensure that all the 'tangible' indicators referred to earlier are being adequately achieved. From the head is demanded all this, and more. To take a rough parallel, the situation demands that heads work (at least) at a level which would be expected of a trained, experienced social worker or senior social worker at Level 2. (Undoubtedly, there are homes demanding Level 3 or even 4 work, but to simplify the argument the writer will focus primarily on that which seems to be considered by departmental staff the broadest and most pressing issue.)

Level 2 workers are expected to exercise judgement about methods and attitudes to work and 'real' needs in specific concrete situations. While expected to judge what 'output' to aim for (implying accountability for carrying a case), they will probably not be expected to commit the organisation on how future possible situations are to be dealt with.

Does this sound too remote, too idealistic? It might be argued that there are just not enough residential staff capable of working at this level. Perhaps, but first we might consider some alternative explanations to the lack of resources argument. Are the available staff being permitted to function at their optimum level? Are there heads who are forced into acting primarily as book-keepers, hotel keepers, and the like, not by personal inability, but by virtue of an absence of departmental policy and guidance? To what extent have they been given the scope to develop and implement their real abilities? In how many departments are there realistic job definitions with suitable discretion clearly delineated? And to ask an even more sensitive question – are there homes where unexploited ability is left untapped and unhelped beneath the shadow of a head who, by any objective assessment, ought not to be occupying that post? If 'standard of care' is firmly within the province of the individual head, then equally so the creation and maintenance of overall departmental standards lies somewhere else. All the questions raised earlier have not yet been tackled but it is clear that this path of analysis leads inexorably to an examination of the higher-level structure of the department.

We began by reaffirming that residential 'management' is essentially about people. We continued by emphasising the critical role of the head of the home. We have now reached the final strand of the argument. Departments must look hard at their own headquarters and supporting structures.

ROOM NEAR THE TOP

This article started by wondering what impact the creation of the new social services department has made on residential care. Perhaps one of the main differences between the two 'eras' (before and after integration) was summed up – with obvious feeling – by one assistant director (local authority population one million) discussing residential care with another assistant director (population 90,000), at a Brunel conference: 'What managed to pass for flexibility in the small departments can really be seen as confusion in the large authority'.

Whether this sweeping and pessimistic evaluation is valid for all large departments can be disputed. What is hardly open to doubt is the elongation of the hierarchy. The days when the head of a residential establishment could readily contact a discernible and relatively well-known 'boss' have disappeared. The 'gap' between the head of home and the top officer of his or her organisation has widened considerably.

What then is the nature of the gap, not in terms of salary grades, but in terms of the work to be done? What can be said about the personal qualities of the people who need to fill that gap? What do the answers to these questions tell us about the nature of the work and the role of other headquarters staff? Given the wide variation in the numbers and types of centres in departments, 'answers' can serve only as general guidelines.

If the head is the crucial factor in the standard of care in each home, then the search is not for someone who is 'managing' *homes*, but for someone who is capable of managing a group of heads. Managing is used in the same distinct sense as it was when discussing the role of the head. This time the work is rather different. It remains 'managerial' in that the *group manager* will be expected to appraise performance and ability, help to deal with work problems, arrange suitable training and so on. However, our level of work analysis points to the need for the Level 3 group managers to be primarily concerned with systematic service provision. They would be expected to go beyond responding to specific situations case by case. Services have to be provided which are moulded and shaped according to the needs of a continuous flow of situations. Thus, for example, a Level 2 head's work might be defined in terms of a given population of residents, whereas the Level 3 manager would need to be occupied with patterns of service for a range of homes. The group manager must have the personal ability to judge and respond to the comparative position in a variety of situations. How can these group managers fit into the different departmental structures?

Social services departments have chosen organisational structures which can be broadly subdivided into two major categories:

1 The functional model, primarily divided according to functions such as fieldwork, residential and day care, administration, etc.
2 the geographical model, where the department is first subdivided into a number of 'mini departments'.

The second tier of management from the top is thus either an assistant director (residential) or a divisional director, in the functional and geographic models respectively. With some few exceptions we cannot expect assistant and divisional directors to be managing heads of centres. The scope and breadth of work for both these Level 4 managers is such that they are now far removed from the scene of work of most heads. Yet the gap must be filled in order that the link between departmental policy and its implementation in the home shall be maintained. The gap can now be more precisely defined. The work to be done is to ensure that homes are output-orientated and that policies implemented in individual homes are subject to systematic monitoring, evaluation and support.

The role of the group manager is critical. It is certainly not to depress individual initiative, but to ensure that heads function at a level demanded by the department and by society. We cannot talk of output-orientated residential centres on a departmental basis unless we have an adequate output-orientated structure filled by capable intermediate managers. Of course, departments have created posts (between the assistant or divisional director and head of home) to fill the gap we have been describing. Many of these posts have been given titles such as 'homes adviser'. Whether these roles do in fact represent a genuine link in the chain can be ascertained by analysing the duties, authority and level of work of their role.

If 'advisers' are mainly concerned with functions which we have described as 'supporting', perhaps with some accountability for basic services, the basic social work aspects of output are in danger of not being filled. A vacuum is created, although valiant attempts can be made by departments (area liaison schemes, area adoption schemes) to pump in the missing output functions. We can state emphatically that, unless support, guidance, supervision and assessment of the head's work is made in a systematic fashion by a person generally agreed to have the necessary knowledge and ability, and paid at an appropriate grade, stagnation might continue to be a common feature of the residential scene.

The words 'authority' and 'assessment' appear in our image of the residential group manager. The inclusion is not accidental. It is a nettle which many practitioners and commentators seem unwilling to grasp. Indeed, the Williams Report, in its brief comments on the duties of headquarters staff, is apologetic in the extreme. Large organisations, it is recognised:

> must employ people to visit the Homes in order to ensure that they are run in accordance with the policy laid down and to advise those doing the work. In one sense this might seem to be the function of an inspectorate but in practice it is very much more an advisory and consultative service.
>
> (Williams 1967: 156)

In a perfect world we could relax, no toes would be stepped on, the homes adviser could be essentially a 'sympathetic listener'. But the Residential Services Advisory Group (1973) knows that the reality can be very different.

> . . . unhappily it cannot be denied that some staff are unable to use support. They deny the need for support . . . and cannot be helped to

grow or make constructive progress . . . because of their hardened defences and rigid attitudes they are not the best of caring people.

Probably, and hopefully, only a small minority of staff fall within the advisory group's tactful description. We might also wonder to what extent the advisory group might have encountered and be describing situations wherein Level 2 heads were reacting to Level 2 advisers! Even this report, which contains much valuable material, can only suggest that 'the Adviser must *strive* [my italics] to ensure that such people are not excluded . . . from the common developing aims'. For this reason, we prefer the term 'group manager' to the weaker sounding and unclear title of 'homes adviser'. The manager may need, in the interests of the residents and the community, to initiate unpleasant measures. He, or she, needs the authority's sanctioning to act, as well as Level 3 capacity.

It is difficult to provide anything more than a guide to the number of residential group managers required to maintain an effective residential superstructure. Authorities vary widely in numbers and types of residential centres. As a rough numerical guide, and no more, let us assume that a department has sixty centres. How many heads could a group manager genuinely manage? Eight? Ten? Twelve? If we ignore, for simplicity's sake, the possible existence of other staff who might be aiding the group manager, these are the sort of numbers we should expect to get in reply to our question. (The Residential Services Advisory Group sees the optimum number as one adviser to 8–10 homes, but reduced to 4–5 homes in respect of specialist establishments.) From here we arrive at the sample statistical position that a department of some sixty centres will require not less than six group managers. And, by looking at the highly developed fieldwork structures, we can tighten up the picture. If, as we have already argued, heads should function at the level of experienced social workers and seniors, then the group manager slots into the comparable area officer pay and status. Having said all this, in how many departments is there still not considerable 'room near the top'?

Outline answers have been attempted for many of the questions raised earlier. Nevertheless, by concentrating on the main stream of output flowing through the department to the resident, insufficient attention has been paid to those activities we have named 'supporting'. It is to these we must now turn.

EVERYONE CARES

Everyone cares – and if they do not, a good case can be made out for stating that they ought to. In this sense departmental staff who have no direct contact with residents also wish to feel that their work contributes to the general well-being of clients. The image of the agency administrator as a desiccated calculating machine, uninterested and unconcerned, is a fiction which, as far as my own research experience is concerned, is remote from reality. For these supporting staff caring is an attitude, desirable if it can be obtained, but it is not the main focus of their work.

In contrast, heads are also expected to be capable of ordering supplies, controlling petty cash funds, preparing reports and estimates, maintaining budgets – all included in the supporting classification but in this instance we have suggested that their prime orientation should be towards the resident, i.e. output. The danger, which cannot be emphasised too strongly, is that financial, secretarial, and logistical functions are mistakenly understood to be the totality of 'residential management'.

The argument so far has been based on drawing a continuous systematic path, beginning with the social functioning of the residents, continuing to the duties of the head of the home and the position of headquarters staff. This has been designated an output-orientated path, primarily concerned with basic social work and basic services. The provision of supporting functions *to* the home has been deliberately reserved for the end of this paper.

The output–supporting classification presented here is very different from that which appears to operate in many departments. In our model, central staff working primarily in the various fields of supporting activities cannot manage residential heads and, consequently, *cannot* be held accountable for the standards of care. These staff provide essential services, monitor adherence to financial policy, and may interact with heads in a variety of non-managerial roles.

An alternative to the output–supporting pattern of residential organisation might be classified as the 'fabric–casework' division. In this dichotomy 'fabric', 'bricks and mortar' or just 'management' are broadly identified with the 'hard' activities which are, in the main, supporting or basic services according to our definition. Key elements of basic social work are seen as 'professional' territory, are not precisely defined and can be frequently left in organisation limbo-land. We have already noted, when discussing the role of the homes adviser, some of the measures that are taken to pump professional expertise into the vacuum. Other symptoms of the confusion which can be caused by this casework–fabric bifurcation are the anxiety of heads regarding their links with headquarters, the discomfort of homes advisers regarding the true nature of their role, and the uncertainty of assistant directors in functionally organised departments if, and where, boundaries of discretion can be drawn between professional social work and 'management'. Where departments have moved towards the newer

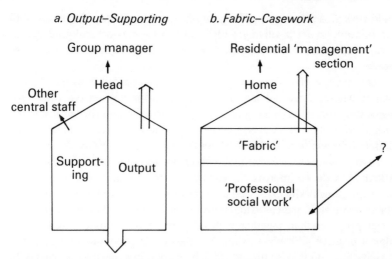

Figure 4.2 Two contrasting patterns of residential organisation

geographically based organisations, the same principle would apply with the output stream leading to the divisional directors. As yet, it is too early to comment on the impact of the decentralised department on residential care.

The distinction between the two types of residential classification is illustrated in a simplified form in Figure 4.2.

CONCLUSION

I have argued elsewhere that policy and organisational structure are interconnected and cannot be divorced from the notion of 'care' (Billis 1973). The existence of either one without the other leaves residential care the prisoner of whim. Aloofness from the debate is a luxury which cannot be afforded in a problem of this scope. Our concern here has been to study the nature of the interconnection and to suggest a particular analytical path.

We have proposed a list of activities carried out in the residential setting and introduced the concept of output and supporting functions in order to trace a direct line from service delivery up through departmental structures. The role of the head is emphasised as the crucial factor in the establishment's standard of care. The creation of residential group managers is seen as fundamental to any hope of a systematic and comprehensive departmental approach to residential care. Unlike the homes adviser role, often found in departments, the group manager is seen as an output-orientated person of experience and status comparable to the fieldwork area officer post. The group manager is envisaged as a role with 'teeth', able to act positively with regard to the support and guidance of heads and in the extreme to initiate measures to replace unsatisfactory heads.

This picture of residential organisation is compared with the 'fabric' pattern wherein 'management' is regarded as primarily concerned with the supporting functions (see Figure 4.2b) and basic services (in contrast to the output orientation of our model). The 'fabric' model is seen to have serious deficiencies and to raise doubts about the nature of its service delivery.

In discussions with residential workers the question has repeatedly been asked: How do we improve the situation of residential work? Most of the answers are naturally expressed in terms of increased resources, better pay, status, more staff, increased and newer homes, improved training, etc. This paper proposes that, together with all these, organisational research can play a positive part when examining the whole panorama of residential activity, including those topics which have, perforce, been mentioned only briefly.

5 Delegation and control

INTRODUCTION

This paper explores the question of delegation and control in SSDs. It begins by reporting the findings of research undertaken with directors and their deputies in the early 1980s which revealed widespread differences of view regarding organisational relationships in their departments. In order to gain a better appreciation of these issues the paper continues with a brief search of the literature. The conclusion is reached that writings from the discipline of public administration have been primarily concerned with democratic accountability and have had little to say about control and delegation within the bureaucracy. Social administrators have focused more on the impact of unsuitable organisation on professional discretion. The fleeting search through the organisational literature suggests that the approaches to control and delegation can be characterised as 'top down' (further subdivided into 'directorial' and 'practitioner king or queen') and 'bottom up'. None of these is seen to resolve the questions raised in the essay, and an alternative structural model is presented.

DIRECTORS AND THEIR DEPUTIES

In 1980 about 80 of the 116 SSDs in England and Wales had deputy directors. Most counties (41), a majority of metropolitan districts (27) and 12 London boroughs had deputies in post. Five counties had 2 deputies (Social Services Yearbook 1980). This paper draws on the results of (a) a two-year research *project* with a senior management team of one SSD and (b) a briefer comparative *study* of a further 6 SSDs involving directors and their deputies. The former involved the director, deputy and 4 assistant directors of a metropolitan borough who collaborated in a research project. In the study, directors and their deputies were separately interviewed regarding their respective roles and 'cleared' documents were obtained.

The work revealed a considerable degree of confusion surrounding questions of the control and delegation of work. Other research has shown similar unclarity at lower levels of the department (Stevenson and Parsloe 1978).

The project revealed a depressing picture. Typical statements from participants were:

- The senior group is seen as a dustbin.
- The deputy does not have a real role.
- I feel I cannot get any co-operation.
- We have a situation of private armies.

The senior management team felt that the roles of the director and deputy overlapped and were muddled. There was a strong feeling of lack of guidance and control which had spread well beyond the confines of the senior management team and the middle managers. During the course of the project it became evident that the director's claim that the deputy was in some way responsible for what was called 'day to day management' was causing widespread confusion. The end result was that neither the director, the deputy, nor those with whom they interacted, could give a clear-cut answer to the nature of the organisational relationships between them. Concern that the problems of control and delegation uncovered in the project might not be the result of individual personalities and abilities, but might be more widespread, led to the comparative study.

The study included three counties, two metropolitan districts and one London borough. The individual discussions with directors and deputies covered the following areas: the core elements of their work, perception of each other's roles and respective authority, and relationships with other members of the senior management team.

On one point there was total agreement between, and within, departments. The single distinguishing feature of the directorial role was its concern with an inner core of issues that directors felt could not be relinquished. This core was variously expressed by directors as:

- dealing with major issues of political sensitivity
- protecting the political and professional environment
- coping with issues that might hit the headlines

Beyond this kernel of activities aimed at the avoidance of political unrest, there were no clear-cut boundaries to the division of work between the two top officers of the department. In one department the deputy was responsible for a functional area. In only one other department did the director see the management of the senior departmental staff as one of his duties. In the other five departments the existence of a deputy led directors

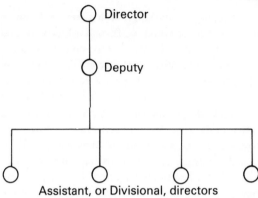

Figure 5.1 The single-line relationship

to posit – at least initially – a single-line relationship between themselves and their deputies. On the face of it, therefore, this would mean that deputies were held accountable for the work of the next tier down, the divisional or assistant directors. This perception, which presumably reflected current local authority wisdom regarding organisational relationships, rarely stood up after the opening discussion. Most deputies had a more complex view of the situation.

The reality of the single-line relationship, depicted in Figure 5.1, can be tested by discovering from directors and deputies which staff they felt accountable for and the nature of the decision-making process.

If Figure 5.1 represents the real position, we would expect deputies to hold their own management meetings with the next tier down at which authoritative decisions could be taken by the deputy in consultation with 'his staff' (all the participants were men). Meetings of deputies with the next tier did take place, but only where the deputy had functional (fieldwork) responsibilities were such meetings unproblematic. Discussion revealed that when deputies did call meetings of the management team in the director's absence they would 'hold over' any matter where it was known that the director 'had particular views and that he might disagree with the particular standpoint'. Directors, in turn, expected that if the issue could 'reasonably wait' it would await their return. In two departments deputies called specific meetings of some or all of the next tier, thus apparently giving real substance to the single-line relationship. In one department this meeting was causing severe problems and its role was felt by the deputy to be 'desperately unclear'. In the other case the director saw his deputy's meetings as dealing with 'practical issues . . . on the understanding that this is the way the director wants it done'.

In short, when pursued with any rigour the single-line model broke down in all the departments. Who controlled which staff, and what work and authority was delegated to whom, remained unclear at the end of the study. A follow-up questionnaire sent three months later to the six departments in the study indicated that the exercise had been of some benefit to departments in clarifying the respective roles. But this should not be exaggerated. Lack of clarity may, it appears, suit both parties! Thus, one deputy felt quite satisfied that at the conclusion of the study a 'grey area' had been left which provided a 'certain room for manoeuvre'. It is, however, rather difficult for the outsider (and perhaps other departmental staff) to feel as sanguine. At a time when the boundaries of the department are being subjected to intense scrutiny and criticism from all sides of the political system, we might wonder whether some of the cosy, relaxed arrangements will survive.

The study confirmed that the project findings were not necessarily personality-based, but that the issues of control and delegation might be widespread. Although other senior departmental staff (the third tier) were not directly interviewed, there were indications, from the statements of directors and deputies, that the confusion over lines of management extended to the senior management teams.

It is not my intention in this paper to pursue the detailed aspects of the project and study. I shall not be arguing that the deputies are unnecessary. The directors of the larger county authorities in particular made a strong case for their retention and even extension. There can be little doubt that the management of complex departments is an onerous job which necessitates a number of headquarters supporting roles.

My main purpose here is to investigate the question of control and delegation, and in order to move forward I shall explore possible models of decision making that might underpin or provide alternatives to the perceptions of organisation provided by staff in the research.

THE SEARCH FOR MODELS

Some clues to possible underlying models, or 'symbolic representations of how things work' (O'Shaughnessy 1972: 120), can be found in the literature of public and social administration. Thus, the issue of delegated bureaucratic decision making has been a chronic concern of public administrators. How can political control be maintained over officials dealing with large organisational machines? In a study of county boroughs in the late 1960s, Greenwood *et al.* (1969: 293) reported that: 'Perhaps the most important fear of members over delegation to officers arises from concern lest they become ignorant of facts that they should know in order to fulfil their duties'. Both the 1967 Maud and the 1972 Bains Committees attempted to resolve the dilemma. The former proposed that officials would be largely responsible for 'administration' with the Management Board of Councillors making policy. The Bains Report declared: 'it has been suggested that extensive delegation to officers is in some way undemocratic, but we do not accept this, provided that the terms of delegation are clear and specific'. Bains found it 'disturbing' to find that five years after the Maud Committee had 'exploded the myth of policy being a matter for the elected members and administration for officers . . . many members and officers still see this as a sufficient description of their respective roles' (Bains 1972: 8). Self saw the hand of 'management theory' at work in the Maud proposals:

> . . . this type of theorising normally favours an orderly chain of decision-making, realised through a grading of decisions according to their intrinsic importance, an allocation of decision-making responsibilities that is as clear and precise as possible, and a stress upon effective delegation subject to such performance tests as can be devised. These managerial notions are certainly out of line with the traditional system of local government which . . . stipulates that in principle all decisions are the responsibility of the part-time elected representatives.
>
> (Self 1971: 272)

Other literature indicates that the dilemma remains unresolved. Two inaugural lectures take this as their main theme. Regan is primarily concerned with what he calls a 'headless state', or the absence of an 'accountable executive' in local government, and argues for a cabinet system in which councils would elect a mayor or sheriff with power to appoint individual members of the council to be the political heads of their ex-council departments (Regan 1980a). This, it is suggested, would overcome the problem of 'democratic accountability'

> since *all* on a local council are responsible for both executive and legislative responsibilities, none is clearly accountable for either. The public cannot easily apportion blame and credit for the stewardship of the council's services when their elected representatives comprise a largely undifferentiated group.
>
> (Regan 1980a: 9)

Regan does not discuss, in this particular paper, bureaucratic accountability – whether or not blame or credit should be apportioned to officers. Jones, however, is concerned to analyse the various meanings of 'responsibility' and its location. He suggests that the notion of 'shared' or 'joint' responsibility is a 'superficially attractive' and 'high sounding' phrase which 'seems to enable a basic problem about the theory of responsible government to be surmounted, namely that in government, people often have to be accountable for more than they decide while others determine more than they are accountable for' (Jones 1977:7). But this can too easily be used to 'justify evasion of responsibility' and a strong plea is made for 'locating responsibility, or at least the main responsibility'. Without such a clarification there is a 'challenge [to] representative democracy itself' (p.6).

Much of the public adminstration debate has taken place around the doctrine of ministerial responsibility and can be traced in the journal *Public Administration*. Baker (1975: 21) pointed out that 'until the appearance of *Local Government Studies* only three years ago, the literature of British local government was largely innocent of theory'. Even a brief excursion into the literature reveals concern expressed by writers such as Self and others over the intrusion of a 'management' approach which does not take into account the characteristic and distinguishing features of the political framework. Work by INLOGOV writers echoes the same point. 'This application of the ideas and concepts from the literature of organisational theory to that of public administration is not a process which receives universal approval.' In their view 'what is needed is a measure of reconceptualisation rather than rejection' (Greenwood *et al.* 1980: 8–9).

A similar wary approach towards organisational theory can be found in some of the social administration literature. Here, the target is what John Smith, writing of the 1970 health and social services reorganisation, refers to as 'this crass managerialism'. He claims that much more use could be made in teaching, research, and practice of the 'largely respectable body about organisational structure, industrial and human relations, and motivation and effort stretching back at least as far as the 1920s' (Smith 1979:447). We should, we are told, move away from the 'framework of Weber's ideal type bureaucracy'. John Smith claims that crass managerialism has not assimilated findings of the many studies of alternative forms of organisation. Similar sentiments and unhappiness with the Weberian dominance are expressed by Rose, who in a paper entitled 'Approaches to the Analysis of Social Service Organisations' concluded that 'we are hardly at the beginning of studying social services organisations as the complex systems they are' (Rose 1976: 238). It may be that social administrators have focused more on the impact of inappropriate organisational forms on professional discretion, compared with public administration's interest in democratic accountability (for example, Thomason 1977), although a number of recent papers indicate a growing interest in professionalism in local government (see, for example, Regan 1980 and Laffin 1980).

In the search for clues to underlying models of organisation that might shed light on the issue of control and delegation we have seen that public administration has little to say about delegation and control *within* the bureaucracy. Issues of political control have taken pride of place and much of the debate has revolved around the policy–administration dichotomy. We might note, in passing, that the participants in our research were not over-concerned with this dichotomy. Their actions appeared to reflect what Jones (1973: 138) has suggested is a 'more relevant line of division: between what is publicly controversial, or potentially publicly controversial, and what is not. Members are to handle the former, officers the latter'. Social administration, on the other hand, offers somewhat more material, although much of the writing appears to concentrate on the defects of current approaches and discusses delegation and control as an aspect of 'professionalism'.

In the following section I wish to explore, equally briefly, approaches from the organisational literature which focus on the same dilemmas of control and delegation.

TOP-DOWN APPROACHES

It seems that the organisational literature often approaches these matters from two opposing directions which may be characterised as 'top down' and 'bottom up'. Thus:

> Those who work from the top down regard the organisation as a system of subdividing the enterprise under the chief executive, whilst those who work from the bottom up, look upon organisation as a system of combining the individual units of work into aggregates which are in turn subordinated to the chief executive.
>
> (Gulick 1937: 11)

I have found it helpful to distinguish two variants of the top-down approach which might be called (a) the 'directorial' model and (b) the 'practitioner king or queen' or practitioner control model.

The directorial model

In the directorial model accountability and authority are initially vested at the top and are then 'delegated' down the organisation. As Wilfred Brown put it:

> Historically, a manager was a person who was put in charge of a venture . . . His delegation of part of the work in no way affected his

total responsibility . . . He was, in fact, completely answerable for any failure on the part of his subordinates.

(Wilfred Brown 1960: 72)

The top-down directorial model is probably the dominant local authority organisational paradigm. This might be exemplified by the following extract from the section on delegation of powers to chief officers from Oxfordshire County Council (1980). The council 'delegates' powers to chief officers who:

. . . may authorise the exercise of these powers by other officers in his department . . . provided that (i) the chief officer shall himself retain responsibility for any action by any officer so authorised to act in accordance with such powers, and (ii) the chief officer shall not authorise any other officer to delegate further any power delegated specifically to him by the chief officer.

In this example, Urwicks' 'sub-delegation' is apparently restricted to one step downwards. We might doubt the reality of this limitation when the list of delegated powers to the SSD director of the above department is examined. Apart from the fact that much departmental activity does not appear on the list at all – and we might wonder where it arises from – those powers that are listed are so vast that the reality of the limitation must be questioned.

The practitioner king or queen, or practitioner control model

The dilemma of reconciling public accountability with the management of complex organisations is reflected in the 1946 Curtis Report. In the large counties it was accepted that the Children's Officer would be unable 'to know and to keep in personal touch with all the children under her [sic] care, and she should therefore aim at allocating a group of children definitely to each of her subordinates' (Curtis 1946: paras 441–446).

The Curtis Report thus reluctantly accepts the principle of delegation but appears to hark back to yet another model of organisation still prevalent in the health service – what we might call practitioner control. In this model *all clients*, patients, or whatever, are assumed to receive what I shall call a 'basic expected level of work' from the consultant. They receive a 'consultant level' service which is not 'allocated' or delegated further down the line. For brevity, I propose to call the basic expected work that the client is expected to receive, the *client-impact level* (see Chapter 3). However, at the same time, the practitioner queen or king is expected to deliver a higher expected level of work or 'service' to groups of clients or patients, to

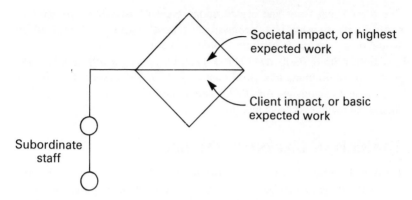

Figure 5.2 The practitioner king or queen

deliver what we shall call a '*societal impact*' (see Chapter 3). This is illustrated in Figure 5.2.

Thus, in the small children's departments (unlike the large departments) the clients, according to the Curtis Report, were presumably expected to receive a 'children's officer' client impact, whilst the local authority was expected to receive a higher 'societal impact' from the children's officer. I have described the 'level' of impact more precisely elsewhere (see Chapter 2). Here a general description may suffice, since the intention is to display broad alternatives rather than to use the concept for detailed analysis.

The practitioner control model has limitations, the most severe being that – if its formal statements are to match actuality – the number of clients it can handle is limited. This is because, unlike the mainstream directorial model, it attempts to resolve the dilemma of control and delegation by retaining practitioner accountability for individual clients.

BOTTOM-UP ORGANISATION

An alternative approach to the issue of control and delegation can be seen in a paper by Dorothy Smith (1965) who coined the rather more elegant phrase 'front-line organisation' in preference to 'bottom up'. She suggested, from her research in one state mental hospital in California, that there are three main characteristics of front-line organisation:

1 The locus of organisational initiative is front-line units.
2 The task of each unit is performed independently of other like units.
3 There are obstacles to the direct supervision of the activities of such units.

She argues that front-line organisations present distinctive problems of control. Her solution is a 'professional type of control structure' which would permit 'some de-centralisation of authority'.

Another Smith (Gilbert) (1979: 37) echoes her views with approval and points to the dilemma of central control units in SSDs where the director ' . . . is held responsible for all children in the care of his department even though he may never have met them'.

TOWARDS AN ALTERNATIVE MODEL

If we exclude the practitioner control model on the grounds of the limited range of clients it can handle, neither the bottom-up nor the top-down approaches meet the needs of large-scale service departments such as SSDs. The dominant directorial model depends on a concept of delegation and sub-delegation which cannot handle the reality of the need for discretion at the front line. The latter (front-line) model does not really answer the problem of political accountability. Both, however, are useful approaches which do succeed in shedding some light on the workings of political bureaucracies. The director does have special responsibilities and the professional social workers in SSDs do have considerable autonomy. Is this autonomy 'delegated' from the director (as the top-down approach claims), or is organisational initiative located in the front line (as claimed by the bottom-up advocates)? These issues, as we have seen, remain unresolved. Delegation does exist, but it is insufficient to explain departmental organisation and, as others have observed, the view at the bottom is equally confused.

Perhaps the practitioner-control model holds a clue to the production of a further 'structural' model. For the role of consultant, or whatever, not only contains what I have called the client-impact level, but *also* contains within the same role the expectations of a societal impact. This can be contrasted with the dilemma faced by the Seebohm Committee which, in its description of the role of director, could not assume that he (sic) would actually be in contact with clients. In defining the role of the director, it described with considerable foresight what the 'societal impact' (as I have named it) might be. But since Seebohm was still constrained within the paradigm of the traditional directorial model it could not resolve the dilemma of delegation. Thus, area teams would have 'delegated authority to take decisions' (para. 594).

Yet it was obvious that the proposed SSD envisaged a distinct client-impact role for social workers and others which, although it can be criticised for lack of clarity, was not dependent on delegated authority from above. What we might call the *concept* of an SSD included the division between societal and client impact. In like fashion, 'schools' include the implicit role of head and teacher; 'factories' have an implicit concept of factory managers and shop-floor; 'prisons' of prison governors and warders. Police stations, fire stations, airports, coal mines and numerous other large-scale bureaucracies can be similarly defined.

I cannot here pursue the different societal impacts that can be constructed. (We might just note the difference in the impact expected from children's officers and directors of social services.) However, the definition of two alternative client-impact levels are crucial to my attempt to link the earlier dilemmas of democratic control and staff discretion to a structural model.

The concept of one 'front line' is by itself inadequate. For there are at least two qualitatively different front lines. In the first instance there is a client impact provided by staff whose output (not work) is prescribed. It may be highly skilled and need significant training, but the different recipients ought to receive services which could, if necessary, be described in such detail as to make no difference to the end product. Client problems are treated as demands to be met (hopefully in a sensitive fashion). The general flavour of such work is of activities that are fairly straightforward, routine or static. Much social welfare provision could fall under the prescribed output heading. In a nutshell, we know before we begin the work what the end product is going to look like. Thus, provision based on housing waiting lists, social security, bus passes, luncheon clubs, are but a few examples of these front-line 'demand' bureaucracies. There are major advantages to this model relevant to the theme of this paper. The end product – the service – is more or less provided in a demonstrable and equal fashion between recipients. When in doubt appeals can be made to the rule-book. This manifest (numerical) equality of the prescribed output model has another great political attraction in that its end product can be clearly understood by the lay person. The model is thus susceptible to easy political control. Intervention in specific 'cases' can be readily undertaken by councillors.

The competing model has a 'professional' front line. (I am ignoring for the purposes of this paper the possibility of higher client-impact levels, which are certainly to be found in, for example, research and development establishments.) I shall merely define the 'professional bureaucracies' as those where staff are expected to make a client impact of a situational response type. In sharp contrast to the prescribed output bureaucracies, we do *not* know beforehand precisely what the end product of the work is going to look like. The problems are not regarded as demands, but as situations which are allocated and have to be dealt with one by one and whose 'real needs' are to be investigated, appraised and judged. As Bartlett expressed it when discussing the nature of professional judgement, 'the complexity and variability of the situation to be dealt with require the exercise of individual judgement by the practitioner in each new situation' (Bartlett 1970: 140). This presumably is a social work model. It apportions services according to diagnosed needs. Inevitably, in this model, cases are less susceptible to political control.

In the construction of our welfare organisations we have a choice; each model has advantages and disadvantages which seem to echo the Platonic debate between numerical and proportional equality (Rees 1971: 92). Each model necessitates different organisational structures. The problem is the lack of clarity existing across a wide range of provision, for example the client-impact level in residential care. The role of receptionists in the welfare system is another documented example (Hall 1971). Recent research into the position of the under-twos in local authority day nurseries raises doubts, despite national and departmental policy statements, about the real client-impact level. It seems that children are treated without regard for their individual need.

> . . . the care given to the infants was fragmented and failed to meet their individual needs. Physical contact with the child was brief and rarely involved eye contact . . .
>
> (Marshall 1981)

Although it is rarely expressed in this fashion, what this and many other studies, such as that of Dorothy Smith, reveal is the gap between official policy regarding client impact and the research findings. Thus, more often than not, policy declares that services are provided on the basis of professional judgement; whereas the client receives a prescribed output service. The failure to make explicit what is actually being provided perpetuates myths about control and accountability. The patient who is treated for several years by a consultant he has never seen is but one example of this myth. A King's Fund Working Party (1979: 35–36) made a similar point: 'many consultants consider that in their NHS work there are certain tasks which can only be done by subordinate doctors, although it is not clear whether this view is shared by patients'.

But to return to the main theme, how does the structural model cope with the dilemmas of delegation and control and how does it look in the light of the way directors and deputies see their role?

DELEGATION AND CONTROL IN THE STRUCTURAL MODEL

In the first place we can abandon the idea that all work in the department is delegated from the director. The notion that the work of hundreds of home helps, care attendants, domestics, drivers, gardeners, cleaners, nursery nurses, day care instructors, social workers, social work assistants, heads of establishments, etc. is all sub-delegated from the director is difficult to sustain. He or she is paid a rather substantial sum of money to do something else – that which we have defined as ensuring the societal impact. In so doing, they may require *assistance*. The deputy is an obvious candidate for such work. Other 'managerial' roles (see Chapter 4) may also be complex or onerous and also require assistance.

Second, a structural approach implies that the very concept of 'an SSD' implies a basic expected level of work – a client impact. This exists immediately the department is created. This work is not delegated, but forms an essential part of the defining boundary of the organisation. It needs to be *controlled* if political accountability is to be maintained.

I have thus incorporated both the top-down and bottom-up approaches in one model, but in a very different fashion. This can be illustrated by examining Figure 5.3 which is an attempt to display the way in which the model might work in a typical London borough. In this much simplified structure, societal impact is vested in the role of the director. There is a hybrid client impact (see Chapter 3) of social workers and home helps whose work is controlled and managed by area officers and home-help organisers. Because neither area officers nor home-help organisers can cope on their own, they require assistance from team leaders and assistant home-help organisers respectively. In this model social workers are expected to respond at Level 2, but they have no assistants to help them. The line of control moves directly from area officers to the assistant director (fieldwork) who needs the assistance of principal officers. The line of control leads from assistant director to the director who has a deputy in an assistance role.

There are many other possible models, and there is no overwhelming virtue in this one compared to others. However, this type of model building does enable clear statements of control and assistance to be made. Directors should do directorial level work – and that can be defined. They cannot escape in this model the control of their departments.

SUMMARY AND CONCLUSIONS

The research project and study illustrate the continuing problem of bureaucratic 'delegation' and control. In the search for explanatory models, a modest examination has been made of the public and social administration literature. Public administrators often focus on the reconciliation of political control and delegation to officials, whereas social administrators have been rather more concerned with the place of a

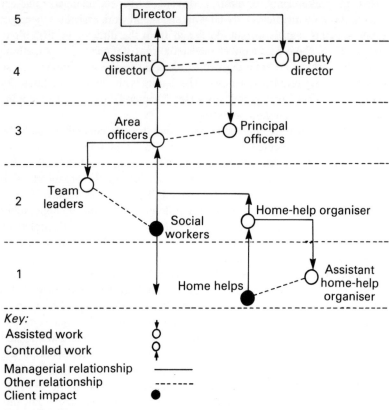

Figure 5.3 Some examples of control and assistance roles in the fieldwork
division of a London borough SSD

professional delivery of service. The statements of directors and deputies in
our study reinforce these dilemmas. Political sensitivity and the importance
of issues likely to hit the headlines vindicate a top-down model. Yet the
lack of clarity over the meaning of delegation, and the divorce from grass
roots of senior management revealed in other research, indicates that the
bottom-up approach cannot be ignored.

I have argued that neither the bottom-up nor the top-down models can
cope with the complexities of large-scale welfare bureaucracies. A
structural model which distinguishes (a) societal from client impact and (b)
control from assistance has been outlined. In passing it has been suggested
that the client-impact level is unclear in many areas of SSD provision. By
distinguishing two different client impacts I have attempted to show links

with the issues of political control and professional discretion. It has not been suggested that one model is 'better' than the other, but that there are advantages and disadvantages that can be made explicit.

6 Development

IN DEFENCE OF HAIR-SPLITTING

It is not often that we have the opportunity to explore in some detail the introduction of a new administrative concept. Sometimes the exploration is not a luxury but a necessity. An organisation, or set of organisations, may embark on an anticipated mild flirtation with the newcomer. The affair becomes more serious. The term spreads, takes root, and over the years its origins become shrouded in mystery. There may even be a correlation between ambiguity and administrative longevity. Portmanteau terms implying much and saying little may suit a particular strategy (Donnison et al. 1970: 118–119). Enquiry into the meanings behind organisational vocabulary may appear to be fruitless, or counterproductive. Why bother? Undertaking the daunting task of analysing the word 'administration', Dunsire (1973:viii) finds it necessary to pose a similar question. 'Does it matter?' After all: 'To a practising administrator, of all men, cerebration about "administration" in the abstract goes decidedly against the grain . . . '.

Dunsire's defence of 'hair-splitting' suits well our own purposes. 'Distinctions are hair-splitting [he argues], only so long as we do not need them for purposes of our own; if we do come to need them, yet do not quite realise it, we may go on using one term in several senses, and fail to communicate' (p.ix). Brown (1971: 19–20) writes in similar vein. He points out that concepts depend on 'shared perceptions', that mental models depend on concepts and that without such models we cannot understand social institutions. Hair-splitting may therefore be seen as an essential component of concept and model building. And on this more general issue of model building we close the defence with a comment of the late Richard Titmuss:

> The purpose of model-building is not to admire the architecture of the building, but to help us to see some order in all the disorder and

confusion of facts, systems and choices concerning certain areas of our economic and social life.

(Titmuss 1974: 30)

Analysis has its dangers. Bell and Newby (1971: 27), discussing theories of 'community', refer to the 'thriving sociological industry' in which the *pièce de résistance* was Hillery's analysis of no fewer than ninety-four definitions. Our discussion of development is not intended to join that particular industrial scene. We are concerned with disentanglement, with hair-splitting as a prelude to model building and organisational problem solving.

DEVELOPMENT AS A PHENOMENON OF SOCIAL SERVICES DEPARTMENTS (SSDs)

Of course, the introduction of a particular term in one context may be greeted elsewhere with yawns of *déjà vu*. The analysis that follows may have, at least in part, wider significance. The main purpose, however, is the attempt to capture a phase in the history of a set of organisations (SSDs) in order to illustrate the way in which new terminology is introduced in response to changed objectives and the ease with which problems become buried and obscured by the new language.

We start by noting that the term we shall be exploring is essentially a 'post-Seebohm' phenomenon. It can hardly be accidental that the creation of SSDs after 1970 brought in its wake a trail of new distinctive phrases. Development, research, planning, training (amongst others) have blossomed in the wake of the main-stream activities. The Seebohm Committee were anxious lest their proposals be seen merely as a reshuffle of existing functions:

> ... we have stressed that we see our proposals ... as embodying a wider conception of social service, directed to the well-being of the whole of the community and not only of social casualties ...

(Seebohm 1968: para. 474)

Whether the brave new role allocated to the departments has in fact materialised is a moot point. These are early days to be passing judgements. The relevant point for our discussion is, however, precisely the organisational consequent of the changed objectives. The Committee itself was quite aware that the leap to 'community tasks' would necessitate a 'community focus' and talked somewhat vaguely about '... developing and utilising research and intelligence services ...' (para. 592). Indeed, one member of the Committee, writing just before the implementation of the

Report, saw the proposed intelligence and research units not only as providing data on 'real needs', but also as a political lever at local and national level. That is to say that local authorities would have an eye on what level of provision their neighbours were providing and central government might also ' . . . encourage the less ambitious authorities to raise their standards' where such authorities were below the average (Parker 1970: 113). Other authors used development as an activity in its own right (Kogan and Terry 1971, Rowbottom and Hey 1970). We are suggesting, therefore, that 'development' is one of those terms that stems from the creation of departments which are not merely *amalgamations* but 'creative innovations' (Shumpeter 1947).

We shall see that the term has now become an organisational pot-pourri whose ingredients are no longer readily identifiable. One of our central themes will be that by establishing duties, posts and sections with a development tag, SSDs might be responding to a number of different phenomena and that the absence of 'shared perceptions' can leave the real problems to fester. The following exploration highlights a number of major situations where development has been utilised as a convenient organisational response – as a response to: (1) criticism of existing standards; (2) problems of organisational structure; (3) absence of new activities. Finally, we shall consider the notion of development as social experimentation.

DEVELOPMENT AS A CRITICISM OF EXISTING STANDARDS

A familiar complaint is that standards of service in SSDs have deteriorated. The accuracy, or otherwise, of this criticism is not a direct preoccupation of this paper (although it is difficult to imagine that standards could be raised without solving some of the acute problems illustrated). Here the important factor is that some departments judge that standards have fallen. Consequently, in an effort to make good the shortfall, new posts may be established. Has a genuine diagnosis been made? Will the new post provide a remedy? In many cases, we suggest, criticisms made about the quality of service delivery are in fact judgements of the work of specific individuals and groups and their inability to achieve expected levels of performance – an inability which might be attributed to a failure in personal capacity or other reasons, such as inadequate resources. These two possibilities are illustrated in Figure 6.1.

In both examples (Figure 6.1a and b) staff X and Y are expected to attain a more or less specific level of performance. As Jaques has shown, all work contains both prescribed and discretionary elements, although:

At times it may seem that so much of the content of responsibility may be prescribed that little or no discretion appears to be left in a job.

(Jaques 1967: 79)

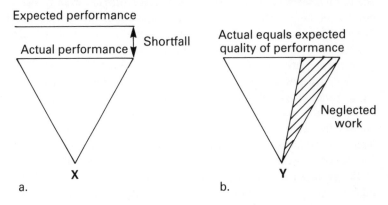

Figure 6.1 Expected and actual performance

If we reduce the discretionary content of a job to near zero we 'dehumanise it. It can be better done by a machine' (p.81). Building on the work of Jaques, the author and colleagues have been engaged in developing a theory of the stratification of work in organisations. From this emerging theory we put forward the thesis that there is a hierarchy of discrete work-levels in which the range of the ends or objectives to be achieved, and the range of environmental circumstances to be taken into account, both broaden and change in quality at each successive step (see Chapter 2). The relevance of our present discussion is that it is only in the lowest level of work (Level 1) that output can be completely specified (as far as is significant) beforehand; i.e. that *output* (not discretion) can be prescribed. At Level 2 and above, the output can be only partially specified beforehand – appraisal and assessment of the situation are required. In social work the critical boundary would be between those staff who are judged to be capable of being accountable for a case (Level 2), and those who are not (Level 1). This is a distinction of considerable significance for departments and society. More detailed examination of this theme would take us far afield; its application for social work in the residential setting is analysed in Chapter 4.

We are now in a position to see that the level of performance expected of X and Y in Figure 6.1 might be more or less susceptible to any form of external measurement. It is only where outputs are tightly prescribed and discretion minimal that measurement of 'standards of service' could be attempted. And even in this case measurement is hazardous and can provide only a crude guideline. Take two authorities whose populations cannot be distinguished in any significant way one from the other in terms of their needs for meals on wheels. Both authorities provide exactly the same number of meals per thousand of the population. Can we deduce that 'standards of service' are identical in both departments? Closer investigation would be required before any conclusion was reached. How, for example, are the meals being delivered? What is the nature of the interaction between the deliverer of the meal and the recipient? Are the meals being provided with courtesy and sensitivity – or deposited on the doorstep as a chore to be completed as rapidly as possible? When we attempt the more difficult task of measuring in quantitative terms outputs which can be partially prescribed – not meals but social work intervention – the link with reality becomes tenuous to the point of illusion.

Diagrammatic representation, as in Figure 6.1, should not be misconstrued. Performance, both actual and expected, assumes the presence of human evaluation – an elementary observation, but one which sometimes gets lost in the rush for the comforting concreteness of mathematical data. Figure 6.1 depicts a situation where an 'area' of work, represented by the clear triangles, needs to be covered by X and Y. But the two examples represent different situations.

In Figure 6.1a the judgement is that X really cannot 'deliver the goods'. Perhaps X has been over-promoted. Narrowing the spectrum of work is not seen to be a solution. The prognosis is that this would lead to less work being performed without any significant improvement in quality. Yet departments sometimes create new posts, possibly graded more highly than X, in the hope that the missing quality will be injected into the scene. In addition to X, who in all probability is retaining his or her original post and title, a new 'super X' is brought in to cover the same area of work. The missing quality (development) may, depending on local custom, appear as part of the new title. Alternatively, or in addition, it may loom large in the more detailed job description. Burns and Stalker refer to the familiar managerial strategy of 'bringing somebody in':

> A new job, or possibly a whole new department, may then be created, which depends for its survival on the perpetuation of the difficulty.
>
> (Burns and Stalker 1968: x)

People in organisations, like battery hens, require a minimum of space to survive. It is a puzzling thought that SSDs with their particular approach and core of staff trained in interpersonal skills appear to be, as yet, as prone to the same bureau-pathologies as other organisations.

Figure 6.1b is different. Here Y is judged to be suitable, but not to have been provided with adequate resources – Y is overloaded. Consequently, an area of work (shaded in the figure) is neglected. Some of the choices available to the department would appear to be:

1 to do nothing;
2 to reallocate Y's workload, some (not necessarily the shaded) functions being neglected;
3 to reduce Y's workload;
4 to increase resources;
5 to provide 'specialist' staff.

This last strategy is of particular interest since it can lead to a second possible use of the word 'development'. Not, as in Figure 6.1a, an injection of required quality; and not, as in choice (4) above, the provision of additional 'conventional' workers: but the introduction of some 'specialist' worker. Specialist is relative. It depends for its existence and meaning on that which is regarded as generalist. If there is no *qualitative* change in the work performed – a move to another work level – it merely means, in the words of Simon (1967: 22), 'that different persons are doing different things'.

So we have identified two distinct and conflicting usages of the term development. In Figure 6.1a there is an infusion of additional quality, a striving to attain an appropriate level of performance. But who is not in this form of the development business? Certainly, if top and middle management are not engaged in development of this sort something may be thought to have gone seriously astray. If, on the other hand, development is equated with a move into specialist work, why use the term at all? Used in this fashion, the word can be misleading, implying that other staff are not engaged in 'development'.

Job titles attract expectations. Advisers will expect to advise, consultants to be consulted, training officers to train. The title may not reflect that which is really expected from the role holder. Advice and consultancy may not be sought, and training officers may be bewildered to discover that there is little direct training for them to do. As yet we have by no means exhausted the situations to which the title development is a response.

DEVELOPMENT AS A RESPONSE TO PROBLEMS OF ORGANISATIONAL STRUCTURE

SSDs are not only much larger than the sum of their predecessors, they are vastly more complex. One director, presumably with some feeling, has referred to them as 'growing monsters' (Westland 1974). They are faced with a wide range of structural problems which are manifested in difficulties in the co-ordination of services, systems, and 'awkward' and small-scale activities. A tempting response has been to label everything that is not easily integrated – development. In other words: 'getting it together' (co-ordination) = development.

Essentially, problems of co-ordination flow from a well-known conundrum. How do we cut organisational cake and still retain its wholeness – and wholesomeness? The more complex and ambitious the work of the organisation, the greater the problems of co-ordinating the various parts (Greenwood *et al.* 1975). When we are discussing departments which are not just growing numbers of staff employed but are also passing through a stage of creative innovation, we discover problems of co-ordinating existing activities – and the 'non-existent'. First we shall examine in this section that which exists.

In general, SSDs have moved towards either a functional or geographical model of organisation. That is to say, that the second tier of operational management is either assistant directors, fieldwork, residential and day care (or some similar titles), or divisional directors of 'mini-departments'. It is not the intention of this paper to enter the minutiae of departmental structures. It is sufficient to note that both models have advantages and disadvantages and that local circumstances play a large part in shaping the preferred structure. In both instances co-ordination can be considered at least at two distinct levels: at the grass roots, the delivery of Level 2 services to clients; and at the level of systems (Level 3) the provision of frameworks within which those services can be provided in an integrated and acceptable fashion. Whilst the different overall structures will lead to variations in the precise nature of service and systems co-ordination, it is contended that the same approach can be adopted. Experience indicates that the term 'development' is primarily used in the context of systems co-ordination. However, in view of the weaknesses in the area of service co-ordination, identified in a number of reports of individual tragedies which have aroused much public concern, a brief digression would appear to be warranted.

Clients receive services from the department in a number of different settings and from a number of different specialist workers and occupational groups. It may well prove necessary to create some mechanism for co-ordinating *cases*, where a case is defined as:

> . . . an instance of the situation presented by a person or family registered by the department as in need of help or action by the department.
>
> (Rowbottom *et al.* 1974: 251)

The mechanism suggested in *Social Services Departments* is that of case

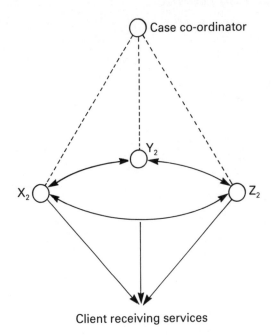

Figure 6.2 Case co-ordination

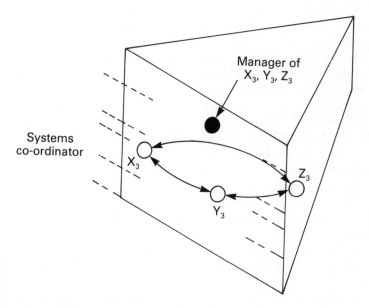

Figure 6.3 Simple systems co-ordination

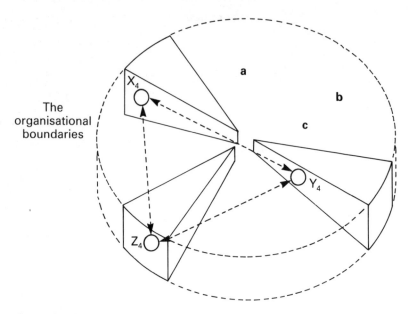

Figure 6.4 Complex systems co-ordination

co-ordination.[1] This is illustrated in Figure 6.2 where X_2, Y_2 and Z_2 represent workers providing services to the client. We turn next to systems co-ordination, a more fertile and complex field for the introduction of development.

If we return to the problem of the division of activities and the analogy of the organisation cake, we can identify two Level 3 (systems) activities – within and across the 'slices'.

The production of 'within-the-slice' systems should be straightforward or simple, resulting from the existence of one clear-cut accountable manager (see Figure 6.3). It is the increasing number of 'cross-slice' or complex interactions which present more intractable problems. The differentiation associated with the division of labour calls forth a wide variety of integrative devices – the ubiquitous working party being an outstanding example. Another possibility, where integration is required on an ongoing basis, is to create a separate role with general cross-slice duties, possibly a common reason for the establishment of 'development officer' posts (see Figure 6.4). This kind of role, which stems from integrative reasons, can be distinguished from the sort of specialist illustrated in Figure 6.1b.

The examples in Figures 6.2, 6.3, and 6.4 attempt to illustrate the propositions made so far. For diagrammatic simplicity the organisation has been represented as a closed system.[2] The diagrams, the single slice of the organisational cake illustrated in Figure 6.3, and the more complex position represented in Figure 6.4, ignore the open-system implications. In reality, systems co-ordinators are likely to be in contact with large numbers of people inside and, particularly in Figure 6.4, outside the department. The point was made that some of these co-ordinative (Level 3) posts have attracted the title development. Figure 6.4 enables us to appreciate the dynamics of organisational change which have led to such titling. We reiterate that it is mis-titling as a symptom of confusion which we are pursuing.

In Figure 6.4 six members of staff are depicted: X_4, Y_4, Z_4, a, b and c. The first three are entrenched in an explicit segment of the organisation – in the case of SSDs, probably functional or geographic divisions. Each has an identifiable boss, a network of colleagues for support and advice, and a chain of command (whatever its problems) which leads to the apex of the department. Now consider a, b and c. Their duties have not been indicated in the diagram for reasons which demand examination.

They (a, b and c) are appointed and expected to work at the same level of work as the other three members of staff. They are expected to provide frameworks within which cohesive service delivery can take place, although they may also, in varying degrees, become involved in the direct provision of services. But, in this example, they have no firm organisational base since the focus of their work does not fit precisely into one of the existing segments, nor is there any real common denominator spanning these 'isolates'. They may be working on their own, or with a few subordinate staff. Their line of accountability might be dubious, the post itself is likely to be new, the result perhaps of a sudden piece of legislation or of the creative innovation. They share only one common feature – organisational indigestibility. They straddle the existing bases of organisation. Sometimes, at one and the same time, they represent the exciting and the awkward. Training, community work, intermediate treatment, voluntary service officers, liaison officers with health – all are candidates for the development tag. In like fashion, organisational bases that have been abandoned, or never implemented, re-emerge in the guise of specialist or 'development' posts (e.g. those based on client group or social work method). These too have now an 'across-the-slice' focus. Co-ordination, integration, policy making (as we have defined it) – this is what all these posts are really about. Why not use a title that provides a less confusing sense of the main thrust of the work?

Further difficulties can arise when a, b and c are integrated into one development division with terms of reference which do not stand up to scrutiny. It is highly debatable whether the small SSD development divisions (usually combined with some additional title) can sustain substantial inner tensions. It might be more logical to link a, b and c into the segment with the closest mutual interest. That, of course, on the assumption that, having removed any obscurity buried by mis-titling, the need for the posts still exists! Combining a number of roles such as those we are now describing into one 'convenient' group causes (in the experience of this researcher) tensions at two levels. Staff at the same level strongly miss the existence of a collegiate or sentient group – it is difficult, if not impossible, to create any 'team spirit', any sense of common purpose. Above this their manager is placed in an invidious position. Where is he or she leading this disparate group? What widespread range of talent is necessary to guide and support these middle-level policy makers (a, b and c)? There *is* an attempt at rationalisation. All are concerned with the development of systems and 'resources'. Some of the individual components of development divisions make strange bedfellows: covering them with a seemingly attractive bedcover may not be a long-term alternative to the provision of a good home. At this juncture the notion of any shared perception about the meaning of development collapses. This would appear to be an extension of the argument used when discussing Figure 6.1. The same answer can be given. Which higher-level staff are not in the development business?

DEVELOPMENT AS A RESPONSE TO THE ABSENCE OF NEW HIGHER-LEVEL ACTIVITIES

Functions or activities can be absent in two senses:

1 We may *state* that they are present; but this manifest statement may not match reality.
2 They really can be absent in explicit form from organisational life.

The manifest–reality mismatch

We have already mentioned cases where recognised work was not being performed. We are concerned in this section with a very different situation. What is absent is a qualitatively higher level of work. Indeed, a large part of the difficulty lies in the absence of a comparative organisational language which would facilitate a constructive dialogue. Sadly, many existing job descriptions raise a hollow laugh from their incumbents. They (job descriptions) would appear to be most effective at the most tangible level – what we would call Level 1 work, where the output is prescribed. Not the least of our research problems is the continuing pursuit, where the need is felt, for a more precise and acceptable language. But more of this later. We are suggesting that some new, expected, qualitatively 'higher' (above Level 2) activities might in fact exist only at lower levels and that part of the trouble flows from the fact that there is no common agreement about the nature of the work. Some examples may aid in the elaboration of this theme.

A cursory glance at the formal headquarters hierarchy of SSDs is adequate to impress us with the bewildering number of permutations of planning, research, training and development (see Social Services Yearbook 1976). Indeed, each of these is often preceded by some qualifying term, e.g. forward planning, capital development, social environmental development.... What do these titles really mean? What is a 'research officer'? Are departments hiring staff who are expected: to collect some prescribed data (Level 1); to respond to some research situation themselves and perhaps instruct others what data will be needed for a specific project (Level 2); to provide a systematic research service, dealing with a continuous flow of departmental research needs and helping to formulate a policy to meet those needs (Level 3); to provide a comprehensive departmental research service, not only encompassing the current flow of research needs, but also dealing with emerging or as yet unmanifested research requirements (Level 4)?

It is critical to be aware of the real and expected level at which an activity is to be pursued. We have illustrated above very briefly the essence of what might be Level 1, 2, 3 and 4 research roles. It would appear that some departments have placed Level 3 or even Level 4 expectations on staff who, by virtue of their experience, could realistically only be expected to produce Level 2 research work. A gap, reflecting the mismatch, is created with widespread consequences. The particular consequence that concerns us is the departmental response that 'fills' this gap by undefined development.

A similar exercise could be repeated in respect of other activities. The newer activities are thus prone to attack on two fronts. Since they are new, their boundaries are unclear. And secondly, when sufficient boundary clarification is achieved, the whole complex question of level of work remains to be analysed. It is all too easy to regard 'development' as the repository of social work aspirations for the future: a future where 'real' needs will be 'researched', agency policy will be 'planned' and staff will be 'trained' – laudable objectives – providing these slogans do not hinder the critical examination of what work is actually being performed.[3]

The absence of relevant high-level activities

A more subtle variant of the absence of higher-level functions seems almost metaphysical. We might, in fact, be inclined to ignore this phenomenon were it not for its obvious importance for administrative problem solving and organisational design. What we are describing is a situation where there is as yet no institutional articulation of 'below-the-surface' unease. Here and there individuals sense that something is awry, that something important is not being done, but no authoritative forum is able to conceptualise the problem and propose a remedy. This is the fertile ground where the invited outsider can work in a collaborative manner with organisational members, analysing their problems. It is by the utilisation of this methodology that the researcher–analyst is enabled to get into the skin of the organisation to obtain shared perceptions. In the absence of internal or collaborative analysis, 'development' can eventually be found in a variety of titles which do not necessarily tackle the real need but are rather a stumbling response to the general sense of unease.

DEVELOPMENT AS SOCIAL EXPERIMENTATION

Is there a case for the utilisation of 'development' as a term in its own right? To answer this question we draw a distinction between development as a *state* or act, and development as the *process* by which the state is reached. Much of the paper so far can therefore be regarded as an examination of the organisational responses intended to achieve a state of 'normality' or 'improvement'. (We have seen that in most cases other and more suitable titles could be advantageously employed.) The responses take the form of processes, activities or strategies. Improvement is regarded as a rather vague new state which is accompanied by specialisation, co-ordination or planning as necessary prerequisites.

There is a more specific usage. This occurs when development is primarily associated with a defined new state or act, i.e. with a project or experiment. To be involved in development is now to be engaged in the production of a new product – to be 'experimenting'. So there are some SSDs where posts have been established with project development duties. Called development officers, their role would appear to be modelled on the manufacturing mode of organisation.

According to the manufacturing model, experiments can be isolated, controlled and guarded. There is an end product which may, or may not, be launched onto the market. Research is the process which, it is hoped, will result in an act of creation, or an idea. Once this is achieved development is the process of conversion of:

> . . . converting an idea . . . into an article which a factory. . . can make in

sufficient quantities and sufficiently cheaply to make the whole venture profitable.

(Burns and Stalker 1968: 158)

This is a simplistic summary of research and development in the industrial setting; there are many problems widely reported in the literature (see Brown 1971: Chapter 23). Nevertheless, the outline is sufficient for our purposes. What we wish to question is the validity of the approach for SSDs or for many service organisations. Do departments really launch experimental projects? It is suggested that they are actually involved in the very different act of social exploration (Marris and Rein 1974: 242–61).

Clients, the department's raw material, cannot be controlled in laboratory conditions, even in 'regulatory total institutions' (Webb 1971: 326). Marris and Rein (1974: 260), in their comprehensive and powerful critique of the American Community Action projects, pinpoint the dilemma:

In practice, then, the projects could not realise their claim to be experiments without abandoning their determination to benefit the communities in which they worked. They were not demonstrations but explorations of the possibilities of reform.

Explorations, the authors point out, are an integral part of the field of operation, they are pragmatic and flexible and consequently need to be retrospectively interpreted in a different manner from an experiment:

The whole process – the false starts, frustrations, adaptations, the successive recasting of intentions, the detours and conflicts – needs to be comprehended.

(Marris and Rein 1974: 260)

Self's (1974: 214) strictures about cost-benefit techniques in examining policy issues may be seen as part of the same broad approach. He points to the predicament of the economist who 'can guard the purity of his research by eschewing all contact with policy making', but if they do so ' . . . the practical utility of their work also dwindles . . . '.

It would seem that labelling social explorations 'experiments' often springs from political motives. In a study of detention centres Hilary Land concludes that:

The controversial detention centre policy gained acceptance by being labelled 'experimental', because it is very difficult to oppose an experiment. Such a tactic allowed its proponents to remain vague about the actual methods to be employed in implementing the policy on the grounds that it would restrict the experiment too much.

(Land 1975: 369)

In passing we might note that the exploration-experimentation conjuring trick is a problem for academic commentators, as well as agencies and practitioners. This is neatly illustrated by Land's interesting study which, as we have seen, although it fully appreciates the political character of the detention centre exercise, still does not question the ground rules. There is the usual emphasis on statistical data; in this instance, since reconviction rates remained high, the experiment, Land states, ' . . . could not, in 1961, be judged a great success'. The unsurprising conclusion is reached that the rapid expansion of detention centre provision in the early 1960s was not 'soundly based on the *successful* outcome of an experiment'(p.369). Since it is patently clear from her own analysis that the centres were never experiments (but explorations) we appear to have an example of kicking down an already open door.

If, as we are arguing, SSDs are concerned with explorations, not experiments, the case for project officer posts, distinct from operational staff, is questionable. Explorations, once embarked upon, become an integral part of the social territory. New explorations, whilst they may have a lengthy planning phase, rapidly become enmeshed in false starts, frustrations, adaptations and associated phenomena. It might be difficult to discern precisely when the exploration moves into a full operational state. Why not involve those who will eventually be accountable for the project, as soon as possible? Overcoming the problems encountered by new explorations might be considered invaluable experience, not to be isolated into discrete project roles. Still, we have here an issue with many more pros and cons than those mentioned. Those who decide have to live with the consequence of their decisions; which leads us back to our main purpose.

SUMMARY – WHAT'S IN A NAME?

The word 'development' poses problems for SSDs (and not just them).[4] Words, titles, can have unintended and unwanted consequences. Unrealistic expectations lead to difficulties. Take, for example, the title 'senior social worker' – a post held at some time by thousands of staff. In a small case study undertaken soon after the Seebohm reorganisation, the author writes:

> No job descriptions had been written and no discussions about their role in the newly-formed department had taken place, leaving seniors unsure of what was expected of them. Such ambiguity and conflict of role expectation encouraged a dissipation of energy and resulted in a lower standard of work.

> (Glasgow 1972: 8)

So it is with development. Dissection of the term causes us to reflect, perhaps to reconsider. A number of possibilities have been uncovered:

1 Development considered as a response to the failure to achieve some desired 'standard'. Assuming that no new qualitatively different level of work is demanded, two types of 'development people' were identified:
   a) those brought in to boost up personal inadequacies (Figure 6.1a);
   b) those who become 'specialists', who concentrate on a narrower range of activities of the same degree of complexity as the 'generalists' (Figure 6.1b).
2 Development can be regarded as co-ordination – responding at different levels to the difficulties encountered in integrating activities of growing and complex organisations. Co-ordination was considered at two distinct points:
   a) at the grass roots, putting together the delivery of direct services to clients (Figure 6.2);
   b) systems co-ordination, providing frameworks within which the grass-roots work can be implemented (Figures 6.3 and 6.4).
3 Development reflecting the absence of higher-level work:
   a) as a response to the mismatch between stated, expected performance and reality;
   b) as a response to a general sense of unease.
4 Development as social experimentation. An implicit manufacturing approach is adopted and project officers launch the new pseudo-experiments.

What then is in a name? Sometimes very little. Certainly not always sufficient to justify the effort of serious investigation. If, on the other hand, there is widespread evidence of distress and unease concerning the usage of a particular term, this surely is a storm signal to be taken seriously by researchers in the field of administration.

Our initial starting point has been the weighty problems faced by staff in SSDs. The question might be raised whether this approach *merely* justifies the *status quo* and makes life easier for departmental staff. Such an assumption would be gross misrepresentation and under-evaluation of the nature of the relationship between 'outsider' (researcher–analyst) and 'insider'. That is a task beyond the boundaries of the present study and is dealt with elsewhere (Rowbottom 1977). We must be content to emphasise that a genuine collaborative relationship is not entered into lightly. There need be few limits to the search for shared perceptions and alternative models. One case study traces the often painful twists and turns which a joint search can invoke; at least one participant was quite explicit that he might be 'talking myself out of a job' (Billis 1973: 459). Uncovering the meanings of the term 'development' may be no less painful. As we have tried to illustrate, departmental aims and objectives might be seen in a different light. In this discussion we have attempted to indicate some of the misconceptions which are already enmeshed in the new social services departments.

We are thus, it is hoped, providing potential tools for administrative problem solving with a set of public service agencies whose impact is already felt by vast numbers of citizens in critical areas of their social lives.

NOTES

1   The definition of case co-ordination provided in *Social Services Departments* (see R.W. Rowbottom, A.M. Hey, and D. Billis, *Social Services Departments*, Heinemann, 1974, p. 252) is as follows:
   a)proposing necessary tasks in relation to the total needs, short-and long-term, of the case; (and then, assuming agreement):
   b)negotiating co-ordinated work programmes and procedures;
   c)arranging the allocation of existing resources to colleagues or arranging the provision of additional resources where necessary;
   d)keeping informed of action and progress in the case;
   e)helping to overcome problems encountered by other colleagues;
   f) providing relevant information to other colleagues, including information on progress;
   g)reporting on progress to superior.
2   For a general background and discussion of closed and open systems, see F. Emery (ed.) *Systems Thinking*, Penguin, 1969.
3   A Working Party set up by the British Association of Social Workers echoes the same theme: 'One of the problems has undoubtedly been a lack of clear definition about the various tasks (and personnel required to perform them) which need to be undertaken by social services departments'. BASW *News*, 24 July 1975.
4   In this connection, see R.S. Milne, 'Bureaucracy and Development Administration', *Public Administration*, Winter 1973, pp.411–25. Whilst he is dealing with a much greater spectrum, some of the similarities are interesting, in particular the different usages of the term 'development administration', pp.411–12.

7   Prevention

'Prevention' in the field of social services, as elsewhere, is an attractive, almost irresistible ambition. It is a slogan which appeals to politicians, academics, social policy makers, practitioners and recipients. Its popularity is easy to understand. For politicians of the left, the concept is part of the progress towards a better society where the social ills of capitalism will be diminished, if not eliminated. For the political right, prevention – by lessening those same ills (if differently defined) – holds out the hope of reduced government intervention and expenditure. For practitioners, 'preventive work' may succeed in attracting new sources of funds and also provide a renewed burst of energy and inspiration to spirits dampened by the apparently endless stream of the sick and distressed. For many social administrators prevention might be regarded as belonging to what has been interpreted as 'the social conscience tradition' – which includes amongst its beliefs a view of the state as 'benevolent', with 'welfare as its aim'.[1] Recipients of preventive services are hardly likely to complain. After all, why suffer tomorrow what can be prevented today?

In general, enthusiasm for prevention might be viewed as part and parcel of the preference for optimistic language in social policy. Thus, we prefer to speak of departments of 'health', 'housing', 'social services', 'social security', when, in the first place, what we are concerned with are problems of ill health, homelessness, social distress and insecurity. Donnison (1979: 17–20), a writer who has spanned the academic and practitioner worlds, expressed this point firmly: bureaucracies 'are organised to formulate and solve particular types of problems'. The logic of 'preventive work' seems so clear-cut, so uncontroversial, that any criticism runs the risk of appearing short-sighted and reactionary. So the concept marches on – and is to be found in most social welfare statements. The Seebohm Report, probably the major welfare document of this period, devotes an entire chapter to the issue. But, as Hall (1976: 10) points out, the pressures for change and the increasing emphasis on 'the need to prevent social ills rather than to merely treat the symptoms' date from the 1940s onwards. These pressures were to find particular expression in the Younghusband (1959), Ingleby (1960), McBoyle (1963), Longford (1964) and Kilbrandon (1964) reports. And an examination of these reports demonstrates that the emergence of the preventive theme in the case of child neglect or ill treatment, for example, in turn stretches back to a series of ministerial circulars issued in 1950.[2]

Advocates of the prevention stance (and the Seebohm Committee present what might be considered a classic exposition) do, however, face a generally acknowledged dilemma. The concept is slippery. Although, as a unifying slogan it is difficult to upstage, as a tool for action in the world of social problems it has proved decidedly inadequate. Honest advocates accept the operational difficulties but frequently march on, usually seeking refuge in the standard call for 'more research'. The logic, or principle, of prevention is rarely scrutinised. It is even rarer to find a discussion of possible disbenefits, or unintended consequences of attempting to translate a confused slogan into service delivery. Whilst the pursuit of illogicality in public declarations can be both easy and trivial, selective hunting can be crucial to the development of competent social policy. It should appeal to theoreticians and hard-headed pragmatists. Prevention in social welfare has spread to the point where culling is required.

This article falls into three parts. It begins by commenting on the way in which prevention might most persuasively be used when discussing causal links in the physical world. These brief comments serve as a backcloth against which the notion of prevention, as it is employed in the personal social services, can be explored in part two. The final section discusses the unintended consequences of the belief in prevention. Overall, the article might be regarded as an attempt to extend the range of 'plausible accounts' of welfare developments – the production of a 'wider range of explanations' (Carrier and Kendell 1977: 287).

PREVENTION IN THE PHYSICAL WORLD

In order to be persuaded that prevention, as used in discussions of social problems, is not merely slippery but misguided, it is helpful first to consider its legitimate usage. Thus, it can be utilised in the physical world where the straightforward meaning is to 'stop'. It is most convincingly employed when considering the impact of one physical factor producing one physical result. Thus, the causal link could be described as follows:

(Physical) Causal *factor* A acts on physical *factor* B results in Problem P_1

$$or (A \rightarrow B) \rightarrow P_1$$

Table 7.1 depicts several of these causal links.

Table 7.1 Prevention in the physical world

A	acts on	B	causes	P_1
Nail		Tyre		Puncture
Deluge		Land		Flood
Frost		Pipe		Crack
Match		Paper		Forest fire

In this first set of examples (as indeed in the second group, given below) a 'non-problem' state B is changed by the impact of another factor A into a situation which may be regarded by an individual or group as a problem. The second, somewhat more complex, set of examples results in an impact being made on human beings, but still with only one causal factor, for example:

snake bites human → illness
mosquito bites human → malaria
spark enters eye → inflammation

We could proceed to get more complex and tenuous interactions such as the link between cholesterol and heart attack, pollen and hay fever, etc. The general point to be made is that in the material world (including the situations where human beings are treated as if they were part of that world) it is indeed possible to talk of 'prevention' as action taken to avoid the occurrence of an anticipated specific problem. From the few examples given so far it can be seen that the problem of control varies; broadly speaking, it entails taking action at one of the three points of the chain. This can involve:

1 *eliminating* or avoiding the causal factor (A) – whilst this is probably not possible for 'acts of nature' (storms, severe frosts, draughts), in other cases it is feasible – swamps can be drained, mosquitoes sprayed, and so on;
2 *isolating*, or erecting a barrier between A and B, e.g. flood barriers, walls, fire trenches, protective goggles;
3 *immunising* or 'treating' B (the non-problem state) in order to minimise the problems should steps (1) and/or (2) not be possible – in the case of humans this may involve taking pills or having injections.

Even in these apparently 'straightforward' examples, it is as well to remember that we live in a world of what Popper (1972) calls 'tentative theory'. We need only recall the difficulties encountered in the attempts to 'prevent' nuclear accidents, or malaria; and the claims made about the adverse and unanticipated effects of fluoridisation programmes. These serve as timely reminders of their essential tentativeness, even when considering apparently persuasive causal statements – and all this is simple stuff when compared with the complex multi-functional processes involved in a discussion of social problems.

If, as is suggested, prevention can mainly be used in the physical world with single factor causes and effects and involves elimination, isolation or immunisation – how then is the term used in the world of social problems and in particular in social services?

PREVENTION IN THE PERSONAL SOCIAL SERVICES

'Prevention' has become so widespread as an acceptable rallying call that a comprehensive analysis of all the usages of the word would be a formidable task. However, many of these usages do not refer to the avoidance of future undesirable states by taking action in a problemless present, but are statements in fact about current problems and the ways in which they should be resolved. Prevention, as used in social welfare, usually means taking action which is judged socially desirable in its own right. (That this is not merely a question of semantics but does real damage will be examined later.) But first, many current usages can, for convenience, be grouped under four subheadings: prevention as

1 dealing with 'at risk' situations;
2 administrative innovation;
3 extra-agency work;
4 the prevention of everything – and everything as prevention.

Prevention and risk indicators

The notion that an individual, group or geographic area is 'at risk' is part and parcel of the belief in prevention and can be subjected to a similar analysis. Since there is an obvious local absurdity in defining a situation as 'at risk' if we already have the problem, it should, like prevention, refer to a problemless present state. Nevertheless, this form of argument is often used. Thus, the Seebohm Committee suggested that the personal social services should adopt as one of its 'main strategies' the extra concentration of effort and resources in specific geographical areas of 'comprehensive high risk'. These would be 'areas characterised by rapid population turn-over, high delinquency, child deprivation and mental illness rates, and other indices of social pathology' – this action would, it was claimed, 'constitute a major contribution to the prevention of social distress' (Seebohm 1968: Chapter 14). Here we have a list of existing social problems which *deserve attention in their own right*; the 'distress' exists already.

In a critical analysis, Rutter (1978), although unwilling to abandon prevention as a useful concept, nevertheless builds up a formidable critique of the way in which what he calls 'risk indicators' are used. In his discussion of the 'prevention of psycho-social disorders in childhood', Rutter points out that there is ample data:

> Showing that children with mentally ill parents, or living in an overcrowded home, or from a low social status family, or from a broken home, or admitted into care, are more likely than other children to develop psychiatric problems or be educationally retarded.
>
> (Rutter 1978: 107)

However, he emphasises that what we have are *risk indicators* and that 'we know far less about *why* children are at risk'. We might add that these risk indicators, like Seebohm's 'indices', also appear to refer to issues deserving attention in their own right.

Rutter moves on to raise further fundamental questions about the general striving to reduce the frequency of 'risk experience' – is, he asks, such striving 'sensible'? May it even be 'damaging'? In different fields, other authors have worried about these issues. Thorpe, Paley and Green (1979), writing about children in trouble, have pointed to what they refer to as the 'hazardous' nature of the 'concept of prevention' – which they too are unwilling to abandon completely. They question 'whether the information generated by preventive work might not make the child more vulnerable if and when he does appear before a court'. These authors make the gentle observation that 'preventive work . . . may have unintended consequences'.

In the light of our earlier discussion of prevention in the physical world, it appears that the use of risk indicators may involve an assumptive leap from *associating* particular problems with some conditions to *explaining* these problems as *caused* by those conditions. Not only is it impossible to posit such emphatic causal links, but it would be wise to consider the possible unanticipated and damaging consequences of any intervention. Carrier and Kendell (1977: 286) make a similar point.

Prevention as administrative innovation – or just doing the job

There is a wide range of so-called preventive work which might all be summed up as – doing the work which the agency was legally sanctioned to perform. Sometimes the word 'prevention' is used when describing additional services, on other occasions when providing alternative administrative solutions, and sometimes just to indicate that investigation and publicity are useful adjuncts to departmental work. The Younghusband Report demonstrates the way in which prevention began to be used to embrace: a widening of functions (para. 200), additional services (para. 201), more intensive work (para. 444), and 'co-ordination and teamwork' (Chapter 12). All this is regarded as 'prevention' – but once again the work is being done with people who already have problems. Smith (1980), in a case study of the concept of 'need', noted a similar tendency to use the term in a variety of ways: 'in practice in this department "prevention" is a residual category for cases in which "general support is deemed necessary"'.

In like fashion, the popularity of that equally slippery concept 'community care' can in part be regarded as an attempt to find alternative organisational solutions to another administrative solution – residential care.[3] Prevention, used in this context, mostly refers to the avoidance of residential care; but residential care is itself an administrative construct and not a disease. In fact, it is possible to visualise a superb standard of care to which there might be fewer objections (say, five-star hotel standards with all the necessary social and medical support that was required). It would be well beyond our present resources but it does make the point that objections to residential care take place within the context of present facilities, and in particular the cost of such facilities. Similarly, fostering is seen as 'preventive' rather than as an alternative, and fortunately cheaper, administrative solution.

Finally, under this section might be included the use of 'prevention' to replace the less exciting and politically acceptable words 'investigation' or 'detection'. What is really happening is that additional efforts are being made to uncover people with problems. This is the emphasis that the Ingleby Report stresses in its discussion of the prevention of neglect in the home (Ingleby 1960: paras 38–45). The report provides a three-stage analysis: the detection of families at risk; the investigation and diagnosis of the problem; and treatment, the provision of facilities and services to meet the families' needs and to reduce the stresses and dangers that they face. The last two stages would appear to be concerned with good practice, rather than any distinct preventive activity. And indeed, it appears to be the first stage (detection) that Ingleby regards as 'genuine' prevention. But here the analysis is muddled. The comprehensive identification of people with problems is interchanged with references to the 'discovery' of situations which are not as yet seen as problems by the individuals concerned. This belief in the professional ability (and right) to intervene in 'pre-problem' states would seem to be the precursor of Seebohm's 'preventive strategy', and leads to what I will shortly describe as 'the prevention of everything'.

Successful detection, as in the case of several surveys done in connection with the Chronically Sick and Disabled Persons Act, 1970, can bring its own problems. The newly discovered clients might actually expect to receive the publicised services!

Prevention as extra-agency work

There is a temptation for those working in one sphere to see preventionist grass growing in the apparently more fertile fields which should be tilled by other agencies. Thus, under its definition of general prevention, the two examples offered by Seebohm are housing and services for the under-fives. It can be argued that nearly all of the detailed activities described under these headings are, or should be, the mainstream work of other departments.

Switching the focus for a moment to another public agency, the police, it is interesting to note the comments of a senior police officer emphasising that 'prevention was also the most important development in police work with youngsters' (Community Care 1980). So, police in that particular area were working to foster activities for young people. (Although in fairness it must be pointed out that the intention was that these activities could then be handed to key people in the locality.)

However, returning to the social services setting, the Seebohm Committee defined 'general prevention' as action aimed at creating environments conducive to social well-being, as service or policy which leads to better or more health, education, housing, equity, and prosperity. So, in its broadest interpretation any policy blueprint, from whatever part of the political spectrum, could be considered 'preventive', since all such manifestos presumably promise a 'better' life.

The prevention of everything – and everything as prevention

It is when 'prevention' is taken to describe intervention in unbounded 'problem-situations' that the term can become stretched to mean the prevention of almost everything. So, we find the Seebohm Report describing a 'preventive strategy' whose aim is to 'assist the individual to achieve a reasonably satisfactory readjustment and avoid the risks which beset him in periods of considerable change'. The school-leaver, the early years of the family, pre-retirement, bereavement, are some of the examples given. But why end here? Equally radical changes might be entering school, examination periods, redundancy, promotion, divorce, appearance of the first brother or sister, change of job, and so on. Indeed Geismar (1969: 123) argues for a 'neighbourhood-wide preventive service' whose main thrust would be on:

- helping families become more effectively related to their environment, and
- dealing with minor intra-familial problems arising out of the normal developmental processes such as childbirth, changing jobs and homes, school attendance, adolescence, etc.

In the current economic climate it is difficult to believe that Seebohm's vision of a 'riskless' future, where individuals will be assisted in periods of 'considerable change', could have been seriously propagated. This example demonstrates the persuasive power of 'preventionism' – the belief that social problems can be prevented rather than resolved.

We have already noted the confusion caused in the Ingleby Report by the failure to differentiate between (a) the detection of actual problems and (b) intervention in non-problem, or 'pre-problem', states. There is a further preventionist stance which is used when intervening to 'prevent' the deterioration of an existing problem into an even more undesirable state. This is a popular approach for those authors who have no difficulty in emphatically positing definite causal links between the most complex social phenomena. Thus, Leonard (1971) has argued that social workers should become involved in what he calls 'primary prevention' – that is to say, 'the pre-conditions, the general circumstances from which social problems develop'. (This argument extends well beyond the more 'modest' Seebohm ambition of extra-agency policy intervention.) But this stance, and the less radical approaches which regard prevention as intervention to 'prevent deterioration' must confront the following question: what operational work in social welfare agencies does not have this (halting further deterioration) as its ambition? Used this way, all work, everything, is preventive.

In this section, several usages of 'prevention' in social services have been explored, for convenience, under four headings. We have noted how – unlike the position in the material world – these usages are not concerned with the avoidance of anticipated specific problems in a 'non-problem' present state. Instead, we have found activities aimed at resolving existing real problems, activities which should be part and parcel of the 'good' organisation, activities which belong to other agencies and, finally, activities which cover just about everything – all variously described as preventive. In the final part of this article it will be argued that preventionism harms clients, staff, and the community as a whole.

THE DANGERS OF PREVENTIONISM

Preventionism, by implying a false dichotomy between 'work' and 'preventive work' within the boundaries of the same department, leads to a built-in predisposition for conflict and contributes to:

1 an unfair deal for clients, those receiving services, and those who ought to be receiving services;
2 confusion and status differentials for departmental staff;
3 problems for the community as a whole.

Preventionism and the client

Preventionism can contribute to inequitable treatment for clients actively receiving services from social service agencies by creating a general culture of two classes of client – those whose problems can be 'prevented' and those who must have needs or problems. Recent research by Holmes and Maizels (1976) convincingly demonstrates how field social workers (who, although a minority of departmental employees, are undoubtedly the predominant professional group) have a distinct order of preference amongst clients. There are, as the authors put it, 'two systems of status hierarchy' operating. Low-status client groups, in particular the elderly and the physically handicapped, are matched with low-status employees, social work assistants and volunteers. Their research shows that over four-fifths of elderly clients, and more than three-quarters of all the physically handicapped clients go to those staff who are unqualified in the social work sense.[4] Here is an example of that dilemma and predisposition for conflict mentioned previously. *Social workers regard ('non-preventible') categories of client as low status.* (Illich (1976:96) suggests that a 'preventive disease-hunt . . . gives epidemic proportions to diagnosis', which in turn requires 'submission to the authority of specialised personnel'.) But at the very least we might question the logic of establishing agencies with a dominant professional group who are unwilling, or at least unhappy, about working with a substantial client group.

Inclusion of preventive work as a category of work distinct from the main operational activities of the department can also lead to inequitable treatment for those who *ought* to be receiving services. What is the justification for the same social services department investing heavily in educational and recreational type intermediate treatment activities with children in 'at risk' neighbourhoods, but at the same time not providing sufficient day care places for its mentally handicapped adults? Is it unfair to suggest that work with the mentally handicapped does not offer the same rewards to professional and political aspirations? The provision of services for 'at risk' pre-problem populations in a situation of departmentally defined budgets is at the expense of those already suffering from severe social problems. Furthermore, many such services have been *ad hoc* and unplanned. It is usually a matter of luck whether particular clients receive day centre facilities. (For example, even in the halcyon years following the Seebohm reorganisation, research by Rowbottom *et al.* (1974: Chapter 7) showed the haphazard nature of day care provision.)

It might be argued – a trifle cynically – that the provision of certain services disguises the real work of social services departments. A little 'prevention' goes a long way and enables agencies to claim to be 'forward-looking', 'progressive', 'creative', and all the other obviously virtuous characteristics. It is doubtful whether the inclusion of these services as peripheral functions within social services departments has stood us in good stead.

Prevention and departmental staff

The dubious culture of preventionism is of importance not only for clients but also for staff, who in turn influence the quality of service. The notion that there is something called 'preventive work', which can take place alongside something which must presumably be regarded as non-preventive work, distorts the status of different types of work. It is not only that, as Holmes and Maizels (1976) have shown, fieldworkers prefer not to work with certain categories of clients whose problems – we have argued here – are regarded as non-preventible. The whole payment and salary structure of the department is biased towards those who work with high-status clients. Despite recent (belated) improvements in the pay of residential staff, they, together with most day centre staff, are paid more poorly, have less training facilities and fewer career prospects.

There is also a wider case to be made against prevention and its impact on staff which relates to the unreal expectations held by the community and by staff themselves. For, if practitioners and policy makers at all levels claim that problems can be prevented, they ought not to feel surprised that the public expects agencies to prevent such problems. Social services, and in particular the social work elements within the department, are caught in a dilemma partially of their own making. The more confident the claims made for professional preventive ability, the greater will be the outcry at 'scandalous' failure; thus diverting attention from the overwhelming mass of solid, mainstream, departmental work. We might also surmise that those trained 'to prevent' might feel considerable dissatisfaction or guilt. Thus, for political and departmental minds, the inclusion of 'preventive' and 'other' work within the boundaries of the same department must lead to a covert or overt dilemma.

The community 'at risk'

Cohen (1979) has argued for scepticism in discussing the 'commonsense' virtues of 'community control'. His words of caution are not inappropriate for 'prevention' – another concept from the utopian stable. He suggests that the 'arcadian vision' of community control should be subjected to 'suspicion' under a number of headings. Two of these, which often overlap in the social welfare context, are of particular interest. They are defined as follows:

– *Blurring* refers to the increasing invisibility of the boundaries of the social control apparatus;
– *Widening* refers to the increasing amount of state intervention – the 'net of social control' is widened.

Interestingly, Cohen gives intermediate treatment as an example of blurring in penal policy, since the same treatment is used for those children who have actually committed an offence and those who are thought of as 'at risk' of committing an offence. Intermediate treatment is an example that is perhaps even more relevant when considering blurring (and widening) in the social welfare context, since it is social services departments that have taken on board the major responsibility and staff associated with this new policy.

My own research into the way in which intermediate treatment is implemented illustrates how the process of blurring and widening takes place (Billis *et al.* 1980: Chapter 9). Analysis of departmental policy making demonstrated that there were a number of categories of children coming within their scope. That is to say, those children:

1 under court orders;
2 departmentally defined as 'at risk';
3 in 'at risk' neighbourhoods.

Thus, it can be seen how, by the introduction of the ubiquitous notion of 'at risk', preventionists increase the invisibility of the social control apparatus by providing the same treatment facilities, such as day centres, for those who have committed an offence and those whom the department has defined as 'at risk' (categories 1 and 2).

Preventionists *widen* the amount of state intervention by creating 'at risk' neighbourhoods (category 3), as in the case of intermediate treatment, or in other instances by classifying entire statistical populations as 'at risk'.

The 'correctional continuum' of criminology is paralleled by the 'continuum of care' in social administration.

These processes make it difficult to escape the professionally defined 'at risk' situation. Even if we are fortunate enough to avoid territorial risk, most of us leave school, have a family, retire and die. Widening can extend to the point where classification of the clientele itself becomes an absurdity for departments which, since they are involved in selective intervention, must classify who is within their province. This has driven more than one department to devise in desperation a new category of client – the 'able elderly'!

CONCLUSION

In this discussion of prevention (and its ally 'at risk') in social services, caution has been urged on two broad counts. Firstly, that as a possible tool for social policy it is intellectually confused. Secondly, that the attempt to attach meaning to and implement a sloppy idea is not of mere philosophical interest but is dysfunctional for clients, staff and the community.

The abandonment of pseudo-prevention may be a step towards the clarification of departmental boundaries based on the analysis of problems rather than the attainment of ideal states. It may take us towards not only 'workable limits to social work' (Pinker 1979b), but trimmer, more muscular, and defensible, social services departments.

The inclusion of 'work' and 'preventive work' within the boundaries of a single public agency has implications well beyond this present discussion of social services. The preventive umbrella permits an unbounded variety of work to creep into the originally sanctioned agency functions. That body of issues for which the organisation was set up in the first place can be steadily increased. For, since it is difficult to object to the apparent logic of preventive activity, it is consequently difficult to contain the steady encroachment of public agencies into areas of life that might more appropriately be left to other public or voluntary organisations, to the private sector, or to individuals and their families.

NOTES

1   For an analysis of the social conscience tradition, see John Baker, Social Conscience and Social Policy', *Journal of Social Policy*, 8: 2 (April 1979), 177–206.
2   Home Office Circular 157/150, Ministry of Health Circular 78/50, Ministry of Education Circular 225/50, Scottish Home Department Circular 7497. Referenced in Younghusband (1959) *Report of the Committee on Social*

Workers in the Local Authority Health and Welfare Services, HMSO, London, para. 202.

3 For analysis of 'community care' see T. Packwood, 'Community Care: The Universal Panacea' in Digby C. Anderson (ed.), *The Ignorance of Social Intervention*, Croom Helm, London, 1980, Chapter 4; and J. Finch and D. Groves, 'Community Care and the Family: A Case for Equal Opportunities?' *Journal of Social Policy*, 9;4 (October 1980), 487–511.

4 See also O. Stevenson and P. Parsloe *Social Service Teams: The Practitioner's View*, Department of Health and Social Security, HMSO, London, 1978; and E.M. Goldberg and R.W. Warburton *Ends and Means in Social Work*, George Allen and Unwin, London, 1979, Chapter 3.

8   Welfare bureaucracies: reflections and problems

INTRODUCTION

This final chapter of Part I reflects on some of the experiences of welfare bureaucracies in the 1970s and picks up several of the themes of previous chapters. It looks forward to the following decade and contends that two major problems would need to be resolved: the lack of clarity over boundaries, and the weakness of organisational structures.

THE FIRST DECADE

There are many ways of responding to what at any given time and place are thought to be social problems. Some are considered sufficiently important to warrant governmental responses. Some may be tackled by the non-governmental voluntary sector, others are left to private enterprise and yet others are dealt with by the family or informal neighbourhood and community groups. Much human need may never become recognised as a social problem at all. It remains 'unmet' – a possible subject for speculation and research. Precisely what problems are met by what sort of response varies between, and within, countries. Nevertheless, in the developed countries at least, there are usually core problems of social distress to which systematic, organised responses are made by government or dependable, non-state institutions such as trade unions, churches and large corporations. The extent and nature of the core issues and the balance between the different responses (governmental, voluntary, informal, etc.) appears to be largely the result of a mixture of political philosophy, economic capability, historical development and sheer chance.

As far as Europe is concerned, the comparative study of welfare administration has hardly begun. Still, recent experience of the UN European Centre for Social Welfare suggests that European social welfare agencies, their managers and staff face many common problems (see

Chapter 3). For example: what is meant by, and how do we cope with, 'decentralisation', 'participation', 'accountability', 'quality of service', 'specialisation', 'professionalism'? Is there a role for volunteers in social welfare? What should it be? How can services between different agencies be co-ordinated? And how do we organise agencies to cope with these and other problems? It seems reasonable to infer that the struggle for an understanding of welfare and its administration extends beyond national, even continental, boundaries.

This essay is primarily concerned to reflect on the experience of the social service departments (SSDs) in England and Wales. The historical background and pressures that led to the particular recommendations of the Seebohm Committee are admirably described elsewhere (Hall 1976). We need only note that SSDs were expected to be responsible for most of the personal social services previously carried out in children's departments, health departments, and (where separate) welfare departments. The new agencies were large and complex structures with hundreds, and in some cases thousands, of staff. The Seebohm Committee in a widely publicised statement recommended:

> A new local authority department, providing a community based and family oriented service, which will be available to all. This new department will, we believe, reach far beyond the discovery and rescue of social casualties; it will enable the greatest possible number of individuals to act reciprocally, giving and receiving service for the well-being of the whole community.
>
> (Seebohm 1968: para. 2)

In the first few years of the decade it seemed as if the optimistic and confident expectations of the Report would be fulfilled. Hopes were high. SSDs expanded at a feverish pace (though admittedly from a relatively low base compared to other services such as education). Benevolent politicians sanctioned the resources. A battery of additional workers appeared – advisers, consultants, development officers, researchers, training officers. More responsibilities were given to the fledgling agencies by an equally optimistic central government. Some difficulties were caused by the reorganisation in 1974 of parts of the local government system and of the national health service. But, 'in the first flush of exercising authority and power and managing resources, it seems that departments were ready to gear themselves to any social crisis' (Cooper 1980: 16–17).

A decade later the talk, and action, is of 'cuts' and 'retrenchment'. Residential homes and day centres are being closed; charges for services are being imposed and increased; staff vacancies remain unfilled. Fewer contexts were more turbulent than those experienced by SSDs in the 1970s.

In addition to the turbulence generated by political and resource uncertainties, the key departmental professional group, the social workers, were beset by internal doubt. Although only a minority of employees, it was the social work profession which dominated the commanding heights of agency policy. Directors of SSDs were expected to be qualified social workers and the appointment of an unqualified director was guaranteed to lead to protests from the British Association of Social Workers. Problems in social work arose mainly from its inability to persuade itself, and to prove to the wider community, that it had a task which was coherent, logical and essential (BASW 1977). The public image of social work had also been the subject of concern for the profession. By 1979, general frustration welled up into the first national social work strike. Social workers faced the common dilemma of human service employees – strikes could harm the vulnerable. The dilemma was aggravated by the claim to professional status. It was difficult to look 'professional' on the picket line.

The decade ended in a manner that would have been hard to foresee ten years earlier. Several critical issues awaited resolution in the next decade, including two that are the concern of this paper: the boundaries of welfare bureaucracies and the failure to find a satisfactory organisational structure.

THE BOUNDARIES OF WELFARE BUREAUCRACIES

SSDs were established within an era dominated by an interpretation of social policy which has been called the 'social conscience thesis'. European and American writers in this tradition 'see the state as benevolent. The social services have as their aim the welfare of their users; the state provides social services, the state has welfare as its aim' (Baker 1979: 195). The tenor of this thesis is generally optimistic:

- a benevolent state;
- a widening and deepening of our sense of social obligation;
- an increase in our knowledge of needs;
- a belief in cumulative change in the direction of greater generosity and wider range;
- the irreversibility of improvements;
- the belief that the central problems of social welfare have been solved.

Early discussions with staff of SSDs threw doubt on the optimism of the social conscience tradition. In 1974, the general function, or continuing goals, of SSDs appeared to be 'the prevention or relief of social distress in individuals, families and communities, in liaison with other statutory and voluntary agencies' (Rowbottom *et al.* 1974: 43). Critics had complained about the narrowness of the aim and had felt that a more positive phrase such as the 'enhancement of the quality of life' was more appropriate than the seemingly dismal concern with 'social distress'.

Is social distress still an adequate description of the boundary of welfare bureaucracies? While it is not without meaning, it remains vague. Vagueness in itself need not be problematic, were it not for the fact that we may be deceiving ourselves into believing that something is provided that is not – a situation of dubious benefit for the community. Clarification of the boundary may lead to internal consistency, a worthy achievement if the worst abuses of bureaucratic overlap in the various sectors of welfare provision are to be avoided.

I believe that the concept of *social breakdown* would lead to a more useful boundary definition than social distress. A state of breakdown means either that institutionalisation is an immediate response or, if no action is taken, then some form of institutionalisation will result within a specified period of time. The characteristic feature of breakdown is the loss of independence, a transfer of accountability for an individual's basic needs (work, leisure, and sleep) to an institution and its employed staff. Linking breakdown to judgements about institutionalisation, within an explicit period of time, is a possible safeguard against over-ambitious and 'historicist' approaches, according to which specific individuals displaying one set of problems are judged to be on an 'inevitable' decline. The addition of a time boundary is an essential element in the definition of breakdown. Without this, every intervention in human situations can be claimed to be 'preventing eventual' social distress. There would be no defence against the steady advance of professionals and bureaucrats into wider and wider areas of social life.

The dominant problems faced by the clients of present-day welfare bureaucracies are those likely to lead to loss of independence. Responsibility for the provision of basic needs is transferred from the individual or his family to an external agency sanctioned by society. These social breakdown needs can be distinguished from another category which it is proposed to call *'social discomfort'*. Using Maslow's hierarchy of needs, welfare bureaucracies deal with the most basic needs – the physiological and safety needs. Social discomfort refers to needs which are less urgent, i.e. 'the love and affection and belonging needs' (Maslow 1943 in Vroom and Deci 1970: 31).

Currently, SSDs are providing services that, while they are primarily aimed at problems of breakdown, also cater for some citizens whose major problem is social discomfort. It is believed that reducing problems of isolation and loneliness (social discomfort) should be part of the work of government bureaucracies because it will reduce amorphous 'social distress'. But the resolution of problems of social discomfort, where these are the most *pressing* needs, will not necessarily reduce social distress. Social discomfort problems must be resolved *in their own right*, but it is highly questionable whether these could, or should, be the target for systematic governmental intervention.

There exists the desire for a high degree of public accountability for social breakdown. In general, governments will either wish to control directly, or to have strong monitoring mechanisms over, the bureaucracies coping with mainstream social breakdown. Governments may also 'subcontract' the problem to solid, non-governmental agencies, whose public status and reliability is assured. However, there are two broad groups of social breakdown that suffer particularly because of the present lack of clear agency boundaries. First, there are problem categories that (at any given time and place) are considered 'abnormal' such as people who drink too much, take the wrong sort of drugs, or get beaten up by the wrong people. Political reluctance to court unpopularity by dealing with the problems of these groups means they are left to the non-governmental sector. Second, other groups are the victims of the border warfare between the breakdown bureaucracies themselves. Which agency, for example, should be responsible for the mentally handicapped in residential care? Where is the boundary between old people's homes (in SSDs) and geriatric wards?

PROBLEMS OF ORGANISATIONAL STRUCTURE

The second major unresolved problem area surrounds the continued inability to establish viable organisational structures. Two possible explanations are offered: the effects of qualitative organisational change, and the influence of what will be called 'social conscience administration'.

Qualitative organisational change

The Seebohm Committee was anxious in case its proposals were seen merely as a reshuffle of existing functions. 'We have stressed that we see our proposals . . . as embodying a wider conception of social service, directed to the well-being of the whole of the community and not only of social casualties' (Seebohm 1968: para. 474). Reorganisation was not to be just an amalgamation, but a 'creative innovation' (Shumpeter 1947). The cornerstone of the proposed department was to be the area team. It was envisaged that an area team would serve a population of 50,000–100,000 and would consist of 10–12 social workers plus home helps and their organisers.[1] 'Considerable flexibility' was expected. But beyond this, little help was offered to those who would have to establish the new system.

It soon became clear to welfare administrators that they were indeed, as Seebohm had expected, in a new ball game. Successful or not, SSDs were different. Early research indicated that the leap into another league had left many departments with what was first identified as a 'missing level of work'. The widespread phenomenon of missing levels of management might be described as the 'chewing gum effect' of qualitative organisational challenge. It arises from two prime forces. In the first place a director is appointed with executive duties and a senior 'management team' follows. The hierarchy becomes larger. Second, significant parts of the new organisation are scarcely affected by the changes. Much of the grass-roots work carries on as before, albeit in a different agency setting. In the case of SSDs this was particularly true of the work of the large numbers of staff working with clients in residential care (see Chapter 4). Thus, at one end of the organisation were to be found a mass of grass-roots workers 'attached' to the client base; while at the other end the senior management of the new agencies enlarges and grows even more distant. The final product can be two substantial ends with a very thin middle – the chewing gum effect.

The consequences of weak middle management in parts of the agency continue to plague SSDs. 'Bigger' is not just 'more' (see Chapter 3). Lack of control and accountability for operational units, absence of effective policies, doubt over standards of care, 'ad hockery' and staff disillusionment – these were but some of the consequences. Another dimension of qualitative organisational change arises from the absence of guarantees that the qualitative change upwards will be matched by a sudden influx of administrative capacity. The belief that anyone can do anything does not stand up to serious scrutiny even in the most egalitarian of societies (see Billis 1984: Chapter 14). Unplanned, qualitative, organisational change brings with it the 'hot air' effect – the rapid rise to bureaucratic heights of less than competent overseers.

The influence of social conscience administration

In addition to problems attributable to qualitative organisational change, there were specific social welfare problems. The appropriate boundary for state intervention in welfare is confused and the social conscience policy tradition has not provided satisfactory answers. Here I examine briefly a few aspects of a parallel, or doppelganger, process which might be called 'social conscience administration' – a belief in the virtues of 'decentralisation', 'delegated authority', 'staff and client participation', 'public accessibility', 'more information and co-operation', 'teamwork', 'corporate management', 'collaboration'. The underlying basis of this administrative paradigm seems to be an enchantment with Schumacher's 'Small is Beautiful' linked to a preference for two (or more) opinions on any topic.

The Seebohm Report epitomised these beliefs. It also demonstrated the tension between the policy and the administrative beliefs. The social conscience policy (the state has welfare as its aim) logically implied widespread government intervention through increasingly 'comprehensive' (and larger) bureaucracies, whereas social conscience administration yearned for the beguiling beauty of smallness. The resolution of this dilemma and the pillar of the Seebohm Committee's proposals was to be the area team:

> We attach great importance to the comprehensive area team approach in the search for an effective family social service and, as a concomitant, the delegation of the maximum authority for decisions to the area officers . . . the important points are that the social service department can only work effectively through area teams, drawing support from the communities they serve.
>
> (paras. 592, 594)

For clients of SSDs, area teams, which were widely adopted, represented *the* major new administrative construct. But the majority of clients continued to receive services either in their own homes or through the traditional bases of delivery such as residential homes and day centres.

In the event, the area team, as envisaged by Seebohm, cannot be said to have realised the hope of its progenitors. One leading academic and community worker put the matter bluntly: 'The Seebohm vision of social services departments in close contact with small committees has not become a reality' (Holman 1980: 14–15). There would probably be widespread agreement that the 'team' has not consolidated its place as a natural and basic unit of community service delivery. In support of this contention the growth of the so-called 'patch organisation', a movement that has been described as a 'quiet revolution' (Hadley and McGrath 1979: 16–18), can be cited.[2] From the limited material available so far, the revolutionary aims look remarkably similar to the original Seebohm ideals. Patch enthusiasts are *in favour of*: small geographic units of service delivery, autonomy, informal networks, seeing problems 'in context', openness, accessibility; and *against*: centralised and bureaucratic organisation. But, overall, the failure to utilise conceptual language has led to a muddled debate whereby 'areas', 'team', 'sub-teams', 'patches', and the like occupy the same organisational territory and make comparisons, let alone critical evaluation, highly speculative.

Social conscience administration may be criticised, not because its key beliefs are misguided, but because they have rarely been submitted to rigorous analysis. They remain little more than a ragbag of emotive slogans. It is not the Seebohm departments or area teams that have 'failed' (if they have); it is the academic community that has not succeeded in providing the necessary critical debate. In a powerful critique of the discipline of social policy and administration, published at the beginning of the decade, Pinker claimed:

> it is sustained today by the prestige of a few charismatic personalities. The increasing involvement of its practitioners in the actual making of social policy and in the education of social workers tempts us to confuse practical activity with intellectual development.
>
> (Pinker 1971: 12)

Pinker criticised the lack of theoretical material and wondered whether the discipline was 'little more than a motley collection of skills . . .' (p.13). Has anything changed? Writing more recently, Webb and Hobdell (1980:99) have suggested that: 'There is clearly substantial conceptual confusion to be sorted out before we reach the stage of choosing organisation structures . . .'.

It is not surprising therefore to discover a gap between managers of welfare bureaucracies, charged with policy development and implementation, and many of the newly trained professional staff, influenced by the woolliness of the social conscience tradition. In the United States this has been described as a 'double-edged' dilemma for the social work supervisor: 'Today's worker approaches his job seeking autonomy, responsibility, participation in agency operations . . . (this) may conflict with . . . organisation objectives' (Granvold 1977:79). It has been easier to blame bureaucracy and its managers than to re-examine basic beliefs. But as Wilensky (1978) reminds us: ' . . . we cannot assume that all bureaucrats are empire builders' or interested just in their own salaries and survival.

THE CHALLENGE TO SOCIAL CONSCIENCE ADMINISTRATION

There are signs that the dominant social conscience thesis is being questioned. Smith and Ames (1979) raise many important questions, casting doubt on the validity of the area team principle. Relying primarily on a review of the literature, they analyse several basic assumptions, such as improved client accessibility, closer identification with the local area, decentralised decision making, increased sense of colleague support, that form part of the social conscience administrative tradition. Cohen (1979) has examined the disbenefits of 'community care' and Pinker (1979b) has proposed a 'slimline social work'. 'Teamwork' has been explored in a joint project between the United States and the United Kingdom (Lonsdale *et al.* 1980). However, theoretical models are still scarce. Tension remains between policy and administrative beliefs. And, with a few notable exceptions, they are researched in isolation.[3]

The social conscience tradition has not encouraged serious investigation of the links between policy, its administration, and service delivery. Webb and Hobdell (1980: 98) make a similar point: 'We certainly have not begun to construct the equations which would link various types of organisations and professional practice with the quality of service received by the client'. Scholars seem unwilling to risk bureaucratic contamination. Yet, unless the present system, and its clients, are to await the millennium, it is difficult to see how administrative reform can take place in the absence of such theories.

The levels of work theory presented in Chapter 2, in conjunction with previous work on the nature of social institutions, provides the opportunity of re-examining many of the beliefs of the social conscience administrative tradition. They can be transformed into concepts capable of linking social policy with the design and construction of social welfare agencies. For example, 'decentralisation' (and other concepts such as 'planning') can by analysed in the light of the *level* of response required (see Chapter 3). As generally employed, 'decentralisation' is used in a descriptive fashion. Self points out that while most writers, politicians and officials are 'decentralists in principle . . . this favourable sentiment seems often incapable of producing effective action' (Self 1976: 72). The word is usually used to indicate either: (a) the administrative delegation of decision-making authority to lower levels in an organisation; or (b) the rights of territorial units to some measure of self-government. The messy discussion on 'patch', 'area teams' and other administrative nostrums can be made sharper and tougher by asking – what expected level of response to social need is desired? Beliefs in decentralisation can be transformed into precise statements capable of utilisation in the design and construction of welfare bureaucracies.

CONCLUSION

Large-scale, complex welfare bureaucracies dominated the field of personal social services in the 1970s. It was a turbulent and frustrating decade. Established within the optimistic 'social conscience' tradition, SSDs have struggled to meet the expectations of the public and their own staff against a background of a changing political climate and declining economy. The key professional group, like their counterparts in the United States, have been beset by problems.[4] Boundaries to professions and organisations are unclear. The SSDs have not quite worked out as expected, failing to distinguish sufficiently between social breakdown and social discomfort. Indeed, their failure to deal with social discomfort questions the role of government in this area.

Further, there is a chronic state of tension between social conscience administration (epitomised by the Seebohm Report) and its policy partner. The former emphasises smallness and consensus, while the latter implies comprehensive (large-scale) government intervention. The area team, the key Seebohm concept, is an attempt to straddle the gulf between the policy and administrative stances – an attempt to secure comprehensive welfare without 'bureaucracy'. New initiatives (the patch) illustrate the absence of conceptual analysis and the problems of implementation. The academic debate has hardly moved beyond the three 'models' of Titmuss (1974).[5] However, there are signs of progress, particularly in current work which attempts to link organisational response to social need.

The response to social problems does not have to be governmental and it does not have to be bureaucratic. But if it is and if the field is not to be abandoned completely, then additional theories must be developed (Slavin 1978: 39). Welfare bureaucracies are likely to remain with us throughout the 1980s. They, and more importantly their clients, will need, and deserve, additional and better theories of administrative reform if they are to avoid some of the worst traumas of the 1970s.

NOTES

1 In fact, many area teams were to become much more complex affairs, apart from the problem of defining what was an area team. See O. Stevenson and P. Parsloe, *Social Service Teams*, London, HMSO, 1978, p.11.

2 The European position is little clearer. 'Teamwork and co-ordination . . . are often misunderstood. (They) call for more than goodwill', Michael Philibert in *Eurosocial Newsletter* No. 16/79, Vienna.

3 In the British literature examples of exceptions would be D.V. Donnison and V. Chapman, *Social Policy and Administration*, London, Allen and Unwin, 1965; R. Hadley, A. Webb and C. Farrell, *Across the Generations*, London, Allen and Unwin, 1975.

4 Even a cursory glance at the literature indicates the parallels. For example, Scott Briar talks about the 'serious doubts among some segments of the profession about the identity of social work . . .' in *Encyclopedia of Social Work*, 16th Edition, National Association of Social Workers, 1977. See also A. W. Dibelstein, *Politics, Economics and Public Welfare*, Englewood Cliffs, NJ,

Prentice Hall, 1980, p.222. Also Y. Hasenfeld and R. A. English (eds), *Human Service Organisations*, Ann Arbor, Michigan, 1974.

5   This is an edited version of his notes, put together after his death in 1973. As the editors admit, the models ('Residual Welfare', 'Industrial Achievement' and 'Institutional Redistributive') are uneven; 'the book is somewhat unfinished'. Also Harold L. Wilensky and Charles N. Lebeaux, *Industrial Society and Social Welfare*, New York: The Free Press, 1965. See also A. Sinfield, 'Analyses in the Social Division of Welfare', *Journal of Social Policy*, Vol. 7, part 2, April 1978.

Part II

Voluntary welfare agencies

9   Voluntary sector management: research and practice[1]

INTRODUCTION

This paper is offered as a modest contribution to the *social policy debate* about the role of the sector and also as an introductory document which provides some insights or reflections on *current organisational problems* faced by voluntary agencies. Indeed, one of the main themes of the paper focuses on the usually forgotten organisational premisses upon which much of the social policy argument often rests.

THE ARGUMENT

Whilst my main concern is with the voluntary sector I shall also draw on more than a decade of research in social services departments and other governmental agencies. Given the almost total absence of research into the organisation and management of voluntary agencies, this has seemed an obvious starting point. After all, there are those who claim that 'management is management' and that the context – statutory, voluntary or private – is of relative unimportance. Whilst I might have had some sympathy with this view at the start of my work, the intervening years have demonstrated the limitations of such a stance. The accrued experience from other sectors must not be lightly dismissed when discussing voluntary sector management, but I shall argue that a major task for research and practice is the *development of usable theories and models for the voluntary sector* which respond to its distinctive problems.

And at this point I must emphasise the necessarily exploratory and tentative nature of these comments. The argument of the following sections runs something like this:

1 The current well-known stereotypes of the statutory and voluntary sectors, which are important elements in the social policy debate, have a substantial and undervalued 'organisation' or 'management' dimension.

2 There are often substantial management problems in the sector; bringing them more into the open may have an impact on the broader policy stereotype.
3 Voluntary sector management may be more complex than statutory sector management and we will need to develop more appropriate tools and theories.
4 As a contribution to that development a tentative model will be offered which might help our understanding of the particular complexities of the voluntary sector.

CURRENT STEREOTYPES

The first point may perhaps be dealt with rapidly. The state system is seen as bureaucratic, inflexible, costly, remote and insensitive to the needs of clients. The other stereotype is of a voluntary sector which is non-bureaucratic, flexible, more cost-effective and close and sensitive to needs (Hadley and Hatch 1981). Undoubtedly, this major policy debate is fuelled and underpinned by themes of a deeper, more philosophical or ideological kind – the nature of the 'just' society, individual independence and liberty, the place of representative democracy and the meaning of 'community' – to note but a few. However, I merely wish to emphasise that many of the central aspects of the stereotypes belong to a missing, unfashionable territory – 'organisation and management'.

It is not an exaggeration to claim that the debate on the role of the voluntary sector is taking place amidst an almost total ignorance of the management dimension of voluntary agencies. Here, of course, I am interpreting 'management' broadly – as I believe it ought to be interpreted. It encompasses not only issues of skills and techniques, but also – and at least as important – those deeper issues such as questions of values, policies and objectives, the response to social problems, the development of suitable organisational structures, the role of governing bodies, the relationship between centre and periphery, and issues of recruitment, training and career development (Handy 1981). The study of management will also include analysis of the meaning of such words as trust, motivation, communication, participation, public and internal accountability, charismatic leadership and so on.

Why then is management unfashionable in voluntary sector research? In part the answer might lie in the wider scene, in what Bob Pinker has called 'the lack of morale' of social administrators who 'have to face at least in the short term, the prospect of living in a type of society for which they have very little enthusiasm' (Pinker 1979a: 42). The word 'management' conjures up an unpalatable range of images – the *status quo*, inflexibility, control, conservatism, etc. For the voluntary sector there are more specific problems. The unspoken sentiment appears to be that management – if it has any legitimate place at all – should stay in the statutory sector where it belongs! Why can't we manage ourselves on the basis of our obvious stock of goodwill, flexibility, commitment and natural ability? There may be a deep and interesting underlying reason for such an attitude, which I will return to consider at the end of the paper.

UNCOVERING THE STEREOTYPES

And this brings me to the second point: one of the overwhelming lessons of our research so far is that *voluntary* organisations can also face severe problems, although these problems may not be 'publicly visible'. Most confident and vibrant agencies have welcomed the challenge to re-examine *what* they are doing, *why* and *how*; other organisations maintain an atmosphere of organisational insularity and unwillingness to bring problems into the open. In one of our workshops we explored what might be the motivating forces behind this insular stance of some voluntary organisations. Participants provided a variety of answers:

- 'Because we are insecure.'
- 'Because we live on the knife-edge of stability.'
- 'Because we have financial insecurity and charismatic figures.'

In the discussion that followed these statements it emerged that insularity might be an instinctive response to organisational anxiety, stemming from a fear that external intervention would reveal too many skeletons in the cupboard. Whilst it is easy to sympathise with this approach – after all, why endanger a going concern? – the *costs* of insularity are rarely examined. Would organisational openness really threaten organisational stability?

In the first place my experience suggests that agencies that actually admit to facing problems may well be amongst the most dynamic organisations in the sector. For example, one young agency, working in the field of handicap and generally acknowledged to be pioneering and energetic, has been fearless in opening up its policies and organisation for widespread discussion. Needless to say, I am not suggesting that problems and dynamism are positively correlated; but only that the frank *admission* that problems may exist can be the sign of a confident and forward-looking management. In passing, we may note that it may also be necessary to educate donors not to penalise frankness and to help them distinguish problems that flow from a basically healthy context and those which emanate from years of insularity and ineffective committees and staff.

Insularity may therefore be seen as a possible threat to effectiveness and even survival. I can now point to several examples where failure to open up a genuine debate about the policy of an organisation has led to the position where, to all intents and purposes, it might not have existed. I am not arguing for organisational survival *per se* as a 'good thing'. However, if, as is often the case, organisations stubbornly insist on minimal survival, they might as well do something that is less wasteful of scarce resources and more socially useful.

Sometimes it may appear that lack of finance is the real threat to agency survival and, of course, lack of resources is often a severe problem. But, for example, we cannot expect agencies whose committee members and staff are divided between and amongst themselves as to what and why they are pursuing a particular approach or goal to be very convincing in their appeals for funding. I am thinking here of one agency whose unwillingness to open up its problems for debate made it unable to produce a clear and convincing statement of its counselling policy; consequently it alienated both its potential sources of funding. Local authorities and private donors were suspicious of an agency which appeared unable to clarify its approach to 'non-directive counselling'.

The uncovering of the many organisational and management problems of the sector may present an initially uncomfortable challenge to the dominant virtuous stereotype. A growing realisation of the key role of good management will require understanding and greater sophistication from all those in contact with the sector. Thus, a central question for donors, for example, amongst others, will be whether an agency has the appropriate structure, processes and people to develop, implement and change policy.

But the admission that all may not be well on the management scene will also require a change of attitude from trustees and lay management committees. Here, too, what we might loosely call a more 'professional' approach is needed. Without entering into detail, our work with numerous agencies demonstrates an overwhelming need to educate these governing bodies regarding the role they ought to be fulfilling. The transition to greater reality – moving beyond the stereotype – may be painful; but paying attention to the management dimension will, I believe, strengthen the sector as a whole and improve the quality of service.

COMPLEXITY: THE CHALLENGE FOR RESEARCH

Neither the voluntary nor the statutory sector is likely to stand up to serious management investigation. In fact, and here I come to the third point, voluntary sector management may be more complex than the statutory sector and will present a major challenge for researchers.

Many of the ideas which have emerged primarily from work in the statutory sector have, and may continue to have, utility for problems faced by voluntary agencies. However, it seems that the types and intensity of problems presented by participants in our programme differ from those presented by statutory agencies. Some examples of the key areas of difference surround issues of organisational *goals*, *growth*, and *governance*.

I have already provided one example of *goal* unclarity in a counselling agency. Many workshop participants and several of the agencies in the collaborative research projects faced similar fundamental problems. One organisation, much influenced by the Seebohm Report, had attempted to set up a comprehensive social service, a goal which conflicted with the actual demands for its service that flowed from the community it had decided to serve. Another agency tried to implement a policy of client participation in the field of homelessness, a policy which, after interviewing staff and clients, was manifestly in contradiction to what was actually being provided, or in their opinion, could realistically be provided. In yet another agency a 'self-help' philosophy was being propounded but analysis of the work undertaken demonstrated that it was primarily a service-giving agency.

These are not semantic problems raised by academics. In every instance we were invited in because of the strains facing these agencies. In the case of the self-help versus service dilemma, the front-line staff were finding enormous difficulty in day-to-day work with groups of parents, and the groups themselves were unsure whether they were members of a democratic group controlling staff, or clients receiving services.

The strains imposed by attempting to implement goals which apparently do not comfortably co-exist may perhaps be allied to another severe problem of voluntary agencies – turbulent organisational change and, more specifically, rapid and unplanned *growth*. The fact that the voluntary sector is 'non-governmental' has *organisational*, as well as the more obvious legal, implications. Whilst I cannot, in a general and introductory paper, attempt a detailed comparative analysis of change in the statutory and voluntary sector (see Chapter 15), I will offer a few observations to justify the main contention.

What I have described elsewhere as 'qualitative' organisational change in the governmental sector flows from Act of Parliament, often preceded by a lengthy process of public debate and enquiry. A notable example of such qualitative change, that is to say, a major and distinct alteration in the organisational response to social need, was the creation of social services departments (SSDs) that followed the Seebohm Report (Billis 1984). Although few voluntary agencies can compare in size to the large post-Seebohm departments, they can experience frequent and no less dramatic organisational changes. Indeed, the very smallness of most voluntary agencies and the absence of statutory boundaries to organisational purposes permits the well-known 'flexibility' of response to need. One typical example is the self-help group which begins to take on paid staff and slowly changes its focus and becomes primarily a service-delivery agency (see following chapter).

Another major group of problems, obviously closely allied to those concerned with the organisational response to social need illustrated above, revolves around the *governance* of voluntary agencies. After all, the governing bodies ought to have a hefty say in the shape of the response to need. But, as we noted earlier, trustees, management committees and the like are all too often unclear about their role. For their part, paid staff may be no less uncertain regarding the appropriate relationships between themselves and their governing bodies. A 'them and us' situation can prevail which may become what has been described as a 'cycle of expectations' with detrimental effects for all concerned (Harris 1983). Much of our work over the past few years has involved understanding and analysing the delicate and complex issue of voluntary agency 'governance' and in particular this specific problem of the governing body/paid staff relationship. But there are other major problematic areas of governance. Here we might note, for example, the tension evident in many 'national' voluntary organisations between unitary and federal structures.

To sum up this section: the impression is that problems of organisational goals, growth, and governing structures are even more severe for voluntary than statutory management – where another set of problems (the internal structure and processes) dominates.[2] So, I am suggesting not only that voluntary sector management is problematic (which is our second point) but that there are also distinctive problems which must cause us to look very carefully at fundamental assumptions. It is the search for a possible explanation for these claims that brings us to the final and main point.

AMBIGUITY AND VOLUNTARY SECTOR MANAGEMENT

If we are to meet the practice and research challenge we need a deeper explanatory model which would both underpin what we have learnt so far and also generate new ideas. I am not sure whether such a model is best called 'sociological', 'social policy', or 'philosophical'; nevertheless, I am fairly sure that *the existence of a persuasive model is an important precondition for the development of distinctive theories and tools* for the voluntary sector. In other words, management research is not only a missing link in the social policy debate about the role of the sector, it must also make a contribution to those broader themes. Otherwise it will be no more than technocratic tinkering, invaluable though that is. Whilst we must ensure that the sector's plumbing is adequately maintained, we shall be failing in our duty if we do not explore alternative and better systems of water supply. Furthermore, such systems and tools must be capable of addressing the real issues of voluntary organisations and not merely be slogans full of popular appeal but of little real utility.

In this search for a deeper explanation we enter territory perceptively explored by the late Philip Abrams, whose contribution to voluntary sector research will be sorely missed. I am referring here to his work on neighbourhood care. He pointed out that 'the idea of neighbourhood care crosses a frontier between formally organised social action and essentially informal relationships' (Abrams 1978). He warned against the dangers of seeing social care as a continuum running from the 'informal extreme of private two-person relationships, to a formal extreme of large-scale public administration'. Drawing on the writings of Talcott Parsons, he proposed a sharp discontinuity between the public world of the bureaucrat and the private world of, for example, mothers. (He included, by the way, the voluntary agency in the formal sector.) For Abrams these were not abstractions of sociological theory but plausible explanations for the real problems of neighbourhood care that he had uncovered. Thus, whereas the majority of volunteers saw neighbourhood care as an opportunity to develop the informal provision of care, the typical organiser of neighbourhood care saw it as an extension of the formal provision of care. An evaluation of the Home Start Project by van der Eyken (1982), who draws on Abrams' work, points to a similar dilemma faced by the Home Start schemes.

These authors are using a model of distinct sectors. We might imagine this as two circles or hoops. The provision of care then falls in one or other of these circles. The problem of neighbourhood care, as Abrams put it, was that it 'straddled both options'. It is clear that this model is helpful. However, it is insufficient by itself to explain the diversity within the voluntary sector which, it will be recalled, is seen in this model as part of the formal sector. That there is more to the matter than this is evident from the different types and intensity of problems mentioned earlier. For help in furthering our understanding I shall turn to a perhaps unexpected source, the work of the anthropologist, Edmund Leach. He, like Abrams, is also concerned with the issue of frontiers and discontinuities, although not in the field of social policy.

Whilst I cannot enter into the detailed argument, Leach (1976) suggests that when we distinguish one class of things from another, let us say Category A from non-A, there is always uncertainty about where the edge of A turns into the edge of non-A. He uses a simple diagram which I have

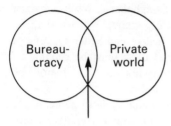

Ambiguous zone

Figure 9.1 The ambiguous zone

found most helpful. If the model used by Abrams may be thought of as two separate circles, Leach brings the two circles together until one overlaps the other. The middle overlapping area he calls the 'ambiguous zone' which he suggests is a 'source of anxiety' (see Figure 9.1).

Now, if we imagine one of these circles as the private world of individuals, friends and neighbours, the other circle might represent the sector of bureaucratic employment organisation. *I suggest that many voluntary organisations occupy the middle ambiguous zone.* The practical implications of this model are that we will not necessarily be able to push all voluntary organisations into one or other of the two sectors. We may have to understand and live with ambiguity. Let us attempt to illustrate the possible validity of this model by comparing the main definitional characteristics of bureaucracy with those of voluntary organisations.

The key features of bureaucracies are, in the main, a clear-cut differentiation between the status of:

1 employer and employee;
2 employee and non-employee;
3 providers and recipients;
4 chairperson and director;
5 director and managers;
6 managers and subordinates.

When we examine many voluntary organisations we can see how all these categories can overlap in bewildering fashion. Most of the 'big battalions' of the sector will have entered the bureaucratic circle, but large numbers are somewhere in the ambiguous zone. Thus, we find situations where employees were previously the unpaid founders of the organisation, where complex funding arrangements make it difficult to identify who really is the employer, where volunteers complicate the neatness of the division between employee and non-employee, where there may be no differentiation between managers and other roles, and where self-help groups confuse the whole caboodle by employing staff from amongst their own members *and* providing services.

I am under no illusions regarding the limitations of the model. Current research is devoted to developing 'better' models which would explain more facts and help resolve more problems. But I have now discussed the model with many people from the voluntary sector and it appears to have sufficient plausibility to be worth pursuing. It seems to help place their problems in context, and provides an explanation for many of the tensions of running voluntary organisations. Agencies are better able to understand where they have come from and where they might be going, and the difficulty of devising 'rules of the game' for the ambiguous middle ground. Moves can be made to diminish ambiguity, if the strain and price is too high, by moving further towards the private or bureaucratic worlds. Alternatively, as reported in the following chapter, the decision can be taken to split the agency. One half moves towards the self-help and private world; the other half becomes a service agency and moves further towards the bureaucratic world with its well-defined statuses and procedures.

I hope that these few examples are sufficient to illustrate the way in which many agencies may differ from fully fledged bureaucracies. In like fashion, it is not difficult to show that they are also very different from the truly private world which is bounded only by terms such as friendship and neighbourliness and where the concept of 'paid organiser', for example, is equally foreign. For that matter, so too is the notion of 'management' alien to this private world. And here we may gain further insight into the reasons for its unpopularity in voluntary agencies and come full circle back to the starting point.

CONCLUSIONS

What then are we to make of all this? I have attempted to stand on the modest mound of our experience in order to peer a little into the distance and seek out some possible challenges for research and practice.

I began by suggesting that management is a vital missing link in voluntary sector research and an undervalued element of the overall stereotype of the sector. If this is so, then research will not only aid in the resolution of technical problems, it will probe into the sensitive core of agency existence and in so doing may question the monolithic virtuous stereotype. There are challenges here for organisations to be more accessible to external intervention, for donors in their appreciation of what is actually happening, and for management researchers to develop suitable ways of working with agencies. I suggested that, despite apparent initial hazards, such collaboration will strengthen rather than weaken the sector.

Still standing on the same mound of research experience, I suggested that the voluntary sector is more complex in its management problems and that there is a different order of priorities amongst these problems. If this is the case then a major challenge for researchers is the search for appropriate tools and theories.

Finally, in an attempt to raise the mound a little higher, I explored the nature of ambiguity. The main implication that emerges from that analysis is sobering. Whilst it can fairly be claimed that management in all sectors is concerned with boundary ambiguity, no other sector has to handle the fundamental ambiguities prevalent in many voluntary organisations. The challenge to practice and theory is consequently more severe. In the 'teeth of the hurricane' will be those agencies that have left the calmer seas of 'non-bureaucracy' and not yet arrived at, or do not intend to seek, what now appears to be the relatively calmer seas of bureaucracy. It is these 'semi-bureaucracies' that might profitably come to the forefront as a major research agenda.

NOTES

1   This is a revised version of a paper originally given to the 1982 Annual Conference of the Association of Researchers into Voluntary Action (ARVAC).
2   Here a warning note is necessary. It is clear that in the last few years the position in local government has changed in many authorities – 'The basically collaborative and harmonious relationships between officers and members . . . are clearly disappearing fast', M.M. Laffin and K. Young, *The Changing Roles and Responsibilities of Local Authority Chief Officers*, Paper for the RIPA Annual Conference, September 1984.

10 Self-help and service

INTRODUCTION

In this paper we report on an action-research project undertaken with a group of one-parent families. Although every participant in the project gave permission for the material to be used for wider teaching and educational purposes, we have decided to call the group 'Riverside' to prevent any inadvertent breach of confidentiality.

We begin by providing some background to the project and the position in 1979. This is followed by a substantial section which reports the views of the participants. This has been included in an attempt to capture the real flavour and intensity of the issues as seen from different standpoints. We proceed by presenting part of the researcher's analysis of the issues (the covering report) and the group discussion which followed the presentation of that report. Next – since this was an action-research project – we report the organisational changes that were set in motion in Riverside. Finally, we reflect on the 'lessons' of the study.

THE RIVERSIDE ASSOCIATION OF ONE-PARENT FAMILIES

In the summer of 1979 an invitation was received from the 'Riverside' Association of One-Parent Families to collaborate with them in examining current organisational difficulties. Two members of the group had previously attended a workshop and had suggested to their colleagues that a longer-term association would be beneficial.

In mid-July a meeting was held with five members of the Riverside group in order to establish a strategy for collaboration with the researchers. It was agreed that the key people involved with the organisational problems of Riverside would be individually interviewed. The action-researchers would then feed back a draft report to each individual. Discussions would be confidential and participants would make additions, deletions or amendments to these draft reports until satisfied that they represented a fair statement of their views regarding the key issues. Individual reports would then be cleared for circulation to the other participants. We decided that, in order to cover the various perceptions of the Riverside position, a total of eight people would need to be interviewed. Therefore, each person would receive not only his or her own report, but also the other seven 'cleared' statements.

The researchers undertook to draw together the individual reports into a 'covering report' whose purpose was to summarise and analyse the main issues. It was made clear that there would be no 'recommendations' for action, but that if all went well alternative 'models' might be produced. It was agreed that the whole group would gather together to discuss all the material. In adopting this approach the researchers were following a well-trodden path of collaborative research.

Individual interviews took place during July and August 1979 and in November of that year the eight participants met together with the researchers to discuss the material.

In March of the following year a letter was received from Riverside which contained details of the proposed organisational changes. For the purposes of this case study this may be regarded as the completion of the project. The three stages – individual interviews, group report and discussion, and organisational change – will shortly be described.

RIVERSIDE – SUMMER 1979

Riverside Association possessed an energetic leadership with keen entrepreneurial skills. Since 1975 full advantage had been taken of the various funding sources. Indeed, at the start of our work with Riverside there were about 30 employees with further grants and employees on the horizon. As we shall see, rapid growth was a not unimportant cause of many problems.

It soon became clear that it was difficult to treat Riverside as one entity. For example, participants continually referred to the 'group' and the 'trust'. What was actually meant by these two terms emerged from the individual discussions. But by way of background we might note that the Riverside Trust was a registered charity established in 1977 and appeared to be the legal employer of many of the Riverside workers.

Looking back, it could be seen that Riverside had gone through a period of dramatic change – from a fairly straightforward self-help group for single parents, to a complex organisation, employing a significant number of staff, who had become increasingly unclear regarding key elements of their organisational position. The first important step had been taken in

1975, when the management committee had decided to set up an advice centre. Funded by at least three different sources, the centre had five paid staff (an administrator, a liaison officer, two counsellors/advice workers and an office junior) and two volunteer workers. As we have noted, the registered charity started two years later and rented a building that was intended to be a centre which would include arts and crafts room, conference room, coffee lounge, etc. The trust was located in that building and once again a variety of funding sources provided employment for a part-time secretary, a field manager, a researcher/development officer and an arts and crafts worker. This was not the end of Riverside's activities. A few years before the action-research project began, a charity shop had been opened and employed a manageress, a driver, plus an assistant in the shop. Furthermore, in 1978 funding had been secured to set up a scheme for painting and decorating the homes of single parents and had employed 19 workers. At the time of our study this had been replaced by another specially funded project employing 18 workers.

So when this collaborative project began, staff saw themselves as divided into two groups: the administrator, liaison officer and counsellors who were seen to belong to 'the office'; and those staff who were based at, and worked for, the trust. Riverside had established a joint management/trust committee composed of the elected members and two staff representatives. The group (the members) had its own finances and treasurer. Riverside's 'official' view of its structure is depicted in Figure 10.1. We shall see how difficult it was to make this structure work.

INDIVIDUAL PERCEPTIONS OF RIVERSIDE

Eight people from Riverside participated in the project:

- one of the counsellors
- the administrator
- the chairman of the group and vice-chairman of the trust
- the former administrator
- the liaison officer
- the building manager
- the trust secretary
- the treasurer

In this section we shall report the main points made by each of the participants. These statements are extracted from the documents which were circulated and finally discussed by the whole group.

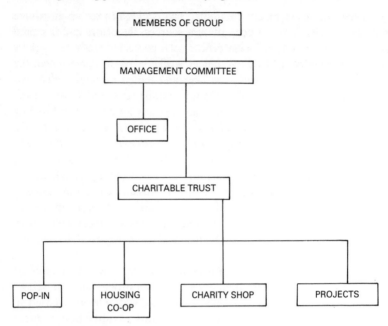

Figure 10.1 Riverside 1979

A counsellor's view

My job is to give advice on matters of income, social security, maintenance, housing and personal problems. I don't see my work as taking over people as cases, but as helping clients to do things for themselves.

I am not clear about the different roles of trust members, the group and the management committee. This has never been made clear to me. Perhaps it is assumed that I know how the organisation functions, but in fact it is all rather vague. I feel that one illustration of the general lack of communication is the fact that I was not informed about this proposed project until today.

I am expected to submit a monthly report to the management committee and have in fact attended a meeting at which I was introduced. This was a shambles. The chairman seemed unable to control the meeting and pull the threads together. I doubt whether the management committee have sufficient information on which to base their decisions. I think that the committee is too large and cumbersome. I don't know who belongs to which committee and it ought to be better structured and more effective.

At the moment I see myself accountable to the staff in the office, but ultimately to the management committee. I would prefer group accountability but I feel that if there were to be a boss that person would have to be of sufficient calibre to really understand the work of the staff. I have a strong sense of commitment to my job but I do not take part in Riverside activities. So, I am in a very different position to some members of staff who live and breathe the organisation. I have got a busy life of my own outside the organisation.

I think that Riverside has developed in a piecemeal fashion and has not as yet come together. I see it essentially as a self-help organisation run by the members – but it also offers a service.

There are frequently personality clashes and dissent. The liaison officer and the administrator are the driving forces behind the organisation and I think it would fold up without them. No one else is committed enough or prepared to perform the work to enable the project to continue at its present level.

The administrator's view

In April we elected a 16-person joint committee to run Riverside. But I think that only about 3–6 members of the committee totally appreciate the responsibilities involved. At the time of the election a number of the committee members did not understand the full significance of their role and four have resigned since then. I am in favour of members of staff being on the management committee. Without them I think that the committee would fail in its job – although the group itself would not collapse. Only a small proportion of the 300 members of the organisation take an active interest in running Riverside.

I think that the trust and the organisation should be regarded as one combined organisation. I am worried about the loss of the self-help approach in Riverside and I see it turning into a service agency. I would like to maintain Riverside as both a service agency and a self-help group. However, I note that the group is ceasing to do things for itself and is relying on the office which is tending to do too much for the group. The dilemma is that if the office doesn't do things then they won't get done.

Indeed, the increase in the number of paid staff is causing me some concern. At the moment I feel that individuals should think for themselves what is to be done. I do not think that everyone is doing a fair day's work and this causes problems. It is difficult to see what can be done. At the moment only other members of staff could initiate a dismissal of an unsatisfactory staff member.

In view of all this I consider that the question of the appointment of a director/co-ordinator is the critical issue which we must resolve. The absence of such a post reinforces the need for the chairman to play a more active role.

The view of the chairman of the group/vice-chairman of the trust

I think it is absolutely essential to distinguish between the activities of the group and the trust. This difference is critical to the problems I want to raise. Prior to this year the committee of trustees ran the trust, and the management committee ran the group and the office. Now the two committees have merged into one – although we retain two separate agenda (trust/group).

I see the group as the members. There is an average weekly attendance of about 15, although there is a big turnover in membership. (Only members can take part in activities.) On the other hand, I think that the activities of the trust are wider and deal with all one-parent families in the area. For example, we provide consultancy services to referrals from the social services departments. However, the group mostly take advantage of the services since these services are only publicised in our newsletter.

I see my role as chairman of the group as calling a halt. I do not feel that I can be clued up in what goes and what doesn't go. My prime interest is not in long-term planning.

We now take on too much, partly because the employees (such as the research and development officer) uncover new needs – for example, short-stay homes for evicted one-parent families. We start projects which are not really established before something else is started up. I would like to prune our activities and I would not bother to apply for some of the grants which are creating employment for people. I would prefer to concentrate on providing facilities – such as a holiday home – for the group. Some of our current endeavours, such as short-stay housing, are unnecessary, because other people are providing those services. I think the fact that we are doing so many things leads to a neglect of the basic purposes of Riverside.

The lack of involvement of members is linked to the above matters. We must offer the group things and we don't ask them to get involved in anything. There is hardly any fundraising done now, and none in the last 12 months. If you ask me, why not? I think that we need someone with the enthusiasm to generate involvement among the members.

Another connected problem is the function and working of the committee. I object to having to sit through four hours discussing issues of one-parent families in general. Few people speak and most just follow the loudest talker. A lot of committee time is spent in clashes of personality.

The former administrator's view

The post that I have just given up has developed from that of office secretary into that of administrator of government grants, buildings, counselling and public relations activities. With the appointment of counsellors my job changed yet again.

One of the main issues facing us is the need for a more definite statement of responsibilities. Too much is left nebulous and unclear, and this creates a lack of professionalism. For example, the appointment of counsellors left me unsure about the boundaries to my own job. Because we don't have any explicit statement, it is often unclear why certain people have a bigger say than others. Thus, it is sometimes suggested that an individual is staying in Riverside only because he or she is in the pocket of a particular powerful figure. The absence of explicit statements can be illustrated by the problem of cars. Is it the office car or the liaison officer's car?

The increase in employed staff has led to the existence of those who are employees only and those who are also members of the management committee. The 'just employees' feel ill at ease, and wonder what happens if they don't get on with the founders. I think that those with dual roles feel that they are on a different plane to the others, and I question whether it is appropriate that there is no clear-cut division between staff and the management committee. Staff interests are beginning to develop which will be different from management committee and trust interests.

Another important issue is the conflict between the group and the trust, which is evident at every meeting of the management committee. I would define the 'group' as the full members who elect the management committee and trustees. The group tends to see the office as being for them; but it has never been clarified whether the services are being provided just for the members' group, or for one-parent families as a whole. I consider it is for the use of all one-parent families, including, of course, group members.

Finally, I want to raise the issue of staff appointments. I am worried about the turnover of staff and the lack of clear-cut methods of hiring and firing. It appears to be a matter of chance as to who interviews potential staff and the appointment procedures are also nebulous.

Looking towards the future it seems that the employment of the present number of staff indicates Riverside's aspirations to a community-wide role. Without this I do not think there would be any need to employ two counsellors. Although it might be possible to separate the group from the wider service provision – this would probably be seen to be too drastic a move at the present time. I would prefer to see other measures adopted, for example the offices of trust secretary and administrator could be strengthened so as to give them genuine responsibility for staff. The post of co-ordinator should be established with more specific control over staff with a duty of putting issues to the committee.

The liaison officer's view

In general, I think that the objectives of Riverside are to further the aims of one-parent families in the area and to help with housing (for those in need), education, finance, day care, and employment. My post is funded by urban aid and I am employed by the management committee. One aspect of my work is to liaise with statutory and non-statutory organisations. So I see myself as an information officer and link-man, attempting to change the attitudes of people towards one-parent families. Outside bodies tend to regard me as a representative of the organisation.

Another aspect of my work is to try and obtain grants for desirable projects. This might really be regarded as research and development work. In some respects my public relations activities might be considered as laying appropriate groundwork for the grant applications.

I feel that the decision-making authority and responsibility of the paid staff should be clarified. We cannot continue in a situation where all are considered to be equal, because no one wants to be unpopular. I have never felt that equality was a true reflection of the position and I have always regarded the administrator as more important than other members of staff. Someone ought to be appointed with authority to deal with issues such as office discipline and days off. This might be a director who would be responsible for making decisions which need to be taken between the monthly meetings and the management committee. The director would be responsible to the management committee for the running of the organisation.

There appears to be a conflict between the group, which operates for its members, and the office or trust which operates for one-parent families as a whole. The management committee see themselves primarily as guardians of the group, rather than as having responsibility for the wider activities of Riverside. Nevertheless, I believe that if the case is well presented then the group as a whole would respond. The management committee seems to have difficulty in appreciating the scale of the financial turnover of the trust and office, which is about £60,000; as compared to the financial burden of the group, which is about £4,000.

I must emphasise that I do not think that the group on its own could fulfil the sort of pressure group role that is at present being performed. And they would not be able to provide the same level of service. I think that it is possible to educate the group in such a manner that the tension between the narrow and wider interests could be overcome.

The building manager's view

I am basically responsible for any building which Riverside owns or has a say in. I have been in post 12 months and I am now also a member of the management committee and a trustee.

I feel that a number of inappropriate issues are brought to meetings of the trust. For example, holiday times should be sorted out by the staff themselves and then presented as a courtesy to meetings of the trust. There are still differences between the trust and the group. It is a major educational exercise to persuade the group that the trust has a wider scope. I think that this is a result of the fact that the activities of the trust are not seen, they are not tangible, in the same way as those organised for the group by the office. But the present split between the two sides will diminish with the opening of the Pop-In, which will be a major benefit for the group. So, despite the present problems of the joint committee, I consider that it would not be correct to split up the committee.

It will be difficult, but possible, to have one person responsible for all the activities of the organisation. Personally, it would not bother me to be accountable to a director. The post of director should be detached from the membership. This would enable schemes to be run visibly and impartially. However, I must emphasise that such a proposition might not be tolerated by the membership. But detachment would, I think, avoid the sort of role conflict that has occurred in the past. I can give a number of examples of this including my own experience of conflict between my role as building manager and as a trustee – for example, when I had to recommend the closure of an unsafe building.

The growth of Riverside should be slowed down. The increase in paid workers has, in my opinion, led to diminution in the concept of self-help. There is an increasing tendency for people to say 'he is getting paid, let him do it'. Riverside is slowly moving away from the notion of a self-help organisation. Things are being done which could be done by the membership themselves, e.g. repairs to the minibus. What will happen if the paid workers leave? Will a vacuum be created after their departure? Although there are fields where Riverside needs paid workers, they ought to be fully exploited by having interested members working alongside them. In this way members could obtain the expertise to take up that job voluntarily. Whilst the paid workers would still be maintained, there will be no void created should grants suddenly be withheld. Are we now truly voluntary in the light of our dependence on external grants? I would propose that we move towards a decreased dependence on these grants.

Finally, I wonder whether the deeds of the trust are really being fulfilled. For example, I think the minibus should be generally available. The opening of the Pop-In will pose a number of questions. At the moment it is necessary to be a member to take advantage of group activities. However, it seems that people could come to the Pop-In without necessarily being a member of Riverside. In this connection I am not sure whether the Pop-In will be publicised throughout the area or advertised just in Riverside's newsletter.

The view of the trust secretary

I see my job as trying to raise as much money as I can. Since the last annual general meeting I am no longer a trustee. I attend the management committee, take minutes, and I am the trust staff representative. I also attend to all the correspondence.

One of the main problems is the small number of people who realise what is involved in terms of responsibility in raising money. Now that Riverside has grown so rapidly there are not enough 'professional' people running it. They need outside and professional help as they are administering a lot of government money. This should be spent strictly in accordance with the purposes for which it was raised. Some members of the management committee who are new trustees do not fully appreciate this and feel that it can be spent in other ways. This can lead to personality clashes and committee meetings deteriorate into personal attacks. When the organisation was small, problems could be worked out by staff. Now with a larger staff, more diversified, there is no one to make an ultimate decision. Grievances should be aired at committees but often feelings run high. Criticisms are often seen as a personal attack.

The organisation has enough on its plate until the Pop-In is finished. They should not commit themselves to any more. There are a lot of little schemes but if too much is taken on at once, ideas fall by the wayside. For example, the boat project – a small boat was bought and left by the canal and vandalised. £750 was raised but the boat sank.

Because of their deep commitment the liaison officer and administrator expect the others to feel the same. Members expect a great deal from them and the other full-time staff. I feel that staff should not be expected to do too much, but should feel free to participate in additional activities if they wish.

At the moment I do not feel myself accountable to anyone particularly and this creates problems. I take on the responsibility for trust staff and usually deal with their problems. I am employed by the trust to make decisions which are then put to the committee, but situations do occur which require immediate decisions and I think I can legitimately take them. On one occasion this was questioned by the chairman and the management committee and was substantiated only after a heated discussion which got well out of hand.

There are often clashes in methods of work. The liaison officer and the administrator, who for so long were the hub of Riverside and the office, are now part of a rapidly expanding staff. Newcomers cannot always accept their authority as of right. I feel that there now needs to be a structure developed for decision making in this new situation.

The treasurer's view

I have been treasurer of Riverside for the past 18 months and in my opinion we are one of the best organisations in the country. I think that the group owes a considerable debt to the administrators. I feel that a lot of the group members do not actually realise what is happening behind the scenes.

I am not happy with the present joint committee. Meetings are too lengthy and I feel that the two committees should be kept separate.

In my opinion Riverside is primarily for the group members, that is to say, those who attend the Wednesday meetings. Although the membership is about 300–400, only 50–60 come to the meetings and there is a hard-core membership of some 15–20. Money is raised by activities such as flag weeks, etc. Only members can come to the subsidised outings.

The committee has changed little over the past two years and it appears to be difficult to get people to volunteer. It seems that new members appear to feel that the committee is a clique.

THE COVERING REPORT

In the autumn of 1979 the eight participants joined together to discuss with the researchers their individual reports and the covering report which consisted of two main sections: the key problems raised by participants; and what was seen as the central issue – self-help or service. The introduction to the report also emphasised that the concentration on problems was not done in order to paint a dismal picture, but was intended to provide the basis for moving ahead.

The main problems raised by participants were grouped, for convenience, into a number of categories. These were not listed in any order of priority and there was an obvious overlap between some of the groupings. Nevertheless, it was felt that these groupings would provide the basis for the model building in the second part of the report. One group of issues appeared to revolve around the role of the *management committee* and the *trustees*. Another group reflected the concern of several of the participants regarding the rapid pace of *growth* of Riverside and the increasing number of commitments that it was taking on board. The issue of *commitment* loomed large in the minds of many of the group. Was it appropriate to expect from more recent paid staff the same level of commitment as that evidenced by the founders of Riverside who were themselves also now paid staff?

Nearly everybody raised questions revolving around the structure of the organisation. Four of the eight participants suggested that a *director* or *co-ordinator* should be appointed. There was also concern about the lack of *accountability*. From the individual reports it is evident that what were described as *personality clashes* were very prevalent in Riverside. (Generally speaking, on the basis of previous experience, the researchers tended not to emphasise these clashes, but rather to see them as manifestations of deeper structural problems that were being raised by participants.) The *committee meetings* were singled out as a particular source of irritation by three participants. Finally, *role conflict* was noted as another problem area. Two examples were provided, the conflict between the role of trustee and employee, and the problem of the 'just employees' – in other words, the uncertainty surrounding the difference between members and employees.

Most importantly, the researchers felt that there was a fundamental and central issue which a number of participants had mentioned and which was *seen to have implications for most of the problems already listed*. This central issue can be expressed as tension between the image of Riverside primarily as a *self-help group* or alternatively as a *service-providing agency*.

The majority of participants noted the conflict, although expressing it with varying degrees of emphasis. In most cases the group – that is to say, the members – were seen to have different interests from those of the trust. Perhaps this was most forcibly stated by the treasurer who declared that Riverside 'is primarily for the group members, that is to say, those who attend the Wednesday meetings . . . whereas the trust is for the benefit of outsiders . . . '. On the other hand, the counsellor and the former administrator felt that it *was* possible to combine self-help and a community-wide service. In the words of the liaison officer, this might be achieved through 'educating the group in such a manner that tensions between the narrow and wider interests can be overcome'.

Two possible alternative 'models' which drew on the real experiences of the group were presented. The two models outlined in Table 10.1 were not produced as an 'academic' exercise remote from the issues, but were intended as first steps in the production of practical alternatives.

One additional, and essential, point must be made with regard to the research approach. The production of alternative models – rather than

Table 10.1 Models of self-help and service

Key characteristics	MODEL A Self-Help	MODEL B Service
Membership	semi-permanent, group	open; potentially to all one-parent families in Riverside; may include group
Main purpose	servicing the group	in response to one-parent families' needs
Size	a 'face-to-face' core, according to needs of group	in response to needs of Riverside one-parent families
Staffing	volunteers, or minimal paid 'servicing' help from members	probably requires paid employees
(Staff) commitment	essential	may be more limited
Staff control	probably unnecessary or informal	co-ordination of activities, financial control and external representation needed
Budget	modest, self-raised	could be significant, including capital investment and external funding
Staff appointment	informal	explicit, formal systems needed
Organisational structure	informal	delineation of staff roles essential
Management committee	hardly needed (as such) – drawn from membership	pressure for 'experts' with standing in the community
Committee meetings	informal, flexible	need to distinguish items of policy, disciplined agenda, communication of decisions needed

'recommendations' for action – was held to be more conducive to securing genuine change. At the end of the day, it was up to Riverside to make decisions based on their intimate knowledge of the real situation, as to which, if either, of the models would be helpful.

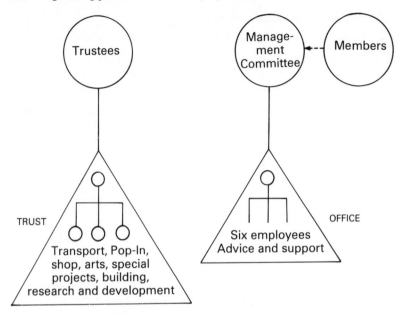

Figure 10.2 The trust and the office

THE GROUP DISCUSSION

During the meeting with the whole group it became evident that there were a number of more specific alternative organisational models which could be developed from the broad self-help and service categories of Table 10.1. Most of these more detailed alternatives involved various permutations of staff groupings. For example, one possibility that was discussed in some detail was to divide the trust with its own governing body of trustees, from those who would be in the 'office' and employed by a management committee elected by the group. Thus, the trust might employ those workers who were involved with transport, the Pop-In, the shop, arts and crafts, the specially funded projects, the building, research and development. On the other hand the office, whose focus was primarily intended to be towards the group of members, would employ about six workers primarily involved in advice and support work. This model is illustrated in Figure 10.2.

Other alternatives were also discussed including the possibility of a three-way split: the office with its own management committee, which would provide counselling services; the trust with its own group of legally defined employees; and the group once again with its own committee who might perhaps employ one or two workers in a direct service relationship

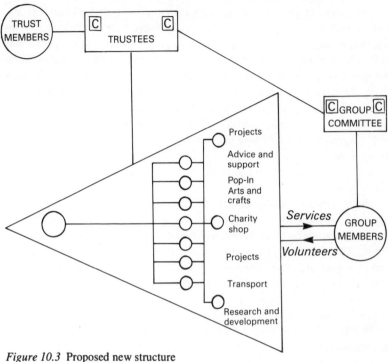

Figure 10.3 Proposed new structure

just for the members. The possibility was also explored of some form of co-ordinating mechanism which would draw together the activities of the three separate groups. In the event, as we shall presently see, a third model was adopted.

TOWARDS A NEW STRUCTURE

In March of the following year a letter was received from Riverside indicating that the organisation was well on the way to adopting a new structure. The administrator pointed out that the legalities of the new structure had been checked with their solicitor and also with the funding agencies and the general response appeared to be that it was an excellent idea. The next step was to bring the suggestion to the committee and this would be followed by a proposal put to the annual general meeting. In addition to an outline of the proposed structure, which is illustrated in Figure 10.3, detailed job descriptions had also been prepared for the key workers.

The essential elements of the new structure were that all services and staff would become part of the Riverside Trust, a registered charity, of which any lone parent residing in the area could become a member. It was pointed out that a non-lone parent could also become an associate member. All the services and staff are shown in the triangle in Figure 10.3. The letter from the Riverside administrator noted that as the number of staff was steadily increasing it had been decided that one member of the present staff should take on the responsibility of co-ordinating the work of all the staff and relaying reports on this to the board of trustees. This is shown in Figure 10.3 by the large circle in the point of the triangle. The circles in a line of seven represent the remaining members of staff and the three circles are the office juniors.

The letter continued by emphasising that although Riverside felt the new structure was a very necessary step, there was considerable concern to maintain the strong links between the Riverside Group and the Riverside Trust. Thus, it was being suggested that two members of the group committee would be representatives of that group on the board of trustees. This is illustrated in Figure 10.3 by the small squares marked C. In addition, any member of the Riverside Trust (with the exception of staff) would be eligible for nomination to the new board of trustees.

This is perhaps an appropriate point to leave Riverside and offer a few reflections on the case study. In passing, we might note that limited contact was maintained with several members of Riverside and, three years later, it appeared that the new structure was performing reasonably well.

DISCUSSION: SELF-HELP OR SERVICE?

Before offering some reflections on the main 'lessons' of the case study, a few words of caution are necessary with respect to the *strategy and process of change* that we have been discussing. Despite the rather gloomy impression that might be gained from the case material, probably due to its emphasis on problems rather than on achievements, Riverside possessed many attributes which should not be underestimated. In particular we might emphasise the openness, awareness and determination of its three key actors. Notwithstanding the bitter fashion in which disputes were some- times conducted, there was an openness about the organisation which is in stark contrast to the situation sometimes found in other comparable agencies. There was no attempt to avoid the inclusion in the collaborative project of people whose views might have been unpalatable or awkward. All the problems and possible areas were included as potential topics for the agenda.

The leading spirits of Riverside were alert to the dangers of their current position and had the necessary energy and determination to push ahead with agreed changes. From our experience with other agencies in similar action-research projects, it seems that these important ingredients can be rather rare. Too often, despite the best efforts of both sides, little occurs after the stage of analysis. Why this should be so remains a topic for speculation and further research.

The contribution of a modest case study to the furtherance of our understanding of any particular area must always be approached with caution. Indeed, one of the reasons for not publishing this case study earlier was to provide time to explore some of the issues in other settings. What we can now say with a somewhat greater degree of confidence is that the *central finding* of the case study – the tension between self-help and service – is one that is not confined to Riverside. The key characteristics illustrated above in Table 10.1 have been utilised in a number of workshops. The most that should be claimed at this stage is that the models appear to make explicit what are often felt to be confusing and overwhelming problems. In so doing, they serve an important purpose of *practical* model building, that is to say they point the way towards ameliorating action.

Two important inter-related questions to which no emphatic answer can as yet be given are: to what extent are these models clear-cut and self-contained alternatives? What are the organisational costs of the long-term maintenance of the sort of combined models that Riverside was implementing at the onset of the project? In attempting to answer these questions little help is available from the few British studies of self-help groups which have taken a rather different focus from the problem-orientated work in Riverside.[1] For example, those studies have, in the main, not been collaborative, and the questions asked by the researchers have been different. Their concern has not been to develop alternative usable models, but to answer an initial set of questions which have been posed by the authors or sponsors of the research. The most interesting of these studies is probably the work of Richardson and Goodman (1983). Many of the issues the authors raise echo the points made in the Riverside project. Thus, they emphasise that the idealised picture of self-help groups may be false and that the reality can be very different. However, despite the considerable contribution which this study makes to a scant literature, its prime social policy focus does not lead naturally to a consideration of alternative organisational models. Whilst we can sympathise with their view that the 'typologies' of self-help groups that have been offered by other authors have been 'misleading' and 'inappropriate', we believe that practitioners, managers and social policy makers will nevertheless continue to have an urgent need for *usable* models or typologies.

If we return to our own study of Riverside we can highlight the significance of the employment of paid staff in self-help groups. We have pointed to the possibility of organisational tension between the two models (self-help and service), which might act to the detriment of clients and staff. Is it 'better' to face up to this tension and follow the path eventually taken by Riverside? The table of key characteristics (Table 10.1) suggests that, along a number of parameters, the requirements of the two models are very different. Thus, the pure self-help group primarily faces inwards, it is highly informal and, although it undoubtedly needs a degree of 'organisation', it is not at all clear that it needs more than minimal paid 'servicing' help.[2] Although it may have one or more paid staff, the problems of commitment and control would probably be minimal. Budgets will be small, staff appointments may be informal, and the need for organisational structure modest. Whilst there will undoubtedly be some need for a management committee and possibly other committees, the meetings are likely to be informal, flexible and possibly frustrating events. These are essentially vulnerable organisational forms which both profit and suffer from the absence of bureaucratic procedures and structure.

Unless the membership has a clear view of its own needs, it can rapidly find itself led by paid staff away from the pure self-help model outlined above and into wider and more extensive territories. We might hypothesise that the better and more qualified the staff the more likely it is that they may find that 'just' servicing a group of members is rather frustrating and they may look to a wider market for their energies. New staff may be employed and the problems of control and co-ordination of activities begin to become severe. The gap between staff and membership grows and it is no longer possible to continue along the previous cosy path. The new staff may not have the same degree of commitment, or at least they may not wish to devote their entire life to 'the cause'.

As the organisation grows, so too does its financial responsibilities and its budget. The problems of accountability to funders arises as a major issue. The staff would be looking to a management committee which is, at the very least, capable of sanctioning, if not initiating, policy issues. There can develop an imbalance in the level of decision making by staff and the level of understanding and ability to comment which can be provided by management committees. All these questions arose in the Riverside study and led that organisation to prefer to move along the path we have outlined.

In the previous chapter I attempted to summarise some of the main issues which have emerged from our research programme and began to develop a tentative theory of voluntary agencies. It was suggested that many voluntary agencies might be regarded as situated in an 'ambiguous zone' between the purely private world of friends, neighbours, family, etc. and the fully fledged bureaucratic world with its clear-cut differentiation of structures into, for example, employers and employees, providers and recipients, managers and subordinates. We further suggested that voluntary agencies could decide to cope with the strains of ambiguity, or perhaps move towards the less ambiguous, private or bureaucratic worlds. Alternatively, as in the Riverside case study, they could decide to take the drastic step of separating organisationally the 'group' (the private world of self-help) from the trust (the more bureaucratic world of service).

As we have already stated, it is now clear that many self-help organisations face not dissimilar issues to those we have been discussing. Perhaps the experience of Riverside, the analysis of its problems and the first development of alternative models may make some contribution to our understanding of this important area.

NOTES

1   The lack of serious British literature is noted in *Mutual Aid and Social and Health Care*, S. Hatch (ed.), ARVAC Pamphlet No. 1, 1980.
2   For a discussion of the role of co-ordinators in setting up, maintaining and developing 'externally-supported' self-help groups, see N. Miller, *Setting-up for Self-Help*, Contact a Family and The Mental Health Foundation, 1984.

11   A theory of the voluntary sector

INTRODUCTION

The research which underpins this paper falls within a tradition which has
been regarded as 'action research' or 'social analysis' (see Chapter 1). The
relevance for this present essay is that it is argued that tentative usable
models and theories for understanding the nature of voluntary organisation,
and the implications for policy, can be generated from the problems posed
by those organisations. This paper begins therefore by noting in the first
part some of the problems of voluntary organisations and moves on in the
second part to make a brief and partial presentation of an emerging theory
of voluntary organisation. Finally, implications for practice are discussed.

DISTINCTIVE ORGANISATIONAL PROBLEMS

Since one of the objectives of this paper is to make a contribution to the
definitional debate, the description of voluntary organisations as
non-governmental and non-profit-seeking organisations, primarily in the
broad field of welfare, will suffice as a preliminary general boundary.
Furthermore, many but not all of the groups that participated in the research
programme employed some paid staff to undertake the services that the
organisation is in existence to provide – its 'operational' work. In practice
these have proved comfortable and fruitful boundaries for research
projects, workshops and seminars.

The problems summarised in this paper are drawn from about twenty
studies undertaken in the past decade. Additional, more limited, work has
been carried out in workshops with nearly 200 voluntary organisations in
the same period. Thus although the list of problems has the benefit of
drawing on a substantial body of experience, it has the disbenefit of
considerable compression.

For convenience the total agenda of problems can be divided into three broad groupings: *constitutional, governance* and *work organisation*; with a fourth, important overarching grouping, the problems associated with *organisational change*. We are concerned here with what Handy (1981) called 'second level' deeper problems; rather than the more technical and ephemeral (albeit important) 'presenting first level' problems; although it must be noted that the deeper problems may emerge after analysis of the more obvious and immediate problems.

First, the heading 'constitutional' is intended to cover those fundamental issues concerning dilemmas of organisational character and survival. Thus the viability and long-term survival of an agency can be explored by asking painful test questions such as: who really cares whether it lives or dies? More frequently, problems arise with regard to organisational identity and control where one of the most familiar sets of problems surrounds the question: what is the real business of the agency? For example, is it primarily a self-help group or a service delivery agency? With regard to control, the question may be put: whatever the constitution says, who really controls the organisation? Clearly, basic questions of this sort are inextricably bound up with resources (see Chapter 12) – although we can in this paper only note in passing how rarely resource issues have been the most severe or the real problem. More often than not, resource constraints have reflected tensions in constitution, governance or work organisation.

Second, governance is probably the most distinctive area of voluntary organisation problems and revolves around the question of accountability for the constitutional (survival and identity) questions. In voluntary organisations the governance function is complex and usually shared in a changing and often inexplicit fashion between a number of groupings in addition to the Boards, trustees and elected management committees and the like. In particular the relationship with paid staff has been a source of major tensions and has led to the largest body of research (Herman and Van Til 1989, Harris 1990). To this can be added the relationship between headquarters and local groups (Young 1989).

Third, under the heading of work organisation can be included all those problems associated with organising the operational work of voluntary organisations. Although many of these problems might be regarded as more superficial than the constitutional and governance issues, two critical questions have emerged. The first is the tension and 'overlap' between the various groupings or 'statuses' (governing body, paid staff, volunteers, members, users) that together make up the organisation. In part we have covered one aspect of this problem under the heading of governance, but the reality is not so convenient, and there are many strains between the statuses which belong to the area of operational work. The second is the tension between what are regarded as 'bureaucratic' and 'democratic' forms of organisation. Both questions will need to be addressed by any tentative theory of voluntary organisation and both go to the heart of the academic challenge to develop better theory for practice and policy.

Fourth, we must note the major question of organisational change which can be regarded as an overarching problem interacting with the previous categories. Voluntary organisations can stumble into dramatic changes without serious consideration of the longer-term implications. This appears especially true in an era of rapid change in governmental policy. For example, the case of the small group running a modest club for the mentally ill that suddenly 'found itself' a substantial provider of day care services.

On the face of it many of the words and phrases used in the foregoing summary of problems appear similar to those used in the private and public sector. And it must be emphasised that, particularly in the larger agencies, familiar bureaucratic problems of paid staff role relationships may be significant. However, closer investigation reveals that it is really a different language, the nature of which will occupy a large part of the discussion in the second part of this paper. Here a few examples may be sufficient to justify the general claim. Thus when agency staff talk about problems of *governance* it does not occupy the same place in their realm as for their colleagues in governmental agencies. It seems to be far more intense and immediate. When they talk about *accountability* they are apt to challenge the concept itself, and not regard it as a straightforward case of managerial accountability. When they raise problems about relationships between '*headquarters*' and *local groups*, voluntary agencies will rarely be referring just to the problems of teasing out accountable staff roles. Other more fundamental constitutional questions about 'autonomy' and membership will form part of the dialogue. So, too, when talking about 'clients' or 'users', the discussion is certain to range well beyond questions of quality of service. When nonprofits talk of managing volunteers it is not some indulgent appendage, as is usually the case in government agencies.

The argument so far is, therefore, that the problems faced by voluntary organisations are sufficiently distinctive to warrant usable theory that relates to those problems.

A THEORY OF VOLUNTARY ORGANISATION

This paper contends that in order to understand the voluntary sector – the new welfare panacea – it is necessary first to distinguish three different 'worlds', each with its own 'rules of the game'. These three worlds are:

1 the personal;
2 the associational;

3 the bureaucratic – which is further divided into the governmental and profit-seeking bureaucracies.

Secondly, and crucially, it is suggested that all three worlds (and their subdivisions) overlap, and that the overlapping areas form 'ambiguous zones'. It is contended that this model – which limitations of space necessitate a rather 'telegraphic' presentation – may prove fruitful in explaining many of the sources of tension in voluntary organisations which must be taken into account in the development of social policy.

Unambiguous worlds: personal, associational and bureaucratic

It will be argued that there are three 'worlds' (personal, associational, and bureaucratic) that have reasonably clear terms of reference, or what may be called 'rules of the game'. The term 'world' in its dictionary definition as a 'scene of human existence' is particularly appropriate to describe these phenomena. Whilst no rules or terms of reference are static, the inter-relationships in these worlds are relatively stable, and are underpinned by theories and explanations that are either well understood and accepted, or can, when necessary, be made explicit.

Notwithstanding the crudity of those rules, and the turbulence and chaos that often seems to dominate our life in these three arenas of human existence, the worlds will be described as 'unambiguous'. Most, if not all, humans are now part of, or are affected by, all three worlds. They always were members of what we shall shortly define as the personal and associational worlds, and the internationalisation of bureaucracy has brought most of the globe's inhabitants within the sphere of influence of the bureaucratic world. We shall move quickly through these descriptions of the unambiguous worlds since the objective is to arrive as rapidly as possible at the point where we can return to look again at the voluntary sector.

The personal world

What might be called the 'personal world' is the most pervasive and familiar of the unambiguous worlds. It is perhaps stretching terminology a little to describe the first of our three groupings as a 'world' – which conveys the impression of a bounded entity – when a key characteristic of the 'personal world' is that it is not tightly bounded. For this reason it is depicted in Figure 11.1 (see p. 163) by a dotted line to indicate its unorganised and free-flowing nature. Indeed, earlier papers (see Chapter 9) treated the personal world and its adjacent associational world as one entity.

Nevertheless, its distinct qualities and differences justify the description of a 'world'.

In the personal world social problems are resolved by relatives, friends, neighbours, on a private basis. It is not usually found necessary or appropriate to establish contractual arrangement between the parties for the resolution of social problems. This does not preclude the State from the need to pass laws governing aspects of the relationships between, for example, parents and children, and it will attempt to enforce those laws through its bureaucratic organs. But the overwhelming character of these relationships is that they are inexplicit. The 'problem-solver' is not given a special 'title' or status by virtue of the efforts made. Problems are responded to without recourse to categorising either those who have the problem or those who respond. It is seen as natural, perhaps as part of being a 'good' parent, or later on in life as part of being a good child in relation to an elderly parent. Or, it is seen as being a 'good neighbour', friend, colleague, etc. The real bonds between the two sides (the problem holder and the solver) are those which are based solely on individual qualities such as loyalty, affection, love, humanity . . . .

There are other characteristics of the personal world. As an account of the work of the late Philip Abrams in the field of neighbourhood care pointed out: ' . . . informal care, particularly in the family, has no beginning or end unless relief is available' (Bulmer 1986: 214). This absence of a 'beginning or end' is very different from the organised worlds of associations and bureaucracies.

The world of voluntary associations

The personal world may be distinguished from the formal world of 'voluntary associations' which may be defined as comprising groups of people who draw a boundary between themselves and others in order together to meet some problem, to 'do something'. The literature usually refers to this as having an 'objective' or 'purpose' (see Sills 1968, Smith and Freedman 1972). The concept of membership is important – without this the boundary cannot be maintained.

The association will need a name; outsiders crossing the boundary will need to adhere to the purposes of the association and be 'members' of that named group. Even the smallest formal association – if it wants to do anything significant – will find it necessary to act as, or create, some form of 'governing body'. The governing body need not be distinguished from the members, and within this definition of association will be included small groups, such as trustees, who function primarily as governing bodies and who would not necessarily regard themselves as an association of members. The absence of a genuine membership in voluntary organisations is returned to later.

The association may rapidly face the need to establish a legal identity since by differentiating itself from the external environment it must – if it wishes to negotiate with that environment, and at the very least exclude non-members – give itself a name. Thus, if it becomes necessary to open a bank account, write letters to 'others', and in general negotiate as a corporate entity, the group moves out of the personal world and becomes an association. The 'rules of the game' in the world of voluntary associations are based on concepts such as voting and elections. The reality of life in associations may be very different to the theory, but that theory serves as a rationale and legitimating force for the existence of the association.

The bureaucratic world

'Bureaucracy' will be defined as a system of paid staff who are organised into hierarchical roles (Jaques 1976). In brief we can note that bureaucracies are bound together by concepts such as accountability and authority. Managers are not elected by their subordinates but appointed by superior authorities. The hierarchical chain of command is the cornerstone of bureaucratic organisation. At the moment the concern is only with unambiguous bureaucracies: those where the fundamental ground rules assume clear-cut differentiation between a large number of 'statuses' such as employer and employee; employee and non-employee; providers and recipients; chairperson and director; director and managers; managers and subordinates; owners and governing bodies.

In the past I have treated the bureaucratic world as sufficiently homogeneous to warrant analysis by common theories and concepts (see Chapter 1). And indeed this is the assumption of most management approaches. Here governmental bureaucracies will be differentiated from the business bureaucracies since the distinction is important in order to develop the model of the voluntary sector. Both government and business share the fundamental characteristics of bureaucracies – the differentiation into statuses, such as directors, staff, customers/clients, etc. However, they have very different 'roots'.

We shall return to consider the nature of 'roots' of voluntary agencies later (see Chapter 12), but for the moment it may be sufficient to suggest that governmental bureaucracies draw their strength from the legitimising philosophy or theory of representative democracy and their resource base from the 'right' to raise money from their particular political territory. Business bureaucracies, or the commercial sector, have a similarly 'straightforward' integrated combination of legitimising theory and resource base. The legitimising philosophy is to be found in the theory of the market which submits that the efficient firms will survive and gather profits. These profits – the 'bottom line' – in turn provide the resources for staff to be employed to undertake the work of the corporation.

Ambiguity

It is suggested that there is a large area of voluntary sector activity that falls between the three unambiguous worlds described above. These 'ambiguous zones' hold the clue to the resolution of the puzzles of the voluntary sector and in particular, my main concern, the voluntary agencies. It is necessary therefore to commence this part with an outline of the notion of 'ambiguity'.

We draw here on the work of the anthropologist Edmund Leach which makes it possible to understand further what ambiguity might mean. He too faced the problem of 'blurring' and unclear boundaries. Of particular help is his diagram of two overlapping circles and his statement that:

> There is always some uncertainty about just where the edge of Category A turns into the edge of Category not-A . . . markers of boundaries . . . are ambiguous in implication and a source of conflict and anxiety.

> (Leach 1976: 34, 35)

We can now combine Leach's definitions of ambiguity, and the distinction between the bureaucratic, associational and personal worlds (see Figure 11.1). It is still assumed that the bureaucratic world is homogeneous. From this it can be observed that there are now two ambiguous 'areas' between the unambiguous worlds. One of these will be called the area of unorganised groups (UG) and is cursorily discussed below. The other section, falling between the associational and bureaucratic worlds, is a large area of voluntary sector activity and a focal point of interest of this paper and social policy developments. This is the territory of the ambiguous voluntary agency (AVA). We shall describe the general features of both these areas before returning to examine in more detail the different zones of ambiguous agency.

Unorganised groups

These groups represent the first step from the personal to the associational world. They may be differentiated from the latter by the fact that they do not have a constitution, or legal identity. People just come together on an informal basis to resolve their own or others' social problems. If any

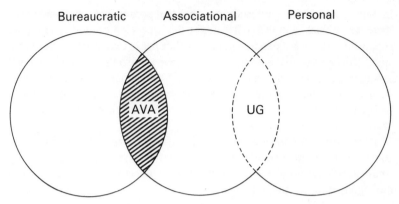

AVA Ambiguous voluntary agencies
UG Unorganised groups

Figure 11.1 The personal, associational and bureaucratic worlds

significant activity is to be undertaken, they will find it necessary to move across the boundary into the world of formal associations.

Unorganised groups are part of the world of associations because they are trying to achieve some objective, to resolve some social problem. But they find themselves with multiple roles flowing from their occupation of the ambiguous area between the personal world of friends, neighbours, etc. and their membership of the 'group', which has purposes (as an association) above and beyond being an individual good neighbour, etc. Although unorganised groups probably play a major role in social welfare in its broadest sense, their lack of stable structures makes them unlikely candidates for the substantial resolution of severe social problems.

General characteristics of ambiguous voluntary agencies

In this section we describe the general characteristics of the shaded area in Figure 11.1: that territory that falls between the bureaucratic and associational worlds which we have referred to as occupied by ambiguous voluntary agencies. An association may or may not employ paid staff to carry out its work. We have called those that do not employ paid staff 'pure' or unambiguous associations.

However, in certain circumstances, even if an association does employ paid staff it may still be considered unambiguous. This arises where the paid staff only help the unpaid membership who undertake the real operational activities (those activities for which the association was set up).

In this instance the paid staff are in a supporting role and undertake 'non-operational' activities. We might think of such groups – with paid supporting staff – as 'standing at the door' of the bureaucratic world. Thus, small local groups that employ part-time secretarial help, or larger regional and national groups that have substantial headquarters staff for activities such as providing information and services to members, financial and budgetary matters, arranging transport and provisions, might still be classified as unambiguous associations.

If an association decides to move to a further stage and employs paid staff to carry out the operational work, then it may be described as entering 'bureaucratic territory' and having become an 'agency' or 'nonprofit'. Thus the argument so far suggests that:

1 if groups decide to move from unorganised to bureaucratic forms, then this is accompanied by increased differentiation of roles or 'statuses', as categories such as 'member', 'committee member', 'volunteer', 'staff', 'director', and so on, emerge;
2 the dominant characteristic of voluntary *agencies* (AVA in Figure 11.1) is the ambiguity of many of these statuses, and the consequent tension between the 'formal' characteristics of the bureaucratic world and the more 'informal' characteristics of the associational and personal worlds.

The three zones of ambiguous voluntary agencies

We now move on to explore the component parts of the territory.

Changes in British social policy demand a model that more accurately reflects the alternatives to the State domination of welfare. Thus, in Figure 11.2 the bureaucratic world has been further divided into the governmental, and profit-seeking or business, 'sub-worlds'. This appears to reflect organisational reality in that there is once again an ambiguous zone between the government and profit-seeking agencies, only part of which is of interest to this paper. We can now combine Figures 11.1 and 11.2 to produce the ambiguous zones of voluntary agency activity shown in Figure 11.3:

> GA – Government-orientated associations
> PA – Profit-orientated associations
> EA – Entrepreneurial associations

The zones (GA, EA, PA) are depicted with dotted lines between them. Again this is intended to indicate a more fluid boundary, one that is not as firm or dramatic as the first entry into the bureaucratic world. But even if the boundary is less rigid it will still be seen to be critical to know in which

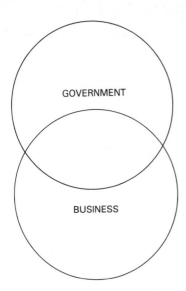

Figure 11.2 Government and business bureaucracies

zone an agency really 'belongs', and what factors determine its placing. A few words about the 'roots' of voluntary agencies may set the scene.

I shall define 'roots' as the twin philosophical and resource sources of agencies. That is to say that the analysis of organisational roots requires both an exploration of the inspirational sources upon which agency policies are developed, and an exploration of the critical resource foundations of agency survival. Such an exploration will also lead to an analysis of the harmony between the two sources and the consequences of disharmony. Whilst some agencies will readily see themselves belonging to a particular zone, others will find that the exploration does indeed go to the roots of their problem.

Government-orientated associations

This group (GA) is perhaps the one that has grown the fastest in the UK in the 1980s. The most straightforward examples of occupants of this zone are agencies where both the resource and philosophical aspects of roots look towards government. Thus government represents the prime source of revenue, and staff and governing body regard government as the appropriate funder. Governmental support would be seen as appropriate because the social problems that the voluntary agency was tackling were those that the agency believed should be the responsibility of government. Thus, in the UK many of the larger housing associations see themselves as

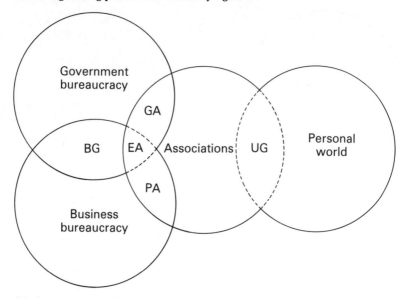

GA Government-orientated associations
PA Profit-orientated associations
EA Entrepreneurial associations
UG Unorganised groups
BG Business/government bureaucracies

Figure 11.3 The worlds of the voluntary sector

belonging to this zone. Many agencies funded by the former Greater London Council would also belong here. A critical question for occupants of this zone is the extent to which their roots are based solely in the world of government bureaucracy.

Many GAs, especially those which in practice owe their establishment to governmental sources, may have only flimsy, even artificial (inspirational) roots. The absence of a philosophy stemming from deep associational roots means that their strength and survival is highly dependent on the degree to which their bureaucratic and, usually, staff-driven philosophy matches that of the government of the day. It can be a hazardous basis.

Profit-orientated organisations

Because of the British Welfare State tradition, this is a relatively modest zone of voluntary sector activity. However, all this may be changing. The basic characteristics of organisations in this zone (PA) is that their inspirational roots come from associations where the mutual self-interest of the members/staff is expressed through the market philosophy. Through its occupancy of the profit-seeking bureaucratic world, the voluntary agency in this zone is primarily dependent on fees. However, unlike the position in the governmental-orientated agencies, these are 'genuine' fees, not indirect payments from government. That is to say that the 'clients' of such agencies are in the main just as likely to choose a firm from the pure profit-seeking world.

This paper is concerned with organisational, rather than legal, entities. Consequently the role of 'charities' has not been the focus of the discussion. We might just note that, according to the organisational approach adopted here, serious questions might be raised regarding registered charities that could not demonstrate some minimum genuine associational roots, as voluntary organisations. This would be the case both for those that were entirely the creatures of government, as well as those that were solely dependent on fee income. For example, the Charity Commissioners (the body that registers charities and can investigate abuses) came to the conclusion that the independent school which it was investigating, and which had charitable status, was ' . . . essentially a commercial and competitive business' (Home Office 1987: para. 55). Whether or not this could be regarded as a voluntary agency would require knowledge about its resource base (endowment funds, donations, etc.), and the extent to which there were genuine 'belief' and associational roots (for example, religious, political). Or was it essentially a 'business', solely concerned with providing educational services for profit?

The appeal to legitimacy of agencies in this zone requires further examination. Where are their true roots? Are they derived from the various professional associations, resting on a philosophy of 'professionalism' and 'professional' standards? Or is it all a charade? The Housing Association movement, mentioned earlier, also has associations founded by groups of architects and other professionals, primarily for their own self-interest, and happy to see fee income as a prime resource base.

Entrepreneurial associations

It may at first sight seem rather perverse to describe this group of agencies (EAs) as 'entrepreneurial', rather than the profit-orientated sector described above. Since these agencies stand at the centre of a number of different worlds and 'sub-worlds', it is suggested that they are more genuinely thought of as entrepreneurial.

In the first place they are clearly in the world of associations. Then they are in the bureaucratic world (since they have paid staff delivering operational activities). Further it can be seen from Figure 11.3 that they are in both the government and profit-seeking worlds. The EA often has strong roots with sometimes a strong associational base, and is resourced from the association by means of membership fees, donations, legacies, endowments. Typical examples of such entrepreneurial associations might be Oxfam, Barnados and the NSPCC.

Those EAs that do have genuine and strong associational roots can be the real entrepreneurs, exploiting changing government policy or charging fees for services, secure in their 'deep-rootedness'. This is perhaps the most interesting of the three ambiguous bureaucratic areas and is also one that is seen as a highly desirable resting place for the bureaucratic, energetic, voluntary agency. It gives diversity of resources and, providing there is, amongst other factors, a talented leadership, continuous possibilities for new initiatives.

Some EAs may have their origins in voluntary associations that we earlier described as 'standing at the door' of the bureaucratic world. Thus Milofsky suggests that:

> Rather than starve, many community organisations have taken on organisational characteristics which allow them to compete better in the mass social system . . . . Recognizing their survival problems, boards of directors count themselves fortunate to be able to hand control of their organisations to aggressive, entrepreneurial directors who are able to build contacts to new sources of funding and radically restructure the organisation.
>
> (Milofsky 1987: 30)

There are other occupants of this zone. Lack of leadership can result in agencies that, despite their original deep roots, slumber on, content to depend on resources from a wide variety of sources, but incapable of bending with the wind and seizing opportunities. Then there are the agencies with much weaker roots: organisations where to all intents and purposes the association is the small governing body or perhaps the paid staff. In some instances changing circumstances have forced agencies to abandon original philosophies and to adopt a value-less, opportunistic existence. Survival is the prime and almost overt purpose. Their roots lie everywhere and nowhere and philosophy and policy bend with the prevailing winds.

SOME IMPLICATIONS

This presentation of an emerging theory of bureaucracy and voluntary organisation originated from the realisation that the traditional bureaucratic paradigm left too many unresolved problems. That paradigm, still widely held by policy makers and managers, assumes that there is clear-cut differentiation between the main statuses: (a) the 'owners' and controllers of the organisation (shareholders, boards, elected representatives, committees, etc.); (b) the paid staff or bureaucrats; and (c) the users (clients, customers, patients, etc.). Of course, the traditional paradigm recognised the fudging at the highest levels: private sector boards that were really managerial meetings in disguise, and political appointees at the top of the paid staff. Nevertheless, the division stands as an, often implicit, fundamental principle of organisation which has underpinned social policy approaches to welfare. Practitioners, policy makers and consultants continue to find the bureaucratic paradigm a highly plausible explanation.

Whether or not the recent move to 'opting out', and the apparent blurring of the sector boundaries, will materially alter the ground rules of bureaucracy will be the subject of a few speculative comments in the final chapter. For the moment we shall concentrate on the implications of the theory of voluntary organisation for the internal management of voluntary agencies, and social policy.

Voluntary agencies and the management of ambiguity

The first, and most obvious, implication of the theory is that an explanation is provided for the genuine management complexity of voluntary agencies noted by so many commentators. The management of such agencies, which operate in the ambiguous territory between the formal bureaucracies and the associations, can with justification be regarded as more complex than governmental or business management.

The 'management of ambiguity' thus requires an understanding of the ground rules of both worlds. Elected leaders and paid staff must appreciate that bureaucratic organisation means paying attention to issues of managerial authority and accountability, levels of decision making, career progression, staff development, conditions of service, explicit policy making, and all the other essential accoutrements of modern bureaucracies. At the same time agencies must absorb the essential concepts of the association: membership, mission, informality and democracy.

The degree of formalisation – the balance between the demands of bureaucracy and association – will reflect the stage of development of the agency, and the balance of power between the various constituencies or 'statuses' in the agency, such as committee members, staff, users or clients, funders, volunteers, members and others. All combinations of statuses are possible, and we must emphasise that these are real fusions of roles not to be confused, for example, with representative arrangements such as worker representatives on boards, or local government representatives on voluntary agency management committees.

Ambiguity can manifest itself in many ways, for example, in the tension between:

- (informal) charismatic leadership versus the pull to authority-based roles;
- (informal) unbounded commitment (the expectation that paid staff should work 24 hours a day) versus (formal) negotiated conditions of service;
- volunteers (be they members of the governing body or service deliverers) versus paid staff;
- the desire for collective, co-operative or 'democratic' forms and styles of organisation, versus standard bureaucratic forms.

An example of the tension stemming from ambiguity is the self-help versus service dichotomy. In one study of a group of one-parent families it was seen how the arrival of paid staff to the self-help group exacerbated the tension between two competing organisational models (see Chapter 10). In voluntary agencies, every possible combination of statuses can be found. These are a basic feature of the agency and are not just some artificial 'graft' or a manifestation of the familiar 'informal' organisation. We have 'clients' (the term is used to describe the recipients of services) who are also members of the governing body, or clients who are part of the paid staff. We find the member of the governing body who can be the executive director of the agency, or a paid subordinate member of staff. We can find volunteer service deliverers who can be clients or members of the governing body. In general therefore the model demonstrates why the pull between the different worlds is so central a feature of voluntary agencies.

Another example is that of those national organisations that have tens or even hundreds of 'branches'. The tensions between headquarters and local groups are legion in many agencies. Closer examination may reveal that different parts of the organisation lie in different 'zones' (as defined earlier). Thus some branches of national organisations may be unambiguous associations, whilst others may be operating in any of the three ambiguous zones. If we examine the headquarters of such organisations, they too can be anywhere. In some cases they may be in a purely supporting role to the main work which is carried out by the membership. In other instances central staff may drive headquarters into the bureaucratic zones, and become almost a separate agency.

Finally, the concept of ambiguity helps to explain why relations between management committee and paid staff are such a familiar and vexed problem for many agencies. This is the front line where bureaucracy meets association. The introduction of paid staff who are expected to undertake operational work represents the move into bureaucratic territory. These staff may or may not share the sense of mission to the same degree as the committee who may still be doing part of the operational work. Or vice versa! The paid staff may be the genuine roots of the agency, representing in reality the only membership, and performing not only the operational work but also in effect undertaking the core survival and legitimating work of the committee, and acting as *de facto* guardians of the future of the agency. In this instance it is the paid staff who really 'appoint' the committee.

It is not surprising therefore that committee–staff relationships are often so tricky. At any given time both sides will need to share the same associational and bureaucratic values. That is to say they must both share the same sense of mission which is in itself a considerable challenge; they must also share a similar view of the degree of bureaucratisation that is needed. Should the agency, for example, take a particular government grant, or employ more paid staff on short-term contracts and possibly jeopardise its recruitment of volunteers?

No model or theory can resolve more than a limited number of problems, but there are important consequences of a theory of voluntary organisation for social policy and these are discussed in later chapters.

12   The roots of voluntary agencies

INTRODUCTION

It is tempting to view voluntary organisations rather like fragile 'black boxes', adrift on a turbulent sea and at the mercy of powerful environmental pressures. The direction of their journey and their very survival is, according to this view, predetermined (by life cycles or various iron laws), or largely dependent on the strength of governmental (funding) currents. The metaphor is not too fanciful. The fledgling discipline of nonprofit studies contains many writings which recognise the lack of knowledge about the workings of voluntary or nonprofit organisations (the two terms will be used interchangeably in this paper).

Although the spate of more recent international papers and books has undoubtedly advanced the state of knowledge of voluntary organisation, it would be foolhardy to claim that we are at anything other than the beginning of a long and challenging search. In fact we know little about the internal composition and operation of the black boxes and even less about the way in which internal factors interact with the environment. This paper presents a model of the 'roots' of voluntary organisations in order to assist in the exploration of the black box. It is contended that the model can be utilised by those working in the voluntary sector in order to facilitate planned organisational change. The conclusion is reached that agencies have choices – the journey is not predetermined and inevitable.

The paper draws together the findings from a series of action-research projects with UK voluntary organisations. The organisational and management problems faced by each group served as the starting point for each project. We commence therefore by presenting sketches of four organisations. These are used throughout to provide some background to the development of the roots model, and to illustrate the relevance of the theory to the organisational problems.

A presentation of the main body of theory is followed by a brief examination of relevant literature. The final discussion returns to the starting point of the paper – the problem of choice and change in voluntary organisations – and indicates several issues for further research.

TOWARDS AN ANALYSIS OF ROOTS: CASE STUDIES

Using four thumb-nail case studies based on collaborative research projects undertaken with voluntary organisations, this section explores some of the factors that might lie beneath the initial problems presented for investigation. The methodological approach used in the research has been extensively used for about forty years by specialists in organisational development (see Chapter 1).

The four organisations examined in this paper are drawn from some twenty studies undertaken in the past decade. Further, more limited, work has been carried out in workshops with nearly 200 voluntary organisations in the same period. Accordingly, although these four groups cannot be regarded as a 'sample' in the precise sense, they have been chosen in the light of this wider research experience. The problems they encountered are typical of many small and medium-sized organisations. The studies illustrate the way in which (tentative) theories about voluntary organisation illuminate one set of problems but leave a further set of unresolved problems. The model of roots was produced in order to deal with earlier unresolved problems, but in turn leaves a further set of issues to be explored.

A pregnancy-advice organisation

One of the intriguing features of work with many organisations is the limited extent to which lack of resources has emerged as the 'real' problem. Of course, the need to raise funds can be a recurring nightmare but, more often than not, apparent lack of resources can obscure deeper confusion. This proved to be so in the case of a small national organisation in the field of pregnancy advice, facing what was presented as a financial crisis. Originally an association of people opposed to abortion, it had attempted to become a service-delivery counselling organisation. Somewhere along the way, non-directive counselling had been adopted as one of several 'operational public explanations' – statements regarding the organisation's stance on abortion. This action seemed to be an opportunistic tactic for the attainment of immediate funding objectives, and not the consequence of any deeper desire to secure 'legitimacy'.

Interviews with staff and trustees, and analysis of documents, revealed that potential funding sources (private and governmental) were uneasy about the organisation and were consequently reluctant to provide support. Some members of the board, once they became aware of the incompatibility between public statements and their own beliefs, resigned.

A self-help agency for single-parent families

It is not only funding that can appear as the presenting, rather than the real, problem. A local group of lone-parent families (belonging to a national organisation) was plagued by internal conflicts which were usually presented as 'personality problems'. In the years preceding the research (see Chapter 10), the organisation had managed, through the energetic and talented efforts of a few of its members, to secure substantial government funding to employ staff.

The analysis uncovered two conflicting models of organisation. The first was a 'pure' self-help group solely concerned with the needs of its own members and content to operate in a highly informal fashion. At most it needed just a few paid staff to service its members. The second model was of an organisation working not just for the benefit of members, but for all the single-parent families in the locality. As such, it required more formal systems of decision making, accountability and governance. Paid staff were an essential component of the organisation. Many of the staff were not lone parents and did not consider themselves 'members'. In this instance the severe strains led to the establishment of two separate organisations: the 'group' of members, and the formal service-delivery organisation which became known as the 'trust'.

A self-help organisation for families

In another organisation, which also defined itself in its operational statements as a 'self-help' group, for families with disabled children, one of the starting problems was the tense relationship between some paid staff and members (families). Most of the funding came from private and public sources and was raised by a charismatic director. A number of local groups of parents were 'supported' by locally based staff employed by headquarters. Analysis revealed that some parents believed that 'self-help' really meant what it suggested, and that they controlled their own activities and the staff. Most staff, however, saw self-help as a method of working in a familiar service-delivery organisation and regarded themselves as 'accountable' to headquarters. It remained unclear whether the parents were really clients or members.

A marriage guidance council

The last, and most complex, case study was undertaken with a large, local, autonomous marriage guidance council (MGC). The National Marriage Guidance Council, to which it was affiliated, had been set up in the late 1930s by a group of doctors, solicitors, clergy and other professionals who were concerned about the rising divorce rate. Similar reasons had led to the establishment of the local group. The main activity of National MGC was the training and supervision of counsellors and 60 per cent of its income came from national government (National Marriage Guidance Council 1987). In response to a severe financial crisis and a management consultancy exercise, the national MGC had decided to move into a wider range of counselling beyond the family, and to change its name to 'Relate'.

The local MGC was unhappy with the change of direction and concerned about the ability of national headquarters to provide adequate training. The local group also had a very different funding base. Client 'contributions' had risen from 7 per cent in 1968 to 57 per cent in 1988. In the same period local government grants had fallen from 62 per cent to 34 per cent. Originally totally based on voluntary labour, a partly paid counselling scheme, whereby counsellors received modest hourly payments after a minimum number of free hours counselling were given, had been introduced in 1968. In recent years several full-time salaried staff, including a director, had been appointed. Approximately 50 per cent of counselling was still supplied by volunteers, 35 per cent by partly paid staff and the rest by salaried staff. Tensions were emerging not only with the national MGC but also within the local group itself.

BETWEEN BUREAUCRACY AND ASSOCIATION

This first part of the theory has already been presented in the preceding chapter. Summarising greatly, there are two central arguments. The first is that voluntary agencies occupy an 'ambiguous' territory where the worlds of bureaucracy and associations overlap. Management within the voluntary sector must, therefore, take into account not only the 'rules of the game' of the bureaucratic world, but also those operating in the associational world. The second argument is that the bureaucratic world can be further subdivided by drawing a distinction between government and business bureaucracies. Within the ambiguous territory in which voluntary agencies operate we can thus distinguish three distinct 'zones':

1 The zone of government-orientated agencies that look primarily to the state for their legitimacy and funding;

2   The zone of market-orientated agencies that look to the market and fee income;

3   The zone of entrepreneurial agencies which may have a strong membership base and also 'play the field'.[1]

The boundaries between zones are more fluid than those between bureaucracies and associations. Movement between zones is less dramatic than, for example, the move from association to bureaucracy. Nevertheless, it is a critical move, and one that can only be understood and planned with the aid of a theory that tries to explain the factors that might lie beneath the movement between zones. That will be attempted later in this paper.

The differentiation of associations from bureaucracies (as defined) and the consequent identification of a middle overlapping territory (with three internal zones), enables a distinctive type of voluntary organization – the agency – to be rescued from broader and less satisfactory bodies of analysis. Voluntary welfare agencies are distinctive because they have both (a) a group of people who are committed to the specific purposes of a particular organisation (this group is not necessarily the official 'membership') and (b) paid staff, who may be part of that group, and who deliver core operational services.

These agencies have probably been one of the fastest growing parts of the voluntary nonprofit sector and are increasingly seen as an important element of welfare state provision. Yet they have scarcely received the analytic attention they deserve. In Olsen's classic (1971) discussion of the theory of groups, the main concern is with large groups which he argues will find it difficult to provide themselves with optimal amounts of collective goods. No place is found for the hybrid agency. Thus 'philanthropic and religious organisations' are not debated because they do not have a 'significant economic aspect' (p.6, note 6). In another footnote Olsen recognises that, when examining charities, his theory ' . . . does not seem especially useful' (p.160, note 91).

Our four case studies confirm the importance of the fundamental distinction drawn in this paper between bureaucracies and associations. Since all of them, with the significant exception of the 'group' of lone parents, employed paid staff to undertake operational activities, we shall refer to them as agencies. The local MGC will also be called an agency, although its changing status is central to understanding its problems.

Many of the problems of the case study agencies can be seen as resulting from the tensions of adhering both to the rules of the game of the associational world (democratic elections, voting, etc.); and to those of the bureaucratic world (managerial command structures, contracts of employment, etc.). Thus the lone parents split into an association ('the group') and an agency ('the trust'). The local groups of parents in the family support organisation thought they were a genuine association, whereas the staff believed in an agency model. The research with the local MGC revealed the tension in its starkest form. Should the group move even further along the path from association to agency? Was it, as some counsellors suggested, losing contact with its 'roots'?

These studies indicate that the organisational theory of the nature of 'agencies' helps to explain some of the core problems encountered in the MGC and other case studies. Associations and agencies could see in broad terms the direction of their development. However, these studies also point to the possibility of taking the analysis further, of beginning to come to grips with the further set of problems of the pressures and forces that might lie behind the analysis of association and bureaucracy.

THE COMPONENTS OF AGENCY ROOTS

In discussions with participants in the case studies (and in workshops and other events) phrases such as 'the absence of roots', or 'losing contact with roots', have struck a sympathetic chord. A useful starting point in exploring further what this phrase might mean, and its connection with the analysis so far, is the dictionary definition which refers to drawing in strength, inspiration and sustenance. It is a definition which serves to remind us that, although resources might be seen as the sustenance element of roots, we must also remember the role of inspiration.

Looking again at the case studies, a number of central variables emerged which together may serve as an initial model of the 'root system', or 'source of strength', of an organisation. And meshed into the web of interacting elements of the root system is the governing body or board, a critical institution in the survival of the organisation. It is the governing body that has a crucial role in the production of what we have called major 'operational explanations' – explicit statements of distinctive organisational responses to problems.

The variables of the agency root system can be identified as:

1 implicit welfare policy
2 non-human resources
3 labour

Implicit policy of welfare accountability

In a succinct discussion of 'organisational goals', Scott (1987: 268) opens by declaring that the concept ' . . . is amongst the most slippery and treacherous of all those employed by organisational analysts'. He might also have added 'policy' as an equally slippery concept. In this paper the term 'operational explanations' has already been introduced, and to this can now be added the notion of *implicit policies*. These are at a broader level than operational explanations and, although they still relate in a general fashion to the activities of the organisation, they do not by themselves offer specific 'solutions'. Implicit policies may sometimes appear in some form of mission statement. More often they lurk in the background as organisational beliefs, influencing organisational policies, and becoming explicit in times of crisis – often as a result of external intervention. Beneath the various operational statements about 'non-directive counselling' were more fundamental beliefs about legal and medical approaches to the problem of unwanted pregnancy. Beneath the operational explanations about helping lone parents and families with handicapped children lay deeper issues about the relative responsibilities of individual, association and State to deal with the *specific* problem. And beneath the explanations about marital breakdown lay beliefs in the utility of specific types of therapy (individual, group, etc.).

Implicit policies may relate to any aspect of the problems being faced by the organisation. They may, in the form of analogy, legitimate and give strength to fragile institutions (Douglas 1987). And beneath these implicit policies lies the even deeper and often impenetrable level of values, views about the world and the nature of life which extend far beyond specific organisational boundaries.

In the case studies one type of implicit policy surfaced as being of particular importance, that is the question of responsibility for the problem to be addressed – what will be called its 'implicit policy of welfare accountability' which denotes a level of implementation between values and operational explanations.[2]

From the case studies, it can be seen that, when faced with the question of who should have prime accountability for resolving a problem, three possible answers could be discerned.

1 Accountability should lie with the individual problem-holder acting in isolation (e.g. individuals and families coming by self-referral to the local MGC);
2 For religious, 'community', pragmatic and other reasons, accountability should lie with like-minded people who may or may not have the problems themselves (as with the self-help groups);
3 the State should take prime accountability (as illustrated by National MGC, and the establishment of the trust in the case of the lone parents).

Financial resources

The second component of the root system is represented by its non-human resource base. Voluntary agencies need offices and buildings, money and equipment in order to provide their services. They raise the necessary funds by a wide range of means. They may receive donations from supporters, dues from members, legacies from well-wishers, fees in payment for services, concessions through the tax system, relief from payment of rates, contributions from payroll schemes, grants and contracts from government, money from special appeals and so on. One approach to the issue of resources has been developed by Weisbrod (1988) who has developed a table summarising 'characteristic relationships among an organisation's institutional form, the type of its output, and its unique source of financing' (p. 90). Accordingly, nonprofits are associated with collective/trust goods and donations; for-profits with private goods and sales revenue; and governmental organisations with collective goods and taxes. A central theme running through this work is the linear relationship between revenue and output: for example, 'an organisation's outputs reflect the sources of its revenues – and vice versa – deciding what society wants from the nonprofits and how the nonprofits should be financed requires joint decisions on activities and financing' (p. 89). There can be seen here, as well, almost a 'corporatist' stance (Williamson 1989).

An alternative approach adopted in this paper is to examine the way in which each of the three implicit policies of welfare is associated with its own typical source of finance. Thus, in (1) above, those with the problem are expected to pay for the solution through fees and the market system; in (2) the group acting on behalf of others or itself raises money through donations, legacies, appeals, membership dues, etc; and in (3) the government provides resources through the tax and allied systems.

Human resources

The third component, or source of strength, consists of the human resources at the disposal of the organisation. These resources essentially comprise (a) paid staff, and (b) volunteers undertaking operational and supporting work. We have argued that when an association employs paid staff to undertake its operational activities (those it was set up to undertake) this represents the most critical of all moves, the move into 'bureaucratic territory', to 'agency'. The move away from association and towards agency is well illustrated in the case of the local MGC which over two decades first introduced a category of 'partly paid' staff, then appointed a director followed by a few paid staff and, in 1989, set up a more substantial hierarchy with the appointment of an assistant director.

THE PROBLEM OF BALANCE

This study suggests that the various elements of the root system and the 'governing body' are in a constant state of interaction and adjustment to each other. We might note in passing that one implication of the analysis is that it is probably more realistic to refer to 'structures' or 'systems of governance' that would also take into account the role of paid and other staff. However, for simplicity, and in order to avoid confusion in the case studies, we shall just refer to governing bodies.

In some, probably newer, case-study agencies (for example, the self-help organisations and pregnancy-advice agency), the process of interaction in the root system can be traumatic. In other agencies with a longer history (the MGC), adjustments may take many years. The organisation's roots themselves interact and, in turn, are both influenced by, and influence, the explanation-producing governance structure. It seems also that a reasonable equilibrium or balance must be maintained between roots and governing body if agencies are to avoid severe problems. A few examples illustrate the interaction and the problem of balance.

In the pregnancy-advice agency, failure to analyse the link between operational explanations, implicit policy, funding and governing body led to resignations of the trustees. The core associational group (strongly against abortion) held beliefs that could, when made explicit, most appropriately be funded from supporters of that group. Local government agencies did not see abortion as a solution which they could support. The tactic of bringing on to the board a few more liberal, prestigious, medical trustees with a different view of welfare accountability did not succeed. Neither did the tactic of producing different statements for different funders. Their ambition of becoming an 'entrepreneurial agency' with varied sources of funding would have required operational explanations that really reflected the broader composition of the board.

In the case of the lone-parents self-help group, the belief that the problem was one which government should support led to applications for substantial funding and the hiring of paid staff. The tensions between different approaches towards responsibility for the problem (implicit policy of welfare accountability), and the consequent human resources required, led to the eventual division into association and agency, each with its own governing body. A new equilibrium of governing body and roots was established and the agency became oriented primarily towards government.

The local MGC study provides a fascinating account of the relationship between governing body and roots. As we saw, the organisation has slowly moved from association to agency. We may now add that one element on the governing body wanted to work closely with the National Health Service and social services departments as a government-orientated agency. However, the analysis of funding and counselling work has indicated the pressures towards other directions. Thus 'fee' income (associated with market operation) was usually more coyly called 'contributions', and was crucial. (On fees and professionalism see Van Til 1988.) Many newer counsellors were in favour of a private sector model of counselling and left the organisation once they were trained. However, a substantial group of the 'old guard' counselled without any payment and represented the associational roots of the agency. The different approaches to accountability for welfare and elements of the root system were pulling in different directions.

The theory presented here takes a very different approach to most studies of voluntary organisations, which appear to assume the existence of powerful and, from the point of view of the individual agency, largely uncontrollable forces. Despite the many important insights and conceptual advances contained in that body of literature, it is difficult to avoid the overwhelming impression that nonprofit organisations can do little to determine their own fate. Thus, to take a few examples, they may be subject to the inevitable march of the well known 'iron laws' of oligarchy (Michels 1962), formalisation (Chapin and Tsouderos 1956), or 'life cycles' (Stinchcombe 1965, Quinn and Cameron 1983, Weitzel and Jonsson 1989). Much of the resource-dependency literature (Levine and White 1961, Aldrich 1976, Benson 1975, Schmidt and Kochan 1977) shares a similar orientation.

Of particular interest, however, is the study by Ben-Ner (1987: 132) who puts forward an economic theory for interpreting nonprofit life cycles according to which 'nonprofit organisations are regarded . . . as strategic collections of self-interested individuals whose interests, and therefore their actions, may change with changes in the environment'. This is a rather limited definition, and would appear to exclude all those philanthropic and charitable organisations which are the focus of this paper. Nevertheless, it is one of the few studies which is based on empirical observation and which also begins to raise questions regarding the response that administrators might make to changes in the environment.

A major problem with the life-cycle literature is the limited role that is given to goals, explanations and policies. A similar criticism has been made by Hall (1987) of the resource-dependency model. He points out that the utility of the resource-dependence model is reduced '. . . since the idea of goals is sidestepped' (p. 308). He further argues that goals '. . . are part of the culture of the organisation and part of the mind set of decision makers' (p. 308) and must be brought back into the study of organisations. This, it can be claimed, must be particularly critical for such a people-dominated organisation as the voluntary agency.

In the roots model, the introduction of the concepts of operational explanation and implicit policy represent an initial effort to grapple with the slippery idea of 'goals' in a usable fashion. But in addition, the model attempts to take account of the link with the structure of governance, an issue which has rapidly occupied a central position in the study of nonprofits (Herman and Van Til 1989, Harris 1990).

CONCLUSION AND IMPLICATIONS

The objective of this paper is to assist in the development of theory that addresses the management problems faced by nonprofit voluntary organisations. The first part of the theory argued that voluntary *agencies* have features of both bureaucracies and associations, and that they can exist in three different zones (government, market and entrepreneurial). The second part portrayed the *root system* of agencies as a system of (a) implicit welfare policy (b) financial resources and (c) human resources. These must be in balance with the governance structure which provides the operational explanations. Each part of the root system was further analysed and examples provided of the tensions that can arise from severe imbalance. We concluded that, whilst all voluntary agencies face tensions flowing from their occupation of the bureaucratic and associational worlds, some strains can become intolerable and impede productive work and the survival of the organisation.

The system of roots was conceptualised as a dynamic interaction of implicit policies and human and financial resources. The analysis of roots is not just an examination of past history, but an exploration of current sources of resources and implicit policies, and their relation to structures of governance. Accordingly, voluntary agency behaviour cannot be regarded as solely, or necessarily primarily, determined by resource acquisition or constraints (Yuchtman and Seashore 1967).

There are important implications for public policy, which, certainly in the UK, does appear to assume a straightforward relationship between public resources and service outputs. Public policy treats the voluntary organisation as the 'black box' of our opening metaphor, as a system that is known only by the results it gives when activated, and not by an understanding of the way it works. Moreover, the repercussions on voluntary agencies of the changes in funding patterns, based on the changing governmental philosophy of accountability for welfare problems are not well understood. There may be profound long-term public policy implications. The connections between public policy, and the structure and processes of the voluntary organisations that are expected to implement that policy, deserve further research.

The major implications of the theory are at the level of the individual organisation. Analysis of the root system and its interaction with the governing body can allow agencies to review the balance of the various elements. It can help them to understand the consequences of decisions which can be taken blindly in rapid response to internal and external forces. Voluntary organisations can *choose* whether they wish to enter the alternative bureaucratic zones.

The model also raises many problems for further research. For example, what are the consequences of moving from the governmental to entrepreneurial zones? Can the same staff still do the job? What sort of governing structures will be required? Finally, this paper may serve to reinforce those approaches which do not view voluntary agencies as helpless bystanders on some larger stage, but as organisations capable of determining their own futures.

NOTES

1   It should also be noted that Hansmann (1980) uses the term 'entrepreneurial nonprofit' in a different fashion.
2   The use of 'implicit policy of welfare accountability' is rather different from the term 'welfare ideology' as used in Kramer (1965, 1985) which refers to a broader set of beliefs that express value preferences applicable well beyond the boundary of a single organisation. Indeed, an earlier version of this paper did refer to welfare 'ideology', but this now appears to be a word too closely associated with the study of membership associations by political scientists and economists.

13 Partnership: a policy in search of implementation

INTRODUCTION

The rise to greater prominence of the UK voluntary, or nonprofit, sector has been accompanied by the gradual and now widespread use of 'partnership' as a policy concept to describe its interaction with government. Is this just political rhetoric? Or can the concept actually be used in policy implementation? Few studies examine these issues from both sides in the relationship and from the perspective of policy implementation. This paper draws on a unique action-research project which enabled partnership to be explored as a policy searching for forms of practical implementation. It analyses the way in which the researcher, together with a local government authority and a large voluntary agency, collaborated in the clarification of interaction. The project led to the consideration of models which began to replace the original notion of 'partnership'. The paper discusses the wider social policy implications and the conditions under which 'partnership' and contracting can co-exist.

PARTNERSHIP AND SOCIAL POLICY

The rise of partnership as a dominant social policy concept

It is difficult to pick up a UK document concerned with the relationship between government (at both national and local level) and the voluntary sector without being impressed by the way in which 'partnership' has become a dominant social policy concept. The concept seems to have crept up on us, at first being used interchangeably with other words such as 'collaboration', 'co-ordination', co-operation' and 'joint' activities. Now a seemingly endless stream of governmental and other semi-official documents are well spiced with appeals to the virtues of partnership.

It is difficult to assess quite when partnership assumed its dominance. In a helpful, if rather unsympathetic, discussion of voluntary sector relations with government, Brenton (1985) notes that a number of central government departments began referring to partnership in 1977. Of particular significance was the government's 'partnership initiatives' in the inner cities which, although initially aimed at the different governmental agencies, recognised the voluntary sector's role as a 'central principle' (Williams 1983).

At about this time the Report of the influential Wolfenden Committee, which, although it included a government 'observer', was established by charitable foundations, suggested that:

> The Ministerial speeches quoted . . . are evidence of a general desire for partnership with the voluntary sector . . . . Central government, as we have seen, officially accepts the principle of partnership with the voluntary sector. . .

> (Wolfenden 1978: 73 and 85)

In fact Wolfenden appears to be rather optimistic. Governmental acceptance of the principle at that time is less evident than suggested. A consultative document called 'The Government and the Voluntary Sector' (Home Office 1978), issued by the government in response to Wolfenden, prefers to talk of encouraging 'closer collaboration'. The word 'partnership' appears only once and perhaps significantly it is the very last word of the document.

A more emphatic view on partnership was expressed by the report of a working party on the role of social workers (Barclay 1982) set up at the request of government by the National Institute of Social Work. The report talks of 'genuine', 'full-blooded' partnership and emphasises the need for joint planning, consultative and collaborative machinery and more explicit agreements. Some enthusiasm for the US system of 'purchase of service contracting' is also expressed.

The national representative body of the voluntary sector itself, the NCVO (National Council for Voluntary Organisations), apparently played and continues to play some part in encouraging the partnership theme. For example, the NCVO actively lobbied for policy involvement regarding the inner city partnership schemes (Williams 1983). More recently, in 1985, they established a Joint Working Party with representatives of the National Health Service (NHS) to produce a report (NAHA/NCVO 1987) which attempted to examine the theory and practice of partnership in the NHS. It should be noted that by this time central government had already begun to speak more often about 'partnership' in welfare, although it was primarily concerned about the relationships between the various governmental agencies, a perennial and unresolved problem. The National Health Service Reorganisation Act of 1973 gave health and local authorities a statutory duty to co-operate with each other in the planning of local services. The main arena for collaboration was to be the Joint Consultative Committee (JCC) which was to consider health, social services, education, housing and environmental health services. The voluntary sector again began to creep onto the partnership scene when in 1985 three voluntary sector representatives were included on each JCC.

It is difficult to determine how and when partnership began to achieve its dominance, and quite what was the influence of the voluntary sector in this process. One thing is quite clear: 'partnership is now a fashionable term' (NCVO/RIPA 1988). It is equally clear that the concept, as currently used in policy documents, can be used to describe many forms of interaction between governmental and voluntary agencies. It can include almost anything, ranging from the provision of financial and other support through to consultation and joint planning (NAHA/NCVO 1987). Indeed we may be forgiven for assuming that, at its broadest, merely standing in the same room or, as Mellor (1985) put it, 'fortnightly talks on the telephone' can be seen as a partnership.

Although we are concerned in this paper with the rise of the partnership concept in the UK, the position in the US would appear to be not dissimilar. It has been suggested by Van Til (1988: 151) that in general 'few themes have seemed more compelling to the organisational politics of the 1980s than the quest for effective partnerships . . . this theme appears to appeal to a widespread desire to "do more with less", to create "win-to-win" relationships, and to "get to yes"'. Another author (Salamon 1987a) refers to 'the "elaborate" and "extensive" partnership arrangements linking government and the nonprofit sector'.

One of the central questions for this paper will be the extent to which partnership could serve as a useful instrument of practical policy implementation. Or is its rise to prominence just political hocus-pocus?

Issues of government–voluntary sector relationships

We have observed so far that partnership has been broadly interpreted to include many kinds of interaction. For the moment we shall assume that, despite its elasticity, policy makers who refer to partnership have the intention, however vague, to describe something closer than formal or informal contracting. Certainly the establishment of JCCs demonstrated governmental intentions to create closer bonds with the voluntary sector. Because of the absence of UK research studies which examine partnership as a term of policy implementation we must turn to allied writings for clues to the main issues that might arise. Most of this neighbouring UK research has centred on the wider problems of collaboration in general (Challis *et al.* 1988, Hatch and Mocroft 1983, Hatch 1980, Billis and Harris 1986); the impact of government funding (Leat *et al.* 1986, Addy and Scott 1987); or the more immediate need to analyse the growth of contracting (Judge 1982).

In a brief summary of the literature on the 'dangers' to the voluntary sector of public funding, Knapp *et al.* (1987) suggest that these take four inter-related forms: bureaucratisation, inappropriate regulation, a threat to autonomy and the mission of the organisation, and financial insecurity. In the US the main problems have been succinctly summarised by Salamon (1987b) as: from the government side, accountability and control; from the nonprofit side, agency independence, distortion of mission and bureaucratisation. It seems that, in both the UK and the US, similar problems have emerged from the general writings on the inter-relationship between government and nonprofits.

There are other similarities. In the US, Salamon (1987a: 30) points out that, despite the fact that nonprofits received 40 per cent of their income in 1981 from government, ' . . . this partnership . . . has attracted surprisingly little attention . . . the phenomenon has been largely ignored in both public debate and scholarly inquiry'. In another study of contracting, Kramer and Grossman (1987) suggest that: 'most of the literature views the contracting process from the perspective of only one of the parties'. As we have seen, it cannot be claimed that the general question of collaboration has been ignored in the UK. Perhaps the traditional pivotal role of government in the provision of human services has encouraged somewhat greater interest. However, closer investigation indicates that most of the more general UK writing on inter-relations suffers from the same problem that Kramer and Grossman note, that is they take into real account only one side of the partnership.

The research reported in this paper revolves around the process of policy clarification in relation to the concept of partnership. We shall see that here too the question of *control and agency autonomy* emerges as a central feature. The paper has several distinctive characteristics. Firstly, it provides an excellent opportunity to study the dilemma of control and autonomy since the voluntary agency in question ought prima facie to have little real independence. Secondly, the action-research methodology adopted placed the researcher in a unique position to study the interaction, and indeed to be part of that interaction. Thirdly, the local authority concerned took the findings seriously and debated and developed the theoretical models developed in the study.

A STUDY OF PARTNERSHIP IN ACTION

Background

In this part we shall provide a brief background to the study, describe the methodology, and outline the main steps in the project. In order to preserve anonymity we shall call the local government area in which the study took place – 'Escot'. For that reason, and because of limitations of space, only essential background details can be provided. We believe that the limitations imposed by these constraints are modest and do not detract from the finding. Furthermore, action research in policy implementation has the particular characteristic that its findings can be and, in our case, were made available and debated in public. Accordingly, in this approach, many 'background' influences and pressures are forced into the open and become part of the process of 'explication' (Billis 1984: Chapter 2).

Escot is an urban area of local government covering a population of about 200,000. The ruling politicians of Escot's council (the body of elected politicians) belong to the Conservative Party and are closely identified with Thatcherite policies of privatisation and 'value for money'. Amongst the services falling within the statutory responsibilities of Escot was the provision of personal social services, primarily directly provided through its Social Services Department (SSD).

This paper is concerned only with the provision of care for the elderly, and the relationship between the council and Age Concern Escot (ACE), an independent charity and part of the national Age Concern movement. Of course much, probably most, care for the elderly is provided by the 'informal sector' of families and friends. In addition the housing department of the council and the National Health Service also provide services for the elderly. However, the provision of organised social services was dominated by the council's SSD and the voluntary agency ACE.

In 1987 the council provided 685 residential places for the elderly, either in its own homes (535 places) or in voluntary and private profit-making homes (150 places). In recent years residential places had declined in favour of more community-based services. About 3500 people received home helps and many thousands received meals on wheels, occupational therapy services, telephones and other communication systems from the council. However, and very significantly, most of Escot's statutory obligations with regard to day care had been 'delegated',[1] without any formal contract, to ACE who ran ten day centres. This is unlike the position in most of the rest of the country where day centres are often under the direct control of SSDs.

ACE was founded in 1947 and undertakes, in addition to its day care provision, a wide range of activities including social provision, community involvement, advice and information, social support and transport provision. At the time of the project (1986–7) there were some 70–80 paid staff and there was the extensive use of volunteers. About 80 per cent of its funding came from the council and several Escot councillors were members of its governing body. Dissatisfaction was expressed by ACE that the council funding did not take sufficient account of the increased frailty and dependency of the elderly in its centres, and the consequent increased resources that were needed. For its part the council was anxious to know whether it received value for money. All this provided the stimulus for the invitation to undertake the research.

Methodology and the study of partnership

We have discussed in detail elsewhere (Billis 1984) the methodological issues involved in the study of policy implementation. We argued there that the approach known as 'social analysis' was particularly appropriate for securing high quality data in sensitive situations. The key features of this approach are: collaboration between researcher and agency participants; focus on the problems posed by participants; the development and analysis of 'usable' theory and models. A central tool employed by the researcher is the problem-driven individual interview followed by the feedback of reports to participants.

The social-analytic approach has been widely utilised in single agency situations, particularly in the governmental and profit-seeking sectors (Rowbottom and Billis 1987). However, the study of policy implementation which ranges across single agency boundaries raises additional methodological problems arising from territorial jealousies.[2] In the project being reported this general approach was reinforced by the study of relevant documents, and group discussions. In this paper the more usual 'action-research' will be used as a convenient way to describe this type of policy-orientated collaborative research.

The changing terms of reference: caught in the middle

It is particularly important to present a short account of the changing terms of reference in this project because it reflects the confused state of the relationship between Escot and ACE, and the changing stance adopted by ACE towards the project and Escot. As we shall shortly see, the emerging weakness of 'partnership' as an implementable concept became reflected in the gradual withdrawal of the researcher from the project as the methodological approach, itself based on assumptions of 'partnership', began to be strained.

The researcher was invited by Escot SSD in February 1986 to undertake a project whose initial objective was to help the SSD and ACE 'to agree the level of service and priorities for the money the Council provides'. In reply the researcher noted the need 'to define quite carefully with yourselves and ACE what precisely' his role would be. At a meeting held in April 1986 with the SSD, the representative of Escot council and the director of ACE, the researcher suggested that a collaborative exercise was the most viable way of continuing. A later letter reported on progress to date and repeated the terms of reference: 'to work in a collaborative fashion with Age Concern in order to produce a middle-range policy document that will enable a constructive discussion to take place between Age Concern and Escot about policies and priorities'. The same letter pointed out that the researcher understood that a 'parallel exercise would be going on in the SSD . . . that a document could be produced, which would indicate the department's own priorities with regard to the elderly'.

The implicit assumption of the participants and the researcher, reflecting the apparent spirit of the April meeting and previous policy declarations, was that Escot and ACE were in some form of 'partnership'. That is to say, that both ACE and the SSD would complete similar exercises on policy clarification, enabling a constructive discussion between partners to take place. So far this project followed a similar path to that taken by an earlier report on ACE, undertaken by a major group of external management consultants, which had also assumed the existence of some form of 'partnership' model of relationships.

Eventually work began with the staff of ACE and key members of the SSD. The development of this level of policy was seen as the responsibility of the bureaucrats. The politicians had background parts and were involved at the critical points of initiating the project, keeping pressure on and making the final decisions.

Although it is not possible within the confines of this paper to provide a detailed account of the work undertaken, it is possible to provide a summary of the main areas of activity as they unfolded during the project. The main areas, which had distinct but inter-related outcomes, were: policy clarification with ACE; the day centre exercise (not reported here); and clarification of SSD policy.

The process of working with ACE in a collaborative fashion to help to clarify their policy was confidential and took place during the early part of the project when assumptions of 'partnership' were dominant. One significant event was a group discussion held with middle and senior level staff in May 1986. At this meeting alternative models began to be identified, a process which was continued in a series of individual discussions with staff of ACE. With the gradual change in the perception of

ACE's relationship to the department, the researcher became more distant from the policy and organisational clarification which continued inside ACE.

The other main strand in this project was the clarification of SSD policy and involved a series of discussions with the senior responsible staff of the SSD. These discussions looked at three aspects of service provision for the elderly: day care, welfare and holidays. It was felt that the SSD needed to provide day care services for those elderly/infirm people who are too well for hospital care, but nevertheless need a great deal of support. Many questions were raised. To what extent did ACE provision meet the requirements of the SSD? What precise work was undertaken by the ACE welfare workers? Were they doing something totally different to the workers of the SSD? Were they 'mopping up' clients not dealt with by the statutory authorities? Or, were their services additional – and perhaps not as high an SSD priority? It became evident to all involved that the SSD had not previously invested the necessary effort in clarifying its own policy in an area of provision which was less politically sensitive than other areas of its provision.

Following the policy clarifications undertaken with ACE as part of the project, and following internal developments in ACE, it slowly became evident during the summer and autumn of 1986 that the basis for a collaborative exercise in policy development between the researcher, ACE and Escot, was disappearing. The partnership assumptions were being replaced by assumptions based on negotiations between two agencies.

The changing terms of reference were in large part influenced by internal developments in ACE. The flow of documents which were received and discussed with ACE during 1986 gave a clear indication of the changes that were implemented, and the serious thought that had been given to the future direction of ACE. Although these documents were naturally confidential to ACE, permission was given for the director's statement of November 1986 to be made public. The key points of that statement were:

- a reminder of the underlying constitutional position – 'ACE is an independent, local voluntary organisation . . .';
- the changes in staff and management committee structure that were in progress;
- the alternative 'models' of policy direction which confronted ACE as possible choices.

In general the director's statement strongly reaffirmed ACE's *independence*, and presented its current position with regard to Escot, which of course was reflected in the changing terms of reference. Thus, the document states that: ' . . . the question for Age Concern must be what are its own priorities. It is then the task of Escot Council to determine the extent to which these priorities reflect its own, and which services and activities it will choose to fund'.

It became clear to the researcher that his role, and the nature of the project itself, reflected a deeper confusion regarding the relationship between the local government (Escot) agency and ACE. A start had to be made to make explicit that which was inexplicit and confused.

PARTNERSHIP IN OPERATION

Alternative models

The researcher's report was presented in May 1987 and included, amongst other things, an outline of four tentative 'models' of possible relationship. These attempted to make explicit the underlying assumptions of the participants in the project and develop them into statements open to critical discussion (Billis 1984). The role of the researcher, according to the methodology adopted, was not to act as a consultant and propose executive action. Ownership of the problem was seen to remain with Escot and ACE. Thus the hope was that the process of explication would eventually lead the participating agencies themselves to make more detailed proposals for implementation. The report noted that there were doubtless other models which remained to be developed, and that each model had its own implications. It was further suggested that 'the extent to which "mixed" models can co-exist, and the relationship of each model to the different categories of need, remains to be explored'. (As we shall shortly see, both these aspects were in fact explored further by the two agencies.) The models – which are now described as they appeared in the original report – were:

- Subordination
- Contracting
- Supporting
- Partnership

In the first model ACE was seen to be in a position of *subordination*, and was essentially an adjunct of Escot Council. Since the council provides the great majority of the funding, it is easy to understand this perception. In this model, however tactfully the relationship is handled, Escot can dictate to ACE what it wants and what it will pay for. 'Partnership' is thus a matter of style rather than substance, there is no real negotiation and the basic approach is 'do as we say'.

The second model is that there is a *contractual* relationship between Escot and ACE. Thus the council and its SSD would need to know what it wanted, and ACE would need to demonstrate that it could deliver the quantity and quality of desired services. The degree of specification might vary, for example, according to the service, so too might the degree of 'monitoring' of adherence to the contract. The basic approach is 'here is what we want, can you provide it?'

The third model is that Escot was regarded as a general *supporter* of ACE. The council feels that ACE as a whole is worth supporting, and provides a grant to ensure the general viability of the Age Concern enterprise. Here, unlike the contracting model, very detailed discussion of services is not essential. Of course ACE must adhere to broad policy limits and retain credibility, but the basic approach might be 'here is your grant, get on and do a good job'.

Finally, the *partnership* model. Here the researcher tried to get to grips with what the minimum conditions might look like for the word 'partnership' to be reasonably employed. The key statements were that: 'An important precondition appears to be that each side respects the contribution of the other and accepts that they are bound together in a common endeavour. Presumably, partners must be able to discuss and plan matters openly on the basis of trust and without the danger of one side penalising the other'.

How did ACE and Escot respond to the analysis?

Implementing the models: the voluntary agency (ACE) position

Although the researcher's formal involvement with Escot ceased in May 1987, documents were later made available which demonstrate the way in which both ACE and Escot Council responded to the analysis.

In August 1987 the executive committee (the governing body) of ACE met to discuss funding and services. It discussed the alternative models and noted that 'at present the dominant model appears to be an uneasy combination of subordination and supporting, which is unsatisfactory for both organisations, and may be the basis for many of the present difficulties'. The executive continued by suggesting that neither model was really satisfactory since subordination 'failed to recognise the contribution of ACE as an *independent* voluntary organisation; supporting fails to define sufficiently clearly the delegated responsibility the council is required to undertake'. As far as the popular partnership concept was concerned, the executive gave it short shrift, considering it to be unrealistic in the current funding relationship.

The executive proposed a mixture of the supporting and contracting models. Thus the council would pay agreed fees for specific services, and in addition the general activity of ACE would be supported by the council through an annual grant as at present. ACE would also continue with its independent fundraising activities.

The executive concluded that having come so far 'it is desirable that ACE and the council continue to work together to develop a joint supporting/contracting relationship'.

Implementing the models: the local government (Escot) position

In September 1987 the director of Escot SSD presented two reports to his politicians – the council of Escot. One discussed 'the relationship with ACE' and the other report began to identify the key elements in the development of a 'partnership system' with the voluntary sector.

The 'relationship' report, perhaps not surprisingly in view of the collaborative nature of much of the exercise, echoed many of the comments found in the ACE executive committee discussion. On the matter of partnership it stated that the researcher 'appears to be equating the concept of partnership with that of active participation or co-operation, although this is not the sense in which it is more generally used, nor in which it is used in other reports on this agenda'. (This report fails to inform us in what different sense the concept had been used.) The director continued by admitting, and thus agreeing with ACE, that 'despite its undoubted attractions', it is unlikely that 'true partnership' as defined by the researcher can ever be effectively developed with ACE unless it had 'substantial independent funding'. We have to look at the second report to discover what partnership, from the local government point of view, might mean.

The report also agreed that (a) the current dominating model was a combination of subordination and supporting and 'might be the basis of many present difficulties', and (b) that the supporting and contracting models offered the best potential for future development. An important further step was taken in the effort to make explicit the relationship with ACE by attaching functions to each of the basic models. Thus it was proposed that a supporting model should be adopted for what were seen as (1) 'developmental' activities – identifying new needs, and developing alternative or innovative responses, and (2) 'quality of life' activities – not essential but designed to improve general enjoyment of life, social interaction or support.

It was suggested that the *contracting model* should be adopted for what were called 'agency activities', e.g. where ACE provided specific services such as day care on behalf of the council. The fourth identified function – campaigning activities – is not mentioned as a possible source of support.

The second report considered partnership as seen by the government agency. Partnership is rather casually explained as: 'formally agreed operating relationships between the key authorities'. The preferred relationship is later described as one in which the larger voluntary agencies, in particular, would 'join in' the planning process with the various governmental agencies. In this document there is a strong emphasis on contracting, no mention is made of the supporting model and no real effort is made to take on board the analysis made in the first report. Both reports were accepted by the council.

So, can there be life for 'partnership' beyond contracting with perhaps a gentle genuflexion towards planning? Does the case study perhaps indicate possible useful meanings for partnership which perhaps do not go quite as far as the 'tough' model presented in the research? What implications can we draw from this case study for control and autonomy? Are there implications for partnership and social policy? We pick up some of these issues in the conclusions.

DISCUSSION AND CONCLUSIONS

Autonomy and control

The Escot–ACE study illustrates the struggle to translate the broad policy concept of partnership into operational terms. It is a struggle, we shall suggest, that may be echoed in many other local authorities and is symptomatic of the current stage of British social policy. In Escot, at one extreme, the process of clarification forced the local authority to the painful admission that it held assumptions and models of voluntary agency subordination. These it publicly rejected. More importantly for the study of voluntary agencies, the process of policy clarification was acknowledged by ACE to have contributed to its process of self-realisation that it was indeed an independent agency. The researcher became only too conscious of this process with the collapse of the partnership assumptions of the methodology.

We therefore have to throw a further factor into the wider debate on autonomy and control (Hartogs and Weber 1978, Kramer 1981, Kramer and Grossman 1987, Leat *et al.* 1986). In the era of increased governmental support, successful voluntary agencies do not only need leaders with entrepreneurial and political talents (Young 1987); they will also need leaders who are educated and prepared to devote the energy to that area of policy formulation and dissection that has traditionally been a strength of the governmental civil service. Voluntary agencies are usually small and specialised compared with governmental agencies. They also have more at stake. They might, like ACE in this project, discover that clarifying policy can be a source of strength and contribute to independence. A similar point is made by Hatch and Mocroft (1983) who point to the advantage of 'having a sophisticated understanding of . . . SSDs . . . and the ability to adapt their own (voluntary organisation's) behaviour accordingly'. Apart from the other potential gains from policy clarification, they may, like ACE, be able to keep several steps ahead of governmental funders who, as we noted in the case of the Escot SSD, have to contend with other burning problems and pressures.

Partnership

And what of partnership? It is tempting to use the evidence from Escot as evidence to support the case against partnership. Certainly, both sides did not only abandon subordination; they also abandoned partnership as used in the research (acceptance of a common endeavour, open discussion and planning, and lack of penalties). Whilst this was not put forward as a tight definition, it was intended to encourage an examination of what a partnership model might look like.

And yet, despite rejecting the tougher view of partnership, Escot continued to search for an operational strategy. Was this just window-dressing or evidence of 'corporatism' (Wilson and Butler 1985a) at the local level? Such views imply a clarity of thought, an agreement of values and ideas, and a coherence of bureaucratic action which are well outside the reality of UK local (and probably national) government. They fail also to take into account changing public opinion and perception of social needs, and the requirement of politicians to make pragmatic short-term responses.

We suggest therefore that Escot, in its search for an operational explanation, was reflecting a real desire for a change in government–voluntary sector relationships. It is a desire which, at the point where we left the story, had not been translated into operational policy. The large general purpose ('block') grant that it gave to ACE had originated from the consensus era when welfare state assumptions of the dominance of governmental services were widely accepted. As we saw, this was generally agreed to be within a model of subordination and there was little pressure to make explicit what was uncontroversial and problematic.

We may hazard a broader proposition that the Escot study, because of its closeness to central government thinking, crystallises and highlights a more general UK position. It reflects the tension between old welfare state assumptions, and newer trends of entrepreneurialism and privatisation which have moved well beyond the narrow boundaries of the Conservative

Party. Thus the Escot dilemma may be that of many other government–voluntary sector relationships, either today, or in the near future. Within the old welfare state paradigm, governmental support for voluntary agencies, excluding purchase of services, was either peripheral, or part of a model of subordination. In this paradigm the general purpose block grant – a gift from government – was a convenient method of finance. In one sense it did represent a 'partnership', reflecting general acceptance of the relative roles of the governmental and voluntary sector in the provision of welfare. If it was not then (in the 1970s) spoken of as a 'partnership', this was also a reflection both of the more modest nature of the support offered at that time, and the absence of any real effort by government to introduce other elements of a relationship that could be even loosely described as a partnership.

The fact that in our study Escot fell back on general sentiments about 'joining in' planning, rejected hard definitions of partnership, and expressed contradictory approaches to adoption of the supporting model with its general purpose grant, need not mean the end of the story. There were sufficient clues provided to enable us to move a few further steps ahead.

It may be helpful at this stage to distinguish partnership, as it might be applied to the voluntary 'sector', and as it might affect an individual agency. In the former usage it would be used as an indicator of sympathetic positive policy towards an aggregation of voluntary organisations who, whilst they share fundamental defining characteristics, also jealously guard their independence and differ amongst themselves in objectives, power and influence. They belong to the sector, but by their nature cannot act as a sector. They can be treated as a sector in implementation terms only insofar as it is possible to introduce policies that are general rather than specific in their application. Thus the introduction of payroll giving in the UK might be taken as an example of the implementation of national 'partnership' policies. On the other hand when the attempt is made to translate and implement partnership policy assumptions into, for example, planning – which necessarily involves treating an aggregation of individual agencies as a coherent sector – then we need not be surprised that inter-sectoral planning shows such little evidence of success (Leat *et al.* 1981, Webb and Wistow 1986, NCVO 1986, NCVO/RIPA 1988).

The use of the same term 'partnership' runs into more difficulties when, as in the case study, it is used both to describe governmental approaches to the sector (as in the second Escot report) and as an operational term at the individual level. Here broad statements of intent will not suffice. At the personal, individual level of inter-agency relationships, partnership must mean something beyond contracting, or even substantial participation in planning specific projects. For example, it is difficult to see quite how partnership could be used in any sensible sense to describe relationships which are based only on contracting. We would be forced to fall back on uncomfortable terms such as 'pragmatic partnership' (Kramer 1971). Indeed, we might hypothesise that, to the extent that the UK follows the US in the introduction of contracting, then partnership will sound increasingly hollow as a national policy theme.

Neither can partnership be salvaged just by adding dollops of participation in planning, or formally agreed operating relationships, however welcome. If it is to survive as a policy at agency level, and consequently perhaps at local and national level, something more will be needed. Government, as the powerful partner, will indeed need to demonstrate reciprocity (Brenton 1985), some tangible evidence of common purposes beyond talking. Here there may be clues in the case study which indicate how partnership, even if it does not extend to the closer relationship rejected in this study, might be developed to mean something more than the purchase of services, or cosy chats. We suggest therefore that the acid test will be whether government agencies provide some degree of funding for general or 'arms length' (NCVO 1984) support, in addition to contracting. Whether they say, in fact, 'Here is your grant – get on and do a good job'. We can expect no less from a partner.

Such mixed models, of specific and general purpose grants, may be more likely to be acceptable within the Welfare State tradition in the UK than the US. They might represent a genuine contribution towards a new balance of welfare provision which ensured that voluntary agencies did not become pale reflections of private or governmental agencies.

Partnership or coalition? Building a research agenda

Partnership might survive for some time as a general policy indicator. We can readily understand why it has appeal for politicians. Not only is it a word of elastic interpretation, always attractive, it is one of a select group of policy slogans that are difficult to dispute. Like, for example, 'prevention', it appears to be a self-evident 'good thing' (see Chapter 7). Such portmanteau policy phrases may be inevitable as indicators of general currents of political sentiment. We can also understand, as we noted earlier in this paper, why the organised representatives of the voluntary sector have sought to forward partnership as a broad brush policy. It reinforces a climate of opinion in which service provision moves away from the governmental agencies and where governmental resources are even more likely eventually to emerge. The growth in government funding of recent years supports their stance.

We have raised more doubts regarding its adoption as a concept for implementation at the agency level, and have raised for discussion whether failure to discover an operational definition at this level might not in time undermine the broader usage of the term. We have speculated regarding the extent to which the supporting plus contracting models utilised in the study might lay the foundation for a view of partnership which synthesised the older welfare state traditions with the newer entrepreneurial trends.

But how realistic is it to envisage partnership becoming a meaningful term of policy implementation? Could UK government and voluntary agencies develop relationships that are not only based on contracting, even with joint planning, but which also provide general support for the wider mission of the voluntary agency?

Clearly, it is not just a wild speculation, otherwise Escot, a tough no-nonsense local authority, would not be giving it serious consideration. Furthermore, careful scrutiny of an important recent report on 'community care' (Griffiths 1988) reveals some intriguing comments. The report emphasises the need for clear agreements and expresses a strong preference for contracting on a fee-per-client basis, or the provision of a given level of service. It also rather grudgingly agrees that voluntary organisations fulfil a 'variety of other roles' (self-help, information, befriending, advocate for individuals, constructive critic, public educator, pilot of new approaches to services, campaigner) which 'can be vital in helping to make the best use of public funds'. Consequently: 'they may often merit some public financial support'. Although these sentiments smack more of public sector expediency than sentiments of partnership, they are worth pursuing and deserve attention.

At the moment, however, local government–voluntary agency relationships may well be better described by the dictionary definition of coalition: 'a temporary alliance of distinct parties for a limited purpose'. They are closer perhaps to what has been identified in the US (Kramer and Grossman 1987) as a 'quasi-market system' which is ' . . . at variance with the more conventional one of a government–voluntary agency "partnership" in which power considerations are minimised'. Closer also to what has been suggested (Challis *et al.* 1988) as the 'planned-bargaining' model.

In this major area we have little idea what initiatives between government and voluntary sector are really under way. As we noted at the start of this paper, there are few research studies of the process of implementation which examine from both sides the way in which the new social policy trends are being integrated into existing systems. What are the factors and pressures that influence the adoption of particular approaches? What is the range and scope of such arrangements? What initiatives represent social policy innovations of wider utility? Will some of these newer systems lead to the domination of the larger agencies, to 'structuration' (DiMaggio 1983)? What, in the UK, will be the impact of community care policies as suggested in the (Griffiths (1988) Report? What impact does all this make on the client? Some commentators (Gutch and Young 1988) have suggested that government–voluntary sector relations are poised between the dangers of an ' . . . environment in which the prospects for survival let alone constructive relationships seem remote' and the opportunities which might lead to 'new and exciting relationships . . .' (Gutch and Young 1988: 12).

The problem is that we just do not know. Our research agenda is thus remarkably similar to that in the US where a study of contracting (Kramer and Terrell 1984) pointed out that we really did not know very much about its magnitude, its general character, or its significance for government, voluntary agencies, and the people using the service. This paper is intended as a contribution to an area of studies which is generally agreed to have been neglected, but which it can be argued should emerge more centrally onto the research agenda.

NOTES

1   Delegation has been defined as: ' . . . situations where authority is delegated to an organisation to carry out an activity. . . whether the delegation is by a formal contract or not' (Smith and Hague 1971, p.79).
2   I have refrained from attempting to include the substantial literature on inter-agency collaboration since this does not take into account either the developing body of knowledge of the distinctive organisational features of nonprofits, or the particular characteristics of the newer governmental–nonprofit relationships (Kramer and Terrell 1984).

14 Exploring government intervention

INTRODUCTION

This paper tries to deepen our understanding about government and the voluntary sector by unravelling some of the key metaphors employed in the policy debate. As Boland and Greenberg (1988: 17) suggest, metaphors draw ' . . . an analogy between one thing that is more familiar and another thing that is less familiar . . . '. Thus metaphors such as 'privatisation', 'colonisation', and 'partnership' conjure up an association with more familiar situations – the independence of being 'private', the authoritarianism and subordination of a 'colony', and the cosy constructive togetherness of being a 'partner'.

For the purposes of this analysis 'voluntary' can roughly be equated with 'nonprofit' or 'nongovernmental' as used in other countries. Most of the voluntary organisations under consideration operate primarily in the field of social welfare, particularly the personal social services. Thus the arts, recreation and leisure are excluded from consideration. Although most of these agencies operate at the local level, we shall mainly be concerned with central government since its power and influence dominate the policy debate.

Some early words of caution are needed. The problems of typologies and precise definition are well-known, difficult, and largely unresolved (Wolfenden 1978, Hatch 1980, Gronbjerg 1989). Any attempt to provide more specific boundaries to this paper is likely to be premature and counterproductive. For example, the analysis might be artificially forced into existing functional categories (such as 'health', 'personal social services', etc.) which largely reflect governmental bureaucratic organisation and which may not take into account the more fluid administrative boundaries of voluntary organisations.

The first part of this paper discusses different forms of governmental intervention and outlines some of the policy metaphors which are used to describe the relationship with the voluntary sector. In the second part, governmental approaches to the component parts of the sector are examined against the main metaphors whose utility is seen to vary from arena to arena. The final part attempts to peer beyond current metaphors.

DESCRIBING THE GOVERNMENT–VOLUNTARY SECTOR RELATIONSHIP

This first section of this part offers a few statistics about the voluntary sector and moves on to discuss different types of government intervention in the voluntary sector. The second section briefly examines several of the metaphors that are used to describe the relationship between the two sectors.

Forms of government intervention in the voluntary sector

Before discussing the ways in which government can intervene in the life of the voluntary sector, a few statistics may be helpful. In fact, most descriptions of the dimensions of the voluntary sector in the UK rely on a few limited studies. Information is usually scarce, limited, and often out of date. It has been estimated (Gerard 1983) that there are more than 350,000 voluntary organisations in Britain (including private schools and trade unions). More reliable figures are available for charities where Woodfield (1987) suggested that there were 'probably' 275,000 of which 160,000 were registered with the Charity Commission, the responsible government department.

Total income of registered charities in 1986 was estimated at £12,650 million (4.1 per cent of GNP): of this the main sources were (a) 61 per cent fees and charges (b) 15 per cent fund raising and donations (c) 11 per cent rents and investments (d) 11 per cent statutory bodies (CAF 1987). Posnett (1988) estimated that the total net income of registered charities had risen by 32 per cent in real terms in the period 1980–85, and that statutory grants represented the fastest growing component of income.

According to government statistics support to voluntary bodies in the period 1980–86 rose in real terms by some 221 per cent (Hansard 14 April 1988). In a slightly shorter period (1982–86) grants from non-departmental public bodies rose from £857 million to £1,649 million. To complete the picture for 1986 we have to take into account £1,048 million to housing associations and societies and £600 million tax concessions. There was also £545 million in grants from local authorities. However, since central government has a massive impact on local government, what central government decides to do will inevitably have repercussions on the voluntary sector.

The overall picture is one of substantial growth of financial resources, particularly in public sector support; the continued domination of fees and charges as a source of revenue; and more modest increases directly attributable to government action such as taxation changes, and payroll giving. Financial support of this type can be regarded as 'primary' forms of intervention.

However, there are other, less visible, but powerful forms of what can be called 'secondary' governmental intervention. Thus government can act to *stimulate* financial resources. For example, politicians may make speeches, write articles, and use the media to encourage individuals and companies to fund specific agencies or classes of organisation. In addition they may make public appearances or act as sponsors for particular causes and thereby give legitimacy to the organisation. Government may reward companies that support charities by the award of knighthoods and other honours.

Yet another secondary type of intervention may be 'exhortation', or the adoption of an 'educational' approach. For example, the government may attempt to influence the pool of volunteers. Thus the Minister responsible for the voluntary sector, when asked whether he saw any objection to politicians 'thumping the tub' to generate greater voluntary activity, replied 'No . . . I certainly regard the voluntary sector as just beginning to realise its potential' (BBC 8 Dec 1988).

In addition to these primary and secondary methods of support, central government influences the activities of the sector through its regulatory powers, through legislation, and through the action and attitudes of bodies such as the Charity Commission and governmental departments. A full study of relationships with the sector would thus also have to take into account the regulatory dimension, and the way in which government can manipulate the levers of power to change attitudes and approaches (Ware 1989).

Even this preliminary and tentative exploration of ways and processes of intervention indicates that they are wider than the present tendency to highlight the highly visible funding sources.

We now move on to examine several of the metaphors that are used to discuss government and voluntary sector. The most popular of these is 'partnership', which co-exists with a more general policy of 'privatisation'. More critical policy observers, in particular from the academic community, have prefered 'corporatism' and 'colonisation'. Recently 'contracting' has become a major theme, and has lost its purely technical meaning by the use of phrases such as 'contracting out culture' (Harding and Thompson 1989: 36). A review of these terms, many of which have attracted a vast body of literature, is clearly beyond the scope of this paper. Nevertheless, some brief descriptions are required.

Privatisation and contracting

Savas (1987: 3) claims that this 'awkward' sounding word (privatisation) first appeared in a 1983 dictionary when it was narrowly defined to mean the change from public to private control of ownership. He suggests that 'privatisation' may now be more broadly defined as a new way of looking at society's needs or as ' . . . the act of reducing the role of Government, or increasing the role of the private sector, in an activity or in the ownership of assets'. In discussing alternative arrangements for providing goods and services, Savas states that 'Privatisation means changing from an arrangement with high government involvement to one with less' (pp. 89–90).

Other authors (Le Grand and Robinson 1984), discussing privatisation and the UK Welfare State, accept a similar definition but suggest that the term must contain some classification of the ways in which the State can involve itself in an area of social and economic activity, and suggest provision, subsidy and regulation.

The broad definition of privatisation is similar to the broad definition of 'contracting' as covering 'all situations where authority is delegated to an organisation to carry out an activity . . . whether the delegation is by formal contract or not . . .' (Smith and Hague 1971: 79). Alternatively, it is possible to take a much narrower definition of privatisation than Savas to mean 'strictly the permanent transferring of services or goods production activities previously carried out by public service bureaucracies . . . ' (Dunleavy 1986).

Partnership

A brief history of the rise of the word 'partnership' as a policy metaphor was provided in the previous chapter. We might just recall that Brenton (1985) points out that a number of central government departments began referring to partnership in 1977. Since then numerous committees, consultative documents, reports and Acts have continued to employ the term as a way of describing the relationship between government and the voluntary sector. As we noted in the earlier chapter, representatives of the voluntary sector have themselves played no small part in encouraging the use of the word.

Corporatism and colonisation

The literature on corporatism has reached 'intimidating proportions' (Rhodes 1985: 288). Rhodes identifies corporatism as a system of government–interest group relations which must contain a number of key features including (a) aggregation – the 'licensing' of groups and the granting of a 'monopoly' in their policy area, (b) incorporation – the *formal* co-option of groups into central decision-making processes, (c) intermediation – the process whereby interest groups not only articulate the interests of their members but also articulate the interests of the centre to their members, and (d) regulation – interest group leaders control their members by regulating demands and ensuring compliance with any agreement struck with the government.

Even scholars from within this school of thought find it essential to explain that 'the corporatist paradigm is not interpreted or employed in any concrete or unified manner by its exponents' (Wilson and Butler 1984: 2). Nevertheless, the authors suggest that relationships between the State, the national associations of the voluntary sector, and the voluntary sector demonstrate a kind of 'selective corporatism' in which the State exerts 'pressure upon voluntary organisations to conform to particular modes of operation in selected domains' (Wilson and Butler 1985a: 25).

Another metaphor, 'colonisation', has primarily been used at the local level to describe situations where statutory (and voluntary) agencies seize social systems and subordinate them to their own needs (Abrams in Bulmer 1986: 129–133). Colonisation was regarded as having a number of different forms: (a) domination – imposing a hierarchy of control, (b) appropriation – redrawing and redefining boundaries so as to change perceptions and bringing what was once informal into the formal, (c) incorporation – the formal agency builds a measure of informality into its procedures.

The intention of this paper is to examine the extent to which these popular policy metaphors further our understanding of developments in the voluntary sector. This is the objective of the next section.

THE METAPHORS IN PRACTICE

Any useful exploration of relevance of the policy metaphors discussed above in the voluntary sector must first get to grips with the nature of the sector itself. In Chapter 11 a theory of the voluntary sector was presented which argued that (a) voluntary agencies occupy an 'ambiguous' territory where the worlds of bureaucracy and associations overlap, and (b) the bureaucratic world can be further subdivided by drawing a distinction between government and business bureaucracies. Within the ambiguous territory in which voluntary agencies operate we can thus distinguish three distinct 'zones':

1 The zone of government-orientated agencies that look primarily to the state for their legitimacy and funding;

2 The zone of market-orientated agencies that look to the market and fee income;
3 The zone of entrepreneurial agencies, which may have a strong membership base and also 'play the field'.

From this it can be seen that there are at least five distinct different arenas for possible government intervention. We now turn to examine developments in the different arenas, and the extent to which current metaphors are helpful. The following comments are offered as speculations, drawing on whatever slender strands of evidence, personal research, and impressions are available.

Intervention in the bureaucratic arena

Although governmental 'welfare bureaucracies' are not the subject of this paper, we must take into account the desire of central government to reduce the service delivery role of the State, especially the local delivery of personal social services. This gives some initial validity to the broad definition (less government involvement) of privatisation. Another argument in favour of privatisation as a useful metaphor has been the decrease in the number of homes for the elderly provided by local government and the rise in the number of private residential homes. However, the move against institutionalisation predates privatisation (Goodwin 1989), and the rapid entry of the private sector into residential care for the elderly appears primarily to have been the unintended consequence of other policy changes.

There are more serious objections to the broad definition of privatisation. Although one element of government intervention – direct provision – may be decreasing, the other two elements (subsidy and regulation) are not (see Le Grand and Robinson 1984). Even if substantial moves are made, following the Griffiths Report (1988) to increase contracting-out, this seems to be balanced by an increase in regulation. How do we weigh the different elements? Is this more or less privatisation?

Government and voluntary agencies

Not surprisingly these 'bureaucratic-associations' have been the central arena for government action. They are what government understands best because they are closest to its own model of hierarchical, accountable organisation. We outline now some of the main trends. We begin by noting the establishment of general and specialist co-ordinating or 'intermediary' bodies at national and local level, a process which was encouraged by the

Wolfenden Report (1978). Several writers such as Wilson and Butler (1985a) have questioned the cosy relationships that have been developed with government. However, as was noted in Chapter 13 the corporatist 'threat' as often presented may not be as great as is sometimes suggested.

The large agencies are getting a larger slice of resources including government grants. This can be demonstrated by extrapolating from the limited statistics (CAF 1987). In 1980 the income (in round figures) of the largest 400 of the 150,000 trusts and charities was £772 million. This represented 10.6 per cent of the total estimated income of the charitable sector. In 1985 the 400 received £1516 million out of a total sector income of £12,650 million, or 12 per cent of the total. In the same five years government grants to the sector as a whole rose by 138 per cent, whereas the top 400 managed an increase in grants of 218 per cent. We have here convincing evidence of the 'structuration' (DiMaggio 1983, DiMaggio and Powell 1983) of the sector.

We may perhaps better understand agency developments by returning to the distinction drawn between governmental and business bureaucracies. It was suggested that there are three different zones of voluntary agency: (1) those who look primarily to the State for their legitimacy and funding, (2) those who look to the market and fee income, and (3) those who may well have a strong membership base and also 'play the field'.

Using this subdivision, a number of significant shifts can be observed, in particular from zone 1, to zones 2 and 3. Agencies that previously assumed a consensus of view and purpose between themselves and government have discovered that they have built their enterprises on shaky foundations. For example, housing associations are now turning to private sector sources of income – 'the fear is that the charitable objectives rooted in the Victorian Ruskinite philanthropy of Octavia Hill will be abandoned and they will end up as the private rented sector arm of some impersonal financial institution' (Travis 1989). Statistics of fees and charges in UK charities display 'surprisingly little uniformity' (CAF 1988) but it seems that agencies, in their growing dependence on fees, are moving in similar directions to those identified in the US (Geiger and Wolch 1986).

The prime policy metaphor intended to encompass all the three zones of ambiguous agencies is 'partnership' which has an uneasy coexistence with 'contracting'. Since most UK personal social services are delivered at local level, both terms would ideally need to be explored in many different localities. However, the rising control and domination of central over local government gives support to modest speculation. Thus it was seen in the case study of 'partnership' at the local level (Chapter 13) that the analysis led to the conclusion that, although 'partnership' was the explicit policy of the local authority with regard to a major voluntary agency receiving most of its money from the authority, the reality was different. In this case the local government authority decided to adopt a mixture of contracted services and general grant support.

Government and the personal world

Here we are concerned with a vast body of individuals who provide the overwhelming proportion of welfare support. They may do this through their role as parent, relative, friend, neighbour, etc. They may also be defined officially as one of the six million 'carers' who look after or provide some regular service for a sick, handicapped, or elderly person living on their own or in another household (OPCS 1988).

We shall also include all those other individuals who *at the moment* may have a modest role in the provision of welfare. We can then see that, although the government has paid little attention to the question of the carers, it has signalled its intention of developing a policy for the personal world through its 'active citizenship' campaign. This is to be achieved through the process of encouraging 'ordinary people . . . to encounter and help solve discomforting problems across the spectrum from individual distress to urban decay' (Patten 1988).

As yet it is unclear where the next steps in this policy of exhortation may lead, but it indicates that 'secondary' forms of governmental intervention should not be overlooked.

Government policy and groups

Because they operate with few manifestations of external presence but mainly through word of mouth and personal recommendation, unorganised groups are almost invisible. Yet they may well be a significant area of welfare provision.

Governments have made some effort to encourage the development of such groups. Thus they were seen as a useful instrument of previous Labour Government policy through the 'creation' of neighbourhood schemes. In this case the metaphor of colonisation has some credibilty (Abrams *et al.* 1981, Bulmer 1986).

The Conservative Government has so far entered this arena primarily with respect to law and order, with the encouragement of 'neighbourhood watch' schemes. It seems likely that its intervention in the personal arena, through the active citizen campaign, will be translated into the 'creation' of similar groups.

TOWARDS A NEW WELFARE CONSENSUS AND NEW METAPHORS

We have unravelled several policy metaphors and examined the extent to which they help to illuminate major developments in the relationship between government and the component parts of the voluntary sector. In this final part of the paper we review some of the major themes and indicate tendencies which have broader implications for the social policy debate.

Inevitability or choice?

The presentation of the model of the voluntary sector in Chapter 11 was not intended to suggest that there is an 'inevitable' process of change from informality to the more bureaucratic forms of organisation. We shall return to this theme more fully in the following chapter. We might note however that groups need never become associations, and associations do not need to become agencies. In like fashion there is no 'iron law' which compels agencies to accept government money. However seductive, contracts and grants need not be, and are not, always tendered for or accepted.

Secondary intervention and industrialism

There is a tendency to concentrate on the more visible aspects of government intervention such as financial support. This inevitably focuses attention on the agency, the main recipient of funds, and distracts attention from the consequences of broader government policy on associations, groups and individuals. Concentration on the tangible indicators also distracts attention from the long-term impact of secondary intervention (such as influencing the climate of opinion) on the agencies themselves.

It can be argued that these secondary interventions will in time have a profound impact on sector leadership, other resources, and the scope, scale and direction of the sector. The most significant policy approaches therefore may not necessarily be privatisation or contracting. Yet another metaphor may be required – that of 'industrialism'. This might be described as the continuous exhortation by the government (and acceptance by the sector) to adopt models of behaviour and organisation today based particularly on the business bureaucracy with its anonymous market and profit-driven imperative. We have already noted the case of housing associations and their move away from their charitable origins. There are other, seemingly innocent, examples which are closer to the academic heartland, for example the award to a university of a 'Queen's Award to Industry'.

The introduction of new metaphors, such as 'industrialism', can, at best, do no more than shed a little additional light on a debate which is still characterised by rhetoric and hunch. New and old metaphors point to questions that can be asked, and indicate gaps in knowledge.

What of the sector metaphor itself? The combination of a historicist approach, the focus on the 'hard' economic indicators of support from government, and the absence of an organisational model which provides some explanation of the mainsprings and roots of the sector, has led some US commentators (Hall 1987) to suggest that the sector cannot be construed as 'independent' but dependent. The analysis in this paper points to a different conclusion. In one sense no sector is independent. All have their roots and their dependencies somewhere. But unravelling the voluntary sector indicates its own deep independent roots in the world of associations. Where no real associational roots can be identified then we can justly ask whether the group truly belongs in the sector.

Turning now to the policy metaphors – corporatism and colonisation are not words that policy makers would themselves choose to describe government approaches. They are mainly used to describe the relationship and impact, and serve as policy-critical stances. By breaking down the sector concept it becomes possible to employ the metaphors in a selective fashion. So corporatism is of interest in exploring the growth of intermediary bodies. For example, it encourages questions to be raised regarding the policy of using major national and intermediary bodies to distribute governmental funds to other voluntary agencies. Colonisation reminds us of the importance of those groups on the borders of the associational and personal worlds. It alerts our attention to the possibility of government support following general policy declarations in favour of 'active citizenship'.

Privatisation is only partially useful. It describes the shift away from public bureaucratic service provision, but it fails to do justice to the powerful countervailing trend of increased government regulation. It is further misleading because it fails to embrace the rise in regulation in the non-bureaucratic arenas.

Contracting is helpful as a technical term to describe a major funding change with respect to agencies, but suffers from similar drawbacks to that of privatisation. It can be used in a narrow sense to involve just the use of contracts, or in a somewhat broader meaning to include government grants (Kramer 1988). However, in the UK context, grants (for general support) may imply a different approach to the voluntary sector than contracts which, as Kramer rightly notes, imply a market orientation.

Partnership is used to describe many forms of interaction between governmental and voluntary agencies. It can include almost anything.

Criticism of partnership has led authors to search for alternative descriptions. British writers (Challis *et al.* 1988) have presented a 'planned-bargaining' model which suggests a balance between traditional left and right-wing political ideologies and approaches.

Towards a new consensus

As yet the battle is not decided between old Welfare State assumptions and the newer trends of entrepreneurialism. It may be some time before the key characteristics of a new approach finally emerge. The 'Thatcherite' approach may yet evolve into a new consensus to replace the previous consensus based on State planning and delivery of services. It may even be possible to breathe new life into the rather battered 'partnership' metaphor. Mixed models of funding may emerge which combine specific contracts with general purpose or 'arms length' (NCVO 1984) grants. Such mixed models might represent a genuine contribution towards a new balance of welfare provision which ensured that voluntary agencies did not become pale reflections of business or, for that matter, governmental agencies.

15 Planned change

INTRODUCTION

Is the nature of organisational change in the voluntary sector different from that in the government sector? What are the main differences? To what extent do existing theories, mainly drawn from public and business sector experience, assist in understanding the question of planned change in voluntary organisations? Is a new theory of voluntary organisation required and what are the possible implications for individual agencies?

This paper addresses these questions by drawing together the experience of research projects in UK governmental and voluntary social service organisations. The first section discusses the centrality of organisational structure in the understanding of planned change. This is followed by a summary of an emerging theory of governmental welfare bureaucracies and voluntary organisation. The similarities and differences of change in the two settings are then briefly explored in the light of those ideas. The paper concludes by examining the implications of the analysis for planned change in individual voluntary agencies.

DEVELOPING IDEAS ABOUT PLANNED CHANGE IN DIFFERENT SECTORS

The study of organisational change can be approached from many directions. Histories of organisations and groups of organisations, the internal and external pressures for change and the balance between them, the role of individuals and groups, formal and informal characteristics, decision-making processes, the place of the external agent in the change process – these are but some of the areas of study that could fall within any comprehensive examination of change. However, for several reasons (discussed below), the focus of this paper on planned change in two sectors encourages a more selective approach which concentrates on organisational structure, auspices and the validity of the bureaucratic paradigm.

The first reason emanates from the intimate relationship of planned change with organisational structure, whose major dimensions (Child 1988) may be regarded as all the official regularly occurring elements of an organisation such as tasks, responsibilities, levels of decision making, spans of control, grouping of units, delegation of authority and discretion (see Chapter 1). It is, I suggest, fruitless to consider planned change without theories and models of organisational structure.

This approach to change has a somewhat uneasy relationship with several major schools of thought. For example, many works in the life-cycle literature examined by Hasenfeld and Schmidt (1989) appear to have an in-built sense of inevitability which contradicts the basic stance of those who believe that organisations have alternatives, and can plan changes (see Chapter 12). The same might be said of the resource-dependency and allied theories (for example, Levine and White 1961, Aldrich 1976, Pfeffer and Salancik 1978, McCarthy and Zald 1977) which also depict organisations at the mercy of powerful and almost uncontrollable forces. Even theories of isomorphism (DiMaggio and Powell 1983, DiMaggio 1983) would attract similar criticism. Writers on planned change would be more sympathetic towards the work of those like Wertheim (1976) who have demonstrated that there can be alternative futures for organisations facing similar conditions. Recent research in multinationals (Bartlett and Ghoshal 1989), although beyond the scope of this paper, confirms the possibility of choice.

The second reason for a selective approach goes to the heart of the development of better theories of change. As Bozeman (1987:42–43) argues in his study of 'publicness' in organisations, most studies are 'generic . . . there is no presumption that differences between public and private organisations are significant . . . typically no theoretical justification is given for observed differences . . .'. A review of the apparent voluntary literature on organisational change (Powell and Friedkin 1986) illustrates the way in which the different auspices (public, business and voluntary sectors) are rarely regarded as essential variables.

Thirdly, even studies which differentiate between sectors appear to accept the traditional bureaucratic paradigm. One of the few specialist studies of voluntary social service organisations urges 'healthy skepticism . . . on knowledge deemed usable in the management of voluntary sector organisations if that knowledge has been derived from the study of other organisational forms' (Tucker 1983: 21).

The nature of the bureaucratic paradigm and the extent to which it is satisfactory for the study of voluntary organisations will be a major question for this paper.

THE ABC OF GOVERNMENTAL BUREAUCRACY

If they were asked, senior managers in government agencies, politicians, and management consultants would probably agree that what we call in Chapter 1 the 'ABC division' is a reasonable, if unrefined, representation of the way in which government agencies ought to, and in the main actually do, work.

'A' represents the political association: national, regional or local electorates who elect their political representatives. The primary 'rules of the game' are those of representative democracy, of a system of elections, majority voting, committees and chairpersons.

'B' will portray the bureaucracy – the hierarchical system of roles occupied by paid staff with its managerial chain of command. Even in agencies with a leading core of professional staff, such as social workers within UK governmental social services departments (SSDs), research indicates the underlying power of the bureaucratic system (Stevenson and Parsloe 1978, Billis *et al.* 1980).

'C' will serve to represent the clients, consumers, customers, users, etc; that is to say, all those who are the target group of the agency.

The mainly Weberian tradition which dominates the study of organisation assumes a clear-cut differentiation between A, B and C. There may be some clouding in the higher echelons of the bureaucracy (B) where it meets the political system (A), but the great mass of the two systems operate according to different and unambiguous sets of rules. This is the case despite the fact that the precise division of activities between the bureaucratic and political systems has long been a subject of controversy: the attempts to separate 'policy' from 'administration' have never quite covered all the situations. In the consideration of policy, there are, as Heclo and Wildavsky (1989: 217) put it so tellingly, ' . . . continual battles in the bowels of the bureaucracy . . . '.

Clients remain outside both systems (A and B). Heroic attempts may be made to bring them into the bureaucratic system of decision making, or to grant them entry as clients (C), rather than as citizens (members of A), into the political committee system. But these can be no more than artificial and temporary transplants onto alien bodies. As a recent government report of assessment systems and community care explains:

Evidence was sought of various practices that would constitute genuine user/carer involvement. It became clear that the vast majority of users and carers were so grateful to receive anything at all that any notion of consumer rights was unrealistic at this stage.

(Social Services Inspectorate 1991: 21)

The basic structure of governmental welfare bureaucracies rests on the division between A, B, and C.

THE VOLUNTARY AGENCY: BETWEEN BUREAUCRACY AND ASSOCIATION

There is no generally accepted term to describe the phenomenon discussed in this section. Nonprofit, voluntary, nongovernmental, social economy, independent sector, indirect administration are some of the terms used to describe individual units or their aggregation. The absence of a generally accepted term reflects both national differences and the absence of a persuasive theoretical explanation for the phenomenon. Many of the essentially negative descriptions have been criticised (Lohmann 1989).

One line of research reported in earlier chapters is to contrast the bureaucratic form of organisation with the membership association. Accordingly, voluntary associations with their crucial concept of membership have 'rules of the game' that are similar to the political association and are based on concepts such as voting and elections (see Chapter 11). However, they have no right to levy taxes, and the typical sources of resources are voluntary labour and contributions from present and past members and supporters (Chapter 12). Membership associations may be regarded as the core distinctive group of the voluntary sector, even though they may not necessarily be at the forefront of social policy concerns (Chapter 14).

If the concept of 'ambiguity' (Leach 1976), as discussed in Chapter 11, is introduced it is contended that the 'worlds' of bureaucracies and associations overlap, and that the middle area can be considered an ambiguous territory which is occupied by voluntary *agencies* that possess the attributes of associations and bureaucracies. This definition of ambiguity is more precise than its usual usage in the literature, for example, Martin and Meyerson (1988) where ' . . . ambiguity refers to that which is unclear' (p.112).

By differentiating associations from bureaucracies (as defined) and the consequent identification of a middle overlapping territory, a distinctive type of voluntary organisation – the agency – can be clearly identified. Voluntary welfare agencies are distinctive because they have both (a) a group of people who are committed to the specific purposes of a particular organisation and (b) paid staff, who may be part of that group, and who deliver core operational services.

What emerges from this analysis is that voluntary agencies do *not* have an ABC division. On the contrary it is possible to find every possible combination of statuses as a basic feature of the structure. Examples of some of these combinations are the recipients of services who are also unpaid members of the management committee, or clients who are members of the paid staff.

We must emphasise that this account of the nature of voluntary organisations is concerned to explore their organisational structure. There are many different sorts of voluntary organisations and many attempts have been made at classification; numerous explanations have been offered for the existence of a voluntary sector at all. (An introduction to some of these can be found in Hatch 1980, Young 1983, Hansmann 1987). But, if the organisation has paid staff delivering operational services, and if it has a group of people committed to its distinctive purposes, then it will be considered an 'agency'.

Voluntary agencies, as analysed here, may be considered as 'neo-bureaucracies' confronting the core structural issue of ambiguity, and it is reasonable to question whether the process of change, and the implementation of change, can be identical to the position in the more familiar and dominant pure bureaucratic form. What are some of the similarities and differences?

COMPARING CHANGE IN PUBLIC AND VOLUNTARY AGENCIES

A fundamental comparison of change in governmental and voluntary welfare agencies awaits a full programme of research. This discussion is intended to sketch out several of the key similarities and differences, and to explore the extent to which the idea of agencies as neo-bureaucracies might help an understanding of the issues.

Change in governmental agencies

In governmental welfare bureaucracies change is sometimes dramatic. Politicians can legislate away entire organisations or services. Change can be equally dramatic in the other direction. The creation of new institutions and services is a well-tried way of indicating the arrival of a new political broom, and of gaining political support. Such drastic change in governmental institutions is usually signalled well ahead in political manifestos, consultative documents and the like. However, looking back on the past twenty years of experience in UK social services departments (SSDs), most change was less severe although no less traumatic for those concerned. It entailed changes at different bureaucratic levels of organisation ranging from overall agency organisation, down through departments and sections.

Change can be initiated by politicians or senior bureaucrats. Certainly, if it is substantial, it requires political sanctioning and eventual agreement. But in the implementation of internal change, the SSD managerial hierarchy reigns supreme. It reigns supreme also in organisational development. External intervention by consultants, of whatever school of thought, is doomed to failure without – at minimum – the active support of key managers. This does not ignore the role of 'street-level bureaucrats' (Lipsky 1980) or of the real nature of policy development perceptively described by Rein (1983). Nevertheless, planned change will require the mobilization of the managerial structure. Clients remain outside the hierarchy and have little explicit direct impact on planned change.

The essential point about these governmental agencies is that the major boundaries of the organisation are relatively stable. The broad societal purposes and main activities are enshrined in legislation and embodied in the role of the most senior manager – the director. Front-line roles are likewise intended to be clear. So too are the relationships of accountability between roles. In practice, none of this works very well, and most SSD staff would undoubtedly regard their organisations as turbulent rather than stable. Yet, seen over a period of several decades, and when compared with the real turbulence of voluntary organisation (soon to be considered), governmental agencies do indeed look stable.

In the short term the typical problem of governmental welfare bureaucracies may be described as *confusion* surrounding the boundaries to roles. Public enquiry after public enquiry into child-care deaths, and other scandals in the UK, have revealed lack of clarity regarding the contribution of various workers in the tragedy being investigated. The problem cannot be seen just as a question of large size. Although many SSDs do employ several thousand staff, the unit of investigation and confusion is often quite small. It can be argued (see Chapter 8) that this role confusion is a direct consequence of poorly thought-through government legislation which fixed unrealistic boundaries to SSD activity. Once fixed by legislation, organisational change could only take place within those boundaries and may be regarded as 'quantitative' or incremental. More commonly, confusion does not result in obvious tragedies but brings with it inefficiency and much personal suffering.

Nevertheless, at the end of the day, the bureaucratic rules of the game, and the ABC division, serve as the touchstone against which current organisation and planned change can be gauged. The position is very different in the voluntary agency.

Change in voluntary agencies

Voluntary agencies, even those that are bound by charity law, are less restricted in organisational boundaries. Client groups, services, professional methodologies of service and geographic coverage can all be changed at short notice. Basic changes in relationships with other agencies can be negotiated and branches and groups founded or suspended. Such change can be 'qualitative' in that it results in distinct leaps in the agency's coverage of social problems (Chapter 3). It is therefore not surprising that much of the classic literature on organisational 'goal displacement' (Sills 1957, Sills 1966), 'transformation' (Zald 1970) and 'ambiguity' (Perrow 1969) appears to draw heavily on the voluntary experience.

The overlap of statuses in voluntary organisations – in particular the unclear division of functions between governing body and paid staff (Harris 1989) – is of great significance for understanding change. Role boundaries are less clear than in governmental bureaucracies, and it is often difficult to identify if, and where, a strategic planning activity (crucial in the planning of change) is taking place. One study of formal planning in voluntary organisations serving 'the mentally retarded and those in the performing arts', suggested that opposition to planning came from two sources. In the former group of agencies ' . . . some board members, often agency founders and relatives of mentally retarded clients . . . eschewed planning because they saw it as a process that would disrupt the informal patterns of decision making . . .' (Stone 1989: 305). In the performing arts agencies, board members saw little need for planning ' . . . because of the tight social relationships that existed among volunteers' (p.305). These findings fit well with the theory of ambiguity. In both instances there was a high degree of status ambiguity, indicating that they were closer to the associational (membership) world where we would not expect planning to be as prominent as those that were closer to fully fledged bureaucracies. It seems that much will depend on specific agency conditions such as the presence of charismatic and capable committee members and/or paid staff, different funding sources, demands for accountability, tradition and ideology (Kramer 1965, Kramer 1981, Middleton 1987). Unlike the governmental position, qualitative boundary change – including crises threatening the survival of the agency – can be swift and radical.

Voluntary organisations with large numbers of paid staff will have greater differentiation of roles and appear to resemble more closely their counterparts in the governmental system. We have little solid UK research in these agencies, but from case studies presented at workshops, limited project work, reports in the media and anecdotal accounts, it seems that the similarity to governmental welfare bureaucracies may be superficial. Ambiguity abounds. In work with a national organisation of parents with handicapped children, with several hundred paid staff, mainly at head-quarters, and hundreds of local groups, a specific project was undertaken in order to examine the strategic planning function. The paid director was himself also a member with a handicapped child (an overlap between 'B' and 'C'). It became evident that the general overlap between board and staff had resulted in a planning vacuum. Dramatic, unplanned change had taken place, resulting largely from the director's charismatic influence.

The idea of ambiguity sheds light on many of the practical problems of change faced by voluntary agencies, which can be seen as resulting from the tensions of adhering both to the rules of the game of the associational world (democratic elections, voting, etc.) and those of the bureaucratic world (managerial command structures, contracts of employment, etc.). This can be seen in the study in Chapter 10 and the examples provided in Chapter 12.

Furthermore, large voluntary agencies considering change have to cope with the chronic problem of the relationship between headquarters and local groups (Young 1989). The notion of ambiguity suggests that local groups may often be pure associations (rather than agencies). This can lead to major differences of interest and perception, since headquarters groups are usually paid staff and consider themselves part of an agency structure. Governmental welfare bureaucracies may have complex relationships among headquarters and local groups; but the latter are 'branches' and part of the line management structure of the overall organisation.

DISCUSSION: THE IMPLICATIONS FOR PLANNED CHANGE IN VOLUNTARY ORGANISATIONS

In view of the dominance of the bureaucratic paradigm, and the substantial experience of change in the business and governmental sectors, we shall in this section be concerned solely with the voluntary sector where ambiguity has important implications for the introduction of planned change.

What do those wishing to introduce a programme of planned change in voluntary organisations need to take into account in order to get to the starting line of the process? (Whether change, once introduced, is 'good' or 'bad' for the client, more efficient and effective, and how the two sectors differ in these matters, are all issues which lie well beyond this discussion.)

The main lesson for those considering planned change is that unlike the comparatively straightforward bureaucratic structure, the voluntary organisation is a delicate balance of statuses (members, volunteers, users, governing body, patrons, paid staff, funders). Many of the action-research projects with voluntary agencies revealed that the balance is far from evident even to those most deeply involved (Billis and Harris 1991).

Paid staff can underestimate the real strength of governing bodies or groups of members. They can fail to realise that they are not just a dedicated band of advocates for the mission of the agency. Not, in other words, just members of an association who can abide by rules of democracy; but also members of a bureaucracy with its accountable role structure. Moreover, it can sometimes be unclear who are the real clients or users of the agency services. The realisation that the employment contract brings with it a dramatic move into bureaucratic territory is painful, and can lead to many familiar problems of young voluntary groups.

Or, new members of the governing body can fail to appreciate the role of volunteers and members. One powerful industrialist, newly appointed to the board of a respected Victorian charity, decided that the director was not 'businesslike' enough. The director, a well-respected and distinguished figure, got wind of the plot and promptly mobilised his many supporters in the local fundraising groups. The businessman retired with burnt fingers. He had assumed, because of the high public profile of the hundreds of paid staff, that he was confronting the familiar bureaucracy and failed to understand the crucial role played by the thousands of local supporters.

There are implications also for organisational development (OD) '. . . a planned, systematic process in which applied behavioural principles and practices are introduced into an ongoing organisation towards the goals of effecting organisation improvement . . .' (French and Bell 1990: 1). The growth of the UK voluntary sector has been accompanied by the widespread use of large consultancy firms and a proliferation of individual consultants. External intervention has become commonplace, and even expected. The question which this paper raises is the appropriateness of the 'principles' being applied, especially by the large firms whose normal clientele is the commercial and industrial bureaucracy. At the very least the anecdotal evidence must be a matter of concern for agencies considering the involvement of consultants.

The analysis so far may help to explain why accidental rather than planned change is a familiar phenomenon.

CONCLUSIONS

The objective has been to contribute to a better understanding of planned change in voluntary organisations by means of a comparison with change in government welfare bureaucracies. The basic structure of government bureaucracy was analysed as the ABC division of statuses or roles between A (the political association), B (the bureaucracy of paid staff) and C (the clients, consumers). Voluntary agencies were seen as ambiguous organisations or 'neo-bureaucracies' which did not have an ABC division. It was argued that the distinctive organisational problems of government welfare agencies revolve around boundary and role *confusion*, that is to say within B. This can be compared with the distinctive problems of voluntary organisations which surround the issue of status *ambiguity*, that is to say the relationships between A, B and C. The conclusion was reached that the type of change that can be introduced, and the problems surrounding its introduction and implementation differ in the two settings. These fundamental structural differences have wide-ranging implications for the administration of individual wefare agencies and for public policy.

The emergence of a new organisational paradigm raises fresh and potentially fruitful questions for research regarding the levers of power and change, and the position of professional and other groups within different organisational structures. Finally, those for whom the organisation was presumably established – the users – may feel only too painfully the consequences of organisational ignorance.

16 Looking ahead: social policy, welfare organisation and sector management

INTRODUCTION

The preceding chapters have raised numerous issues, many of which are likely to endure into the next century as major challenges for practitioners, policy makers and academics.[1] To attempt to produce 'conclusions' from such a broad agenda seemed a foolhardy task and, in any case, most of the essays have their own concluding comments. I have chosen therefore, in this final chapter, to draw on the earlier analysis and reflect on several matters that appear to have wider policy implications.

One theme that emerged strongly in Part I was lack of clarity surrounding the organisational boundaries of SSDs. The first section of this chapter argues that this has now resulted in chronic tinkering with structures, and that it is time to look again at the original reasoning which still underpins the role of the SSD. The second section examines important trends in the development of local voluntary agencies, and questions whether the current preoccupation with contracting is obscuring the consequences of these deeper trends. This is followed by a section which suggests that the government regards the voluntary sector primarily as a tool of public policy. This approach, which is defined as 'instrumentalism', currently rests on an inappropriate business model of organisation. The chapter closes with a fourth section that debates the emergence of the 'sector' – and particularly the voluntary sector – as an important factor in the study of organisations; the issue, in fact, which was at the heart of many of the essays in Part II.

THE FUTURE OF SSDs

Looking ahead, the message for those in active contact with SSDs seems rather depressing. We do not appear to have moved on much since 1970 in resolving basic organisational issues. For example, a recent analysis

(Challis 1990) of 60 reorganisations in SSDs, concludes that local authorities have failed to find 'one self evidently sensible way' of organisation and that many SSDs are 'travelling in different directions' (p.17).

I have argued elsewhere (Billis 1989) that the voyage of the social services ship Seebohm was already coming to an end by the end of the 1970s. Nevertheless the hulk travels on, sustained by a mass of legislation. But for reasons that emerge from the studies in this book, I would not put much money on its safe passage into the twenty-first century. As they approach the next hazard – *Caring for People* (Department of Health 1989) – SSDs may be tempted to find some comfort from the promise of a calm passage contained in the Price Waterhouse study (Department of Health 1991). This report, which provides SSDs with advice on implementing community care, suggests that they 'should not necessarily assume that organisation structures will need major overhaul' (p.1). Other long-standing observers of the social services scene may view such sentiments with scepticism as an unduly optimistic view. Since SSDs have spent much of the past twenty years reorganising, I cannot see why much should change now when there is a really good excuse for another bash.

There are several interconnected reasons why a rethink of the role of SSDs is required. First, the Seebohm vision, as I have tried to demonstrate in several chapters, was not a realistic expectation. An 'effective family service concerned with the prevention of social distress ' (Seebohm 1968: para. 427) has proved to be an undefendable organisational boundary. The fact that no dominant organisational form or 'one self evidently sensible way' of service provision has emerged in more than twenty years is not merely ascribable to 'vested interests' (Allen 1989: 53). It reflects the deeper 'activity' boundary tensions: that is to say, lack of clarity about the business of SSDs.

The second reason for a rethink flows from the first. It is not just that expectations placed upon SSDs are unrealistic; it is that the attempts to implement those expectations have led to large agencies with complex functions. Using the more technical language employed in this book, a Level 5 'societal impact' or 'highest expected work level' (see Chapter 3) has been expected. Such organisations demand a degree of knowledge and resources, and of certainty in the effects of intervention, which have become increasingly suspect. Even in the industrial setting, where there are usually tangible outputs, the operation of Level 5 organisations is, in my personal experience, far from straightforward. Problems of internal co-ordination and communication abound, and senior management can easily become remote from the front line of operations. Meetings proliferate, and the amount of staff time involved in the maintenance of the structure itself can escalate.

There are other associated reasons which argue for a fundamental re-evaluation. Confusion regarding the business of SSDs has resulted in confusion at the front line, with the tension between two different levels of 'basic expected work' or 'client impact' (as defined in Chapter 3) reverberating throughout the departments. The practical manifestation of this is the continuing second-class citizenship of residential workers and others expected to deliver a 'prescribed output' client impact, compared with the more prestigious 'situational response' expected of the fully fledged social worker. The tension between two different levels of response has proved difficult to sustain in one organisation. And the implementation of community care legislation may introduce yet another 'front line' of 'arrangers' and 'purchasers'. Bamford (1990: 161–3) makes a similar point when he builds on the Webb and Wistow (1987) analysis and argues for three different services: social work (in the area of change); social care (primarily support and maintenance); and service planning and evaluation.

Were a major review of SSDs to be undertaken, a few clues with respect to a possible way ahead might be found in the three issues raised in the preceding paragraphs. In other words clarification of the activity boundary, and the client and societal impact, would be essential tasks for the review body. In brief, the analysis undertaken in this book points to organisations which are less complex and have more modest expectations – what we have called Level 4 agencies.

What might these Level 4 agencies look like, and how would they resolve some of the problems of current organisation? In general terms, a Level 4 agency – by definition – would have one less line of management than the present SSD. One immediate result of a shortened management spine would be improved communications between the front line and senior management. It would also reduce the complexity of the 'highest expected work' role – that of the director – who would have a more narrow range of responsibilities. Directors would be responsible for specific kinds of services, rather than a 'general field of need' such as 'social services' (Chapter 2). Cutting the management line would reduce career prospects, but it might also reduce the turnover of directors who, according to reports in the professional press, are apparently unable to cope with the pressures of the job.[2]

Level 4 agencies could be more specialist in focus, and thereby abandon the belief that there was any necessary inter-relationship between the needs of the client groups currently covered by SSDs. This was part of the core 1968 Seebohm argument for the amalgamation of the previous departments into an SSD: 'Since social need is complex it can rarely be divided so that each part is satisfactorily dealt with by a separate service' (para. 142). It is time to challenge what must presumably remain as the major justification for a single department.

Although caution must be urged regarding a too ready acceptance of the lessons of business enterprises, it might nevertheless be wise to take note of Peters and Waterman's (1982: 293) conclusion that: 'The most successful of all (organisations) are those diversified around a single skill'. Organisations, they argue, should 'stick to the knitting'. Would society not be better served by less organisationally problematic Level 4 agencies that had a clearer sense of what they were 'knitting', of what their core activity was, and of what they could do best?

We might recall that such agencies would still be large enough to provide a 'comprehensive service of a specific kind'. A specialist agency based on client groups need not necessarily conform to local authority boundaries. Above everything else, the parents of children with learning difficulties, the relatives and carers of the elderly and disabled, the abused child; all require appropriate and high quality solutions to their problems. It is doubtful that they much care whether that solution is provided by any specific local authority.

New specialist organisations need not necessarily mean just a 'return' to a discarded 'pre-Seebohm' era. Level 4 organisations, if they are to operate properly, require more substantial resources and management structures than was available to most of those earlier departments. Times have changed, and a renewed consideration of agencies organised on the basis of clientele would look very different to the position twenty years ago. But even if client group organisation were treated 'merely' as a return to earlier approaches, there is no reason for embarrassment. The present organisation of social services in the SSD was only one of several alternatives considered by the Seebohm Committee. In the light of twenty years' experience we might well wish to reconsider the validity of the basic approaches of several of the rejected alternatives (Seebohm 1968: Chap. VI).

One argument against the creation of smaller, less all-encompassing Level 4 departments is that there would be more of them, which would result in greater problems of 'co-ordination'. Since such problems can hardly be claimed to have diminished in the last twenty years, this is not a convincing case.

The new Community Care legislation will not get to grips with what have been diagnosed as the underlying problems of activity, front line and highest expected level of work. Indeed, if anything, the proposals may heighten public expectations of the efficacy of SSD intervention in social problems, and continue earlier unrealistic policy objectives:

> They [SSDs] are responsible for meeting social care needs in their areas by arranging the provision of residential, day and domiciliary care services and respite care . . . . The proposals in this White Paper build on those responsibilities.
>
> (Department of Health 1989: para. 3.1.1.)

I do not doubt that the proposed introduction of 'purchaser/commissioning' and 'provider' roles can be made to work. As we have seen from the SSD example, just about any organisational structure can somehow be made to work for a long time, especially if it is underpinned by government. It may take many years of reorganisations and failure to convince government that the underlying tensions can no longer be tolerated. But, as one commentator writing about SSDs declared: 'the departments increasingly resemble beached whales thrashing about but ultimately doomed' (Bamford 1990: 166). To take the metaphor a little further: the tide that has been bringing the whales steadily to the beach is unlikely to be turned back by a Canute-like waving of the 'community care' wand. After two decades the time is ripe for a *post mortem*.

In proposing a re-evaluation of the SSD role I am not necessarily advocating the transfer of services to other sectors. I agree that:

> The real issue . . . is to create systems which encourage or require the people who profit in material terms from them to work in the best interests of clients . . . .
>
> (Webb and Wistow 1987: 231).

Those services can be in the public, private or voluntary sectors. As yet there is little evidence that *transfer* of services increases effectiveness. One of the few studies of transfer of ownership (although not in the social service area) concludes that: 'results . . . failed in most cases to support the thesis that change in ownership improves enterprise performance . . . ' (Dunsire *et al.* 1991: 21).

The argument of this book has been rather different. Agencies must have clarity of organisational boundaries. Using the ideas of Part I, it is crucial that they should be clear about the 'societal' and 'client' impacts they are attempting to make. This is not the case with current SSDs. (It helps also if the other aspects of individual roles, analysed in the early chapters, are clarified, but these will not so immediately threaten organisational viability.) Clarity of structural boundaries and matching individuals to role are challenges facing agencies in both public and voluntary sectors.

The next section moves from the public, to the voluntary welfare sector and notes some of main trends observed amongst local voluntary agencies.

THE FUTURE OF THE VOLUNTARY SECTOR

At an international level, Kramer (1990: 54) has suggested that: 'the next phase of the welfare state will be characterised by a much greater use of voluntary non-profit organisations as service providers'. In this country, the sector, like some remote tribe, has been 'discovered' (or more accurately rediscovered) and encouraged by government to join and play its part in the modern world of welfare. Previous governmental explorers have been aware of its existence, but earlier ventures lacked the fervour of more recent efforts. The government still marches towards the sector along the well-trodden path of 'partnership'; but now it carries the newer banner of 'contracting'. It is a powerful incursion which has produced a mixed reaction of welcome and concern within the voluntary sector. Similar stories are coming in from around the world, although this country is perhaps rather different in the expressions of alarm that have emerged from parts of the sector. Is the concern of the sector justified? Can all the problems of change be laid at the door of government intervention?

Although it is not possible to posit confident causal links between government action and the detailed impact on *individual* agencies, it is possible to identify numerous deeper trends and tensions affecting different *groups of local agencies*.[3] For example, the more established agencies are steadily moving away from advocacy, self-help and community work, and towards service provision. There is also a change in agency activity towards the provision of services for those in more severe need. Many agencies are experiencing an intensification of tension with respect to the place that the individual, the group, or the State should occupy in the resolution of specific social problems. In other words, there are now greater strains regarding 'welfare accountability'. It seems that these may be greatest in groups that have a strong self-help element, or that are heavily dependent on volunteers for service delivery, or that have strong beliefs in empowerment. There are other critical structural changes. Of these the most fundamental are the growth of small agencies with paid staff, and the steady bureaucratisation of the more established groups.

There are many unanticipated organisational consequences for local agencies of changes originally seen as relatively straightforward. For example, hiring paid staff to reduce the burden of work on the agency can lead to a falling off of volunteer commitment, and also to an increased demand for agency services. In short, complex change processes are to be found in many of the variables of what was identified in Chapter 12 as the agency's 'root system'. Nevertheless, despite the complexity of the process, it is difficult to escape the conclusion that central and local government is playing a significant role – usually without any conscious design – in influencing these broad trends.

National voluntary sector leaders are therefore justified in their sensitivity about the role of government. It is an anxiety made more urgent by the position in numerous local voluntary agencies, which are often stumbling into change, or have outgrown their existing structures. Neither governmental nor voluntary sector agencies thus appear to have a clear idea of the longer-term consequences of their actions, a situation that can only be viewed with concern.

The present focus of attention on 'contracting', which is accompanied by a proliferation of handbooks and guides, is unlikely to be a sufficient response to the consequences of the deeper voluntary sector trends we have identified (Billis and Harris 1991). What is required is a broader debate which regards contracting as one important element only in the government–voluntary agency relationship. The debate would require an analysis of the future role of voluntary agencies which took into account their human and financial resources, the make-up of their management committees, and their organisational structures and operational policies. With a few exceptions, most voluntary sector attention is focused at present on day to day funding pressures. Government, on the other hand, has seemed preoccupied with financial probity (Woodfield 1987). A reasonable enough preoccupation, but one which should be matched by a longer term view of trends in the voluntary sector.

Looking ahead to the twenty-first century, there is another trend which may intensify. The move away from the less severe, and towards the more severe, cases of social need has already been noted. This has been accompanied by the exit of government from the provision of many local social, recreational and educational facilities particularly for adults. It will not be surprising therefore if we see the growth of a new generation of low-resource community groups stepping in to fill the gaps left by the more established voluntary agencies and government.

I have argued so far that a broader debate would need to take account of the trends in the voluntary sector, and begin to tease out possible interactions between government and sector. I have further suggested that a focus on contracting is too narrow since it fails to consider the deeper trends. It also fails to take account of the impact of the changing role of SSDs on the future of the sector.

The fate of the welfare agencies in the two sectors may be linked in more subtle ways than can be revealed by the current emphasis on contracting.[4] Here I return to the line of reasoning of the previous section. What might be the impact on the sector of the creation of new specialist Level 4 governmental agencies? Would those voluntary agencies now moving into direct service delivery rethink their policies? Would contracting to the private and voluntary sectors appear such an attractive proposition if the competition was from 'slimline', specialist governmental agencies? Would clients and users prefer to receive services from governmental agencies with a more secure funding base? These are just a few of the questions that await discussion.

The really important message must be sent to those concerned with the future viability of local voluntary action: the members of the board, the staff, volunteers, funders and of course the users. They must be sensitive and appreciate the consequences of actions which, by themselves, seem modest and of limited impact, but which may have long-term and unwanted results. Again, for those in the voluntary sector, like their colleagues in the public sector, the future promises to be no less tempestuous than the present.

INSTRUMENTALISM AND SOCIAL POLICY

The previous section put the case for an examination of the relationship between government and voluntary sector which goes beyond an examination of 'contracting'. We have already noted (Chapter 13) that a popular international policy metaphor for describing this relationship is 'partnership', a suitably vague term which has the considerable political advantage of being capable of expansion to include most policy stances. Here, that earlier discussion is taken a little further. The argument is: (a) that the government's approach to the voluntary sector can be described as 'instrumentalism', (b) that instrumentalism rests on an implicit belief in the inevitability of the ABC division, and (c) there may be unanticipated and unwanted consequences of instrumentalism.

'Instrumentalism' in welfare is a social policy approach that treats voluntary organisations primarily as *instruments* of public policy. It is not a new phenomenon, and is part of a wider desire and well known strategy of governments to move to the 'margins' (Sharkansky 1980). One example of rampant instrumentalism can be seen in the Community Care White Paper (Department of Health 1989) which in various sections (3.4.3 and 3.4.6) talks of the statutory sector 'developing' and 'setting up' voluntary agencies. The 'practice guidance' to SSDs (Department of Health 1991: 4.2.15) states that 'if the SSD is the sole supplier of a service or no service exists, there may be a need to stimulate supply'. Another example of instrumentalism, from a very different political source, is that of the Greater London Council (GLC) which directed its funds ' . . . away from traditionally favoured agencies and functions towards neglected areas and groups, particularly those with a working-class orientation' (Brenton 1985:

219). Instrumentalism may be compared with the more 'hands-off' approach of an earlier period.

> Where Government chooses to spend its money to support the work of a voluntary body, it is deliberately choosing a system which is independent of direct control. The Government values such independence highly. It could not, however, accept the extreme position . . . that having decided to fund an organisation Government in all circumstances stand back and allow the voluntary body untrammelled freedom to spend the money in any way it sees fit.
>
> (Home Office 1978: 7.4)

As the Community Care and GLC examples illustrate, instrumentalism can flow from disparate social and political theories. However, despite these differences, instrumentalism appears to share a common belief in the ubiquity of traditional bureaucratic organisation. This is not surprising. As Hall and Quinn (1983: 18) point out: 'It would probably be fair to say that policymakers and implementers are unaware that a field of organisational theory even exists'. It is therefore perhaps not unexpected that the instrumental approach unquestionably accepts the dominant paradigm, and ignores the very different organisational characteristics (the overlap of A, B and C) of voluntary agencies.

The principal form of organisation used to deliver services in the UK Welfare State is still the governmental bureaucracy based on the broad division between elected representatives, paid bureaucrats, and clients or patients (the ABC division described in Chapter 1). The advent of contracting, with its greater use of external providers of services, will complicate the nature of the relationship between the bureaucracy and the client, but it will not change the basic ABC division.[5] In countries such as the UK – which hope to involve voluntary agencies as more dominant actors on the welfare stage – the assumption is that they are merely smaller and less 'bureaucratic' versions of the large governmental agencies. Alternatively, they are sometimes regarded as small businesses, subject to the familiar pressures of market forces.

Might there be possible unanticipated and unwanted consequences of instrumentalism? The language of the Community Care White Paper indicates that this policy approach does not sufficiently recognise the genuine independent roots of the voluntary sector in the response to social need, in individual and group frustrations. Instrumentalism fails also to understand that voluntary agencies are not the straightforward managerial hierarchies of industry, nor even the more complex structures of professionally dominated government agencies. Hence the continuing criticism by experienced commentators regarding 'crass managerialism' –

' . . . the human services cannot be run like Sainsbury's' (Piachaud 1991: 214). It does not understand that voluntary agencies are subject to more complex forces than those just of the market, or elected political representatives.

A policy based on an inadequate model of the voluntary sector is likely to result in undesirable consequences. For example, there must be grave doubts regarding the viability of agencies which are 'set up' by government, and are not 'rooted' in some genuine group of 'members'. What will be their position in five, or ten years' time? There may be other long-term consequences of an instrumental approach, particularly when it is dominated by a market model of business. Indeed, Ware (1990: 204) has argued that 'the general effect of the expansion of the market system has been to erode altruism'. And in the US it is claimed that the marketplace has led to the 'corporatisation' of welfare with human need being treated as a 'commodity'. The authors, Stoesz and Karger, (1991: 164) warn that:

> . . . competitive practices . . . may become standard organisational procedure, not because they service the public interest in any demonstrable sense, but because the rules of the market appear to require that they be adopted.

The previous section explored major trends affecting the local voluntary sector and suggested that it was difficult to escape the conclusion that government is playing a significant role in influencing those changes. This role has now been further defined as 'instrumentalism' based on a private sector model of organisation. It is, as the analysis in Part II of this book has attempted to demonstrate, a flawed model for understanding the voluntary sector, and a poor basis for the development of social policy.

GENERIC MANAGEMENT

The belief in business virtues, which was noted as underpinning current governmental approaches to the voluntary sector, can also be regarded more broadly as a general approach towards public sector institutions as a whole:

> In the last decade central government policy has placed great emphasis on the need for the efficient use of available resources in the public sector. Efforts have been directed to introducing managerial approaches and cultural attitudes found in the private sector.
>
> (Department of Health 1991: 5.1.3.)

This strength of the private sector model in public policy may be sustained, in ways which lie well beyond the possibility of exploration here, by its commanding position in the academic study of management. In public administration, the rise of 'new public management' (NPM) – with its focus on 'management' rather than policy, on performance appraisal and efficiency, on quasi-markets and contracting out, cost-cutting, output targets and freedom to manage – has also been attributed in part to the international scientific management movement (Hood 1991).[6]

The great majority of research and academic interest has centred on the private sector, with the assumption that the theories and concepts are universally applicable. This 'generic' business-orientated approach dominates management studies and teaching, and the 'sector' is rarely regarded as a prime research variable. Occasionally, the generic approach to management is challenged. A decade ago, Fottler (1981) put the question: Is management really generic? His answer was that the differences between what he called the four sectors (private-for-profit, private non-profit, private quasi-public and public) are significant.

In the UK, the validity of the generic approach has more recently been criticised by Stewart and Ranson (1988: 13). In their opinion: 'whether there is a generic concept of management' is one of 'the challenging questions which confronts both academics and practitioners'. They argue (p.15) that 'the public domain has its own conditions, which are ignored at their peril . . . . [it] is the arena in which values can be realised, which cannot adequately be realised outside it'. Other writers have joined the counterattack against the dominance of the industrial model (see Kooiman and Eliassen 1987).

In addition to these assaults on generic management, there are commentators who express wider disapproval of the idea of management itself, and have coined the term 'managerialism'. This word has been explored by Pollitt (1990) who defines 'managerialism' as an 'ideology': a set of beliefs and practices with a core assumption that 'better management will prove an effective solvent for a wide range of economic and social ills' (p.1). After an analysis of the origins and nature of this 'ideology', Pollitt acknowledges that his book 'has not turned out exactly as its author intended' (p.181). His estimation of the 'difficulty of developing alternative models has soared' (p.182). Those who dislike management – and introduced the term 'managerialism' – have in their turn been severely criticised. Thus, Metcalfe and Richards (1990) have reproached those in political science and public administration for their 'Olympian detachment' which is a reflection of their 'deep-seated resistance to management ideas . . . [they] are, explicitly, saying that things should be done differently even if they are diffident about publicly expressing the views they espouse' (p. 235).

My own view is that business models will continue to dominate social policy as long as they offer the best tentative explanations for organisational problems. What is required now are theories that offer a sophisticated critique of generic approaches. Such new theoretical developments are unlikely to wipe out the entire accrued wisdom of decades of management research.[7] More probably they will provide more specific and 'better' answers to many of the questions rightly raised by the critics of current generic management approaches.

MEETING THE CHALLENGE OF VOLUNTARY SECTOR MANAGEMENT

The theories presented in Part II of this book have attempted to come to grips with the question of the 'sector' dimension in management, and its relationship to the practical problems faced by voluntary sector agencies. During the period of the research covered by this book it became clear that widely accepted ideas about bureaucracies and their management, whilst helpful, were only partially successful as 'plausible explanations' (Carrier and Kendall 1977) when applied to the management problems faced by voluntary agencies. It also became evident that the failure of existing theories to explain the peculiar characteristics of nonprofits was presenting a considerable puzzle for academics from a variety of disciplines (for example, Milofsky 1979, Tucker 1983, Wilson and Butler 1985). Sugden (1984: 70) concluded that 'any economist who tries to investigate the voluntary sector is likely to experience a great deal of embarrassment about the inadequacies of conventional economic theory'. More recently, DiMaggio and Anheier (1990), who are 'sceptical about the plausibility of any *general* theory of "nonprofit organisations" ' (p.154), begin their review of the nonprofit sociological literature by suggesting that: 'For social scientists, the origins and behaviour of sectors that stand outside market and state are tantalizing puzzles' (p.138).

A central theoretical puzzle which continues to reverberate, in some shape or other, throughout the academic literature is the question of sector 'boundaries'. In the UK the puzzle has a long pedigree and is discussed in various forms in, for example, Beveridge (1948), Goodman (1976), Wolfenden (1978), Hatch (1980). In essence there are two questions:

1 What, if it exists at all, is the nature of the boundary *between* the voluntary and other sectors?
2 What explanations can be offered for the diversity *within* the sector?

It is in fact the same central enigma, in another guise, that surfaced as crucial for the understanding of voluntary sector management in the opening chapters of Part II: that is to say, the problem of overlap, blurring, ambiguity, or as Moyer (1981) put it – 'messiness'.

Within the general voluntary sector writings of this period literature began to appear which concentrated specifically on organisational and management aspects of nonprofits (Mason 1984, Young 1983, O'Neill and Young 1988). And in 1990 the specialist journal *Nonprofit Management and Leadership* was established. The rise in interest in voluntary sector management has been accompanied in the UK by several new educational and training initiatives. In the United States graduate training programmes have been developing at a rapid pace. In 1986 the first major conference of academics, funders, and others who had played a leading role in the development of university-based programmes for nonprofit managers took place in San Francisco (O'Neill and Young 1988). Two years later it was reported that

> . . . four years ago, only 36 institutions of higher education could be identified. Today there are 19 academic centers offering degree programs, research, seminars, and more than 300 colleges and universities offering educational opportunities with concentration in nonprofit management.
>
> (Independent Sector 1988: 4)

All this signals perhaps the arrival of a distinct new area of studies – at the very least it indicates the realisation that the concept of a 'sector' may have relevance for the study and practice of management.[8] But will the fledgling nonprofit management area survive? In large part the answer depends on whether persuasive explanations can be developed which will address the dilemmas of voluntary organisation.

I believe that the model of public, private and voluntary sectors presented in Part II begins to address the challenge of voluntary sector management. It illuminates the debate in which some scholars have begun to regard (voluntary or nonprofit) sector boundaries as blurred to the point where the 'sector metaphor' is itself seen to be of little validity (JVAR 1987). I have contended that there *is* a real heart of the sector in its genuine associations, flanked by voluntary agencies and unorganised groups. It is not just a collection of 'hybrids' 'which seem to straddle the public and private divide' (Dunsire *et al.* 1988). The voluntary sector is an 'independent sector' to the extent that it has strong associational roots.

In these final comments I will go even further and argue that an organisation can be considered to belong to the voluntary sector only if its governing body has the power to close down the agency. Agency closure might be a remote possibility, but it does at least provide a yardstick against which to examine other policy trends such as the establishment of 'opted-out' or 'self-governing' institutions. Thus institutions, which may have had grafted on to them associational trappings such as elected representatives, really belong to the governmental sector which decides whether they live or die.

If voluntary (and public) sector welfare management studies are to survive as viable and useful entities, it will not be sufficient just to demonstrate that there are different 'values' in the different sectors. 'Positive' values can all too easily be attributed to individuals and organisations in all sectors. Neither will it be sufficient to concentrate on the attractive stratosphere of social policy whilst ignoring the constraints set by fundamental differences in the structure of organisations.

It will also not be enough to take a purely technocratic approach to organisations. As far as the future of the voluntary sector is concerned, whether or not voluntary agencies are more or less 'efficient' or 'effective' than agencies in other sectors may be irrelevant to the genuine voluntary agency with its devoted stakeholders. Studies which may eventually 'prove' that the public or private sector agency costs more or less than voluntary agencies may persuade funders to pull the plug of public sector support, but it will not stop committed individuals fighting for distinctive solutions to social problems *they* consider important.

NOTES

1 For example, numerous reports and investigations provide details of continuing problems of accountability, co-ordination, and role confusion. (See *Managing to Care: A Study of First Line Managers in Social Services Departments – Day and Domiciliary Care*, Department of Health, Dec. 1988; *Inspection of Child Care Services in Rochdale*, Department of Health, Oct. 1990b; *Report of an Inspection of Collaborative Arrangements between Child Protection Agencies in Cleveland*, Department of Health, June 1990a).

2 For a brief statement of some of the current problems, see *The Development of Senior Managers within Social Service Departments*, Local Government Training Board, 1988.

3 In the following comments on the position of local voluntary agencies I shall draw heavily on recent research (Billis and Harris 1991).

4 Some idea of the quantity of publications devoted to examining contracting can be found by tracing the references in Department of Health (1991) *Purchase of Service*, London: HMSO.

5 For example, the providers of services from the private and voluntary sectors might be regarded as a major category of 'client'. Or, since the SSD will retain 'ultimate responsibility' (Department of Health 1991: 4.2), what will be the position of the 'clients' of private and voluntary agencies acting as providers?

6 See also the special edition of *Public Administration Review*, 'Changing Epochs of Public Administration' March/April 1989, Vol. 49. 2.

7   I have attempted to confront the questions of what business theory has to offer 'nonprofits' in Billis (1991).

8   However, there have been only a few attempts to explore the links between organisational practice and social policy. With the exception of Kramer's (1981) seminal study and later works, the British tradition is more relevant (for example, Hatch 1980, Leat *et al.* 1981, Leat *et al.* 1986, Richardson and Goodman 1983, Hadley *et al.* 1975).

Bibliography

Abrams, P. (1978) *Neighbourhood Care and Social Policy*, Volunteer Centre UK.
Abrams, P., Abrams, S., Humphrey, R. and Snaith, R. (1981) *Action for Care*, The Volunteer Centre UK.
Addy, A. and Scott, D. (1987) *Fatal Impacts? The MSc and Voluntary Action*, Manchester Business School.
Aldrich, H. (1976) 'Resource dependence and interorganizational relations', *Administration and Society* 7, 4.
Allen, T. (1989) 'Managing agencies: a managerial dimension' in I. Allen, *Social Services Departments as Managing Agencies*, London: Policy Studies Institute.
Bains, M.A. (1972) *Report of the Study Group on the New Local Authorities – Management and Structure*, London: HMSO.
Baker, J. (1979) 'Social conscience and social policy', *Journal of Social Policy*, 8, January.
Baker, R.J.S. (1975) 'Systems theory and local government', *Local Government Studies*, 1, January.
Bamford, T. (1990) *The Future of Social Work*, London: Macmillan.
Barclay, P.M. (1982) *Social Workers: Their Role and Tasks*, Report of a Working Party, National Institute of Social Work, London: Bedford Square Press.
Bartlett, C.A. and Ghoshal, S. (1989) *Managing Across Borders: the Transnational Solution*, London: Hutchinson.
Bartlett, H.M. (1970) *The Common Base of Social Work Practice*, New York: NASW.
BBC (1988), Hurd, D. in *Analysis* Radio 4, 8th Dec.
Beedell, C. (1970) *Residential Life with Children*, London: Routledge and Kegan Paul.
Bell, C. and Newby, H. (1971) *Community Studies*, Allen and Unwin.
Ben-Ner, A. (1987) 'Birth, change and bureaucratization in nonprofit organizations: an economic analysis' in *Politics, Public Policy and the Voluntary Sector*, AVAS.
Bendix, R. and Lipset, S.M. (eds) (1953) *Class, Status and Power*, London: Routledge.
Benson, J.K. (1975) 'The Interorganizational Network as a Political Economy', *American Scientific Quarterly*, June, Vol. 20.
Beveridge, Lord (1948) *Voluntary Action*, London: Allen and Unwin.
Billis, D. (1973) 'Entry into Residential Care', *The British Journal of Social Work*, 3, 4.

——(1977) 'Differential Administrative Capacity and Organisational Development', *Human Relations*, 30, 2.

——(1984) *Welfare Bureaucracies: Their Design and Change in Response to Social Problems*, Heinemann: London.

——(1989) 'The rise and rise of the voluntary sector', *Community Care*, 1st June.

——(1991) 'Reflections on the ABC of profit and nonprofit organization: Benefits and hazards in the exchange of ideas', Paper presented to conference at Case Western Reserve University, Cleveland, November.

Billis, D. and Harris, M. (1986) *An Extended Role for the Voluntary Sector*, Brunel University.

——(1991) 'Taking the strain of change: UK Voluntary agencies enter the post-Thatcher period', paper given at conference of Association of Voluntary Action Scholars, Chicago, September.

Billis, D., Bromley, G., Hey, A. and Rowbottom, R. (1980) *Organising Social Services Departments*, Heinemann: London.

BIOSS (1976) *Collaboration between Health and Social Services*, Working Paper, Brunel University, November.

Boland, R.J. and Greenberg, R.H. (1988) 'Metaphorical structuring of organizational ambiguity', in L.R. Pondy, R.J. Boland Jr and H. Thomas, *Managing Ambiguity and Change*, John Wiley.

Bozeman, B. (1987) *All Organizations are Public: Bridging Public and Private Organizational Theories*, San Francisco: Jossey-Bass.

Brenton, M. (1985) *The Voluntary Sector in British Social Services*, Longman.

British Association of Social Workers (1977) *The Social Work Task*.

Brown, W. (1960) *Exploration in Management*, London: Heinemann.

Brown, W. (1971) *Organization*, London: Heinemann.

Brown, W. and Jaques, E. (1965) *Glacier Project Papers*, London: Heinemann.

Bulmer, M. (1986) *Neighbours: The Work of Philip Abrams*, Cambridge University Press.

Burns, T. and Stalker, G. M. (1961) *The Management of Innovation*, Tavistock.

CAF (1988) *Charity Trends*, Tonbridge: Charities Aid Foundation.

Carrier, J. and Kendall, I. (1977) 'The development of welfare states: the production of plausible accounts', *Journal of Social Policy*, 6, 3.

CCETSW (1973) *Training for Residential Work* (Discussion document).

Challis, C., Fuller, S., Henwood, M., Klein, R., Plowden, W., Webb, A., Whittingham, P., Wistow, G. (1988) *Joint Approaches to Social Policy: Rationality and Practice*, Cambridge University Press.

Challis, L. (1990) *Organising Public Social Services*, Harlow: Longman.

Chandler, A.D. (1963) *Strategy and Structure*, Cambridge, Massachusetts: MIT Press.

Chapin, F.S. and Tsouderos, J.E. (1956) 'The formalization process in voluntary associations', *Social Forces*, 34, May.

Child, J. (1972) 'Organisational structure, environment and performance: the role of strategic choice', *Sociology*, 6, 1.

——(1988) *Organization: A Guide to Problems and Practice*, Harper and Row: London.

Cohen, S. (1979) 'Community Control – a New Utopia', *New Society*, 15th March.

Community Care (1980) *Prevention Proves Better than Cure*, 10th April.

Cooper, J. (1980) 'Malaise of mass solutions', *Community Care*, January 3.

Curtis, M. (1946) *Report of the Care of Children's Committee*, Cmnd 6760,

London: HMSO.

Dahrendorf, R. (1968) 'On the origin of inequality among men', in R. Dahrendorf, *Essays in the Theory of Society*, London: Routledge.

Day, P. and Klein, R. (1987) *Accountabilities: Five Public Services*, Tavistock: London.

Department of Health (1988) *Managing to Care: A Study of First Line Managers in Social Services Departments – Day and Domiciliary Care*, London: HMSO.

——(1989) *Caring for People: Community Care in the Next Decade and Beyond*, Cmnd 849, London: HMSO.

——(1990a) *Inspection of Child Protection Service in Rochdale*, London: HMSO.

——(1990b) *Report of an Inspection of Collaborative Arrangements between Child Protection Agencies in Cleveland*, London: HMSO.

——(1991) *Implementing Community Care: Purchaser, Commissioner and Provider Roles*, London: HMSO.

——Social Services Inspectorate (1991) 'Assessment Systems and Community Care', London: HMSO.

DiMaggio, P. (1983) 'State expansion and organizational fields', in H.H. Hall and R.E. Quinn (eds) *Organizational Theory and Public Policy*, Sage.

DiMaggio, P. and Anheier, H.K. (1990) 'The sociology of nonprofit organizations and sectors', *Annual Review of Sociology*, 16.

DiMaggio, P. and Powell, W.W. (1983) 'The iron cage revisited', *American Sociological Review*, 82.

Donnison, D.V. (1976) 'Supplementary benefits: dilemmas and priorities', *Journal of Social Policy*, 5, 4.

——(1979) 'Training for social work', *Social Work Today*, 10, 24.

Donnison, D.V., Chapman, V., Meacher, M., Sears, A. and Urwin, K. (1970) *Social Policy and Administration*, Allen and Unwin.

Dossett-Davies, J. (1989) in *Community Care*, 30th March.

Douglas, M. (1987) *How Institutions Think*, London: Routledge and Kegan Paul.

Dunleavy, P. (1986) 'Explaining the Privatization Room: Public Choice Versus Radical Approaches', *Public Administration*, 64, 1.

Dunsire, A. (1973) *Administration: The Word and the Science*, Martin Robertson.

Dunsire, A., Hartley, K. and Parker, D. (1991) 'Organisational status and performance: summary of the findings', *Public Administration*, 69, 1.

Dunsire, A., Hartley, K., Parker, D. and Dimitriou, B. (1988) 'Organizational status and performance: a conceptual framework for testing public choice theories', *Public Administration*, 66, 4.

Emery, F.E. and Trist, E.L. (1965) 'The causal texture of organisational environments', *Human Relations*, 18.

Eurosocial Report, No. 4 (1975) *Interaction of Social Welfare and Health Personnel in the Delivery of Services: Implications for Training*, November.

Evans, J.S. (1970) 'Managerial accountability – chief officers, consultants and boards', unpublished paper, Brunel University.

Fottler, M.D. (1981) 'Is Management Really Generic?' *Academy of Management Review*, 6.

French, W.L. and Bell, C.H. (1990) *Organization Development: Behavioural Science Intervention for Organization Improvement*, New Jersey: Prentice-Hall.

Geiger, R K. and Wolch, J.R. (1986) 'A shadow state? Voluntarism in Metropolitan Los Angeles', *Environment and Planning: Society and Space*, 4.

Geismar, L.L. (1969) *Preventive Intervention in Social Work*, New Jersey: The

Scarecrow Press Inc.

Gerard, D. (1983) *Charities in Britain*, London: Bedford Square Press.

Glasgow, S. (1972) 'Senior social workers after Seebohm', *British Hospital Journal and Social Service Review*, 8th January.

Glennerster, H. (1989) 'Swimming against the tide: the prospects for social policy', in M. Bulmer, J. Lewis and D. Piachaud (eds), *The Goals of Social Policy*, London: Unwin Hyman.

Goodman, A. (1976) *Charity Law and Voluntary Organisations*, London: Bedford Square Press.

Goodwin, S. (1989) 'Community care for the mentally ill in England and Wales: myths, assumptions and reality', *Journal of Social Policy*, 18, 1.

Granvold, D.K. (1977) 'Supervisory style and educational preparation of public welfare supervisors', *Administration in Social Work*, 1, 1.

Greenwood, R., Hinnings, C.R. and Ransom, S. (1975) 'Contingency theory and the organization of local authorities: part 1. differentiation and integration', *Public Administration*, 53, Spring.

Greenwood, R., Norton, A.L. and Stewart, J. D. (1969) 'Recent changes in the internal organisation of county boroughs', *Public Administration*, 47, Autumn.

Greenwood, R., Walsh, K., Hinings, C.R. and Ranson, S. (1980) *Patterns of Management in Local Government*, Martin Robertson.

Greiner, E.L. (1972) 'Evolution and revolution as organisations grow', *Harvard Business Review*, 50, 4.

Griffiths, R. (1988) *Community Care: Agenda for Action*, London: HMSO.

Gronbjerg, K.A. (1989) 'Developing a universe of nonprofit organizations', *Nonprofit and Voluntary Sector Quarterly*, 18, 1.

Gross, B.M. (1968) *Organizations and their Managing*, New York: The Free Press.

Gulick, L. (1937) 'Notes on the theory of organization' in L. Gulick and L. Urwick (eds), *Papers on the Science of Administration*, New York: Institute of Public Administration, Columbia University.

Gutch, R. and Young, K. (1988) *Partners or Rivals? Developing the Relationship between Voluntary Organisations and Local Government,* London: NCVO.

Hadley, R. and Hatch, S. (1981) *Social Welfare and the Failure of the State*, London: Allen and Unwin.

Hadley, R. and McGrath, M. (1979) 'Patch-based social services', *Community Care*, 11th October.

Hadley, R., Webb, A. and Farrell, C. (1975) *Across the Generations*, London: Allen and Unwin.

Hall, P. (1976) *Reforming the Welfare*, London: Heinemann.

Hall, P.D. (1987) 'A historical overview of the private nonprofit sector', in W.W. Powell, *The Nonprofit Sector: A Research Handbook*, Yale University Press.

Hall, R.H. (1987) *Organizations: Structures, Processes and Outcomes*, (4th edition) New York: Prentice Hall.

Hall, R.H. and Quinn, R.E. (1983) *Organizational Theory and Public Policy*, Beverly Hills: Sage.

Hall, T. (1971) 'Client reception in a social service agency', *Public Administration*, 49.

Handy, C. (1981) *Improving Effectiveness in Voluntary Organisations*, Working Party Report, London: NCVO.

Hansmann, H.B. (1980) 'The role of nonprofit enterprise', *Yale Law Review*, 89, 5.

——(1987) 'Economic theories of nonprofit organization, in W.W Powell (ed.) *The*

Nonprofit Sector: A Research Handbook, Yale University Press.

Harding, T. and Thompson, C. (1989) 'Implications for Voluntary Organisations: Opportunity or Control?', *Social Services Departments as Managing Agents*, London: Policy Studies Institute.

Harris, M. (1983) 'Governing bodies in voluntary agencies: a study of local management committees in the citizens advice bureaux service', M.A. Dissertation, Brunel University.

——(1989) 'The governing body role: problems and perceptions in implementation', *Nonprofit and Voluntary Sector Quarterly*, 18, 4.

——(1990) 'Voluntary leaders in voluntary welfare agencies', *Social Policy and Administration*, 24, 2.

Hartogs, N. and Weber, J. (1978) *The Impact of Government Funding*, New York: United Way.

Hasenfeld, Y. and Schmidt, H. (1989) 'The life-cycle of human service organizations: an administrative perspective' in Y. Hasenfeld (ed.) *Administrative Leadership in the Social Services*, USA: Haworth.

Hatch, S. (1980) *Outside the State: Voluntary Organisations in Three English Towns*, London: Croom Helm.

Hatch, S. and Mocroft, I. (1983) *Components of Welfare: Voluntary Organisations, Social Services and Politics in Two Local Authorities*, London: Bedford Square Press.

Heclo, H. and Wildavsky, A. (1989) *The Private Government of Public Money*, 2nd edition, London: Macmillan.

Herman, R.D. and Van Til, J. (1989) *Nonprofit Boards of Directors: Analyses and Applications*, New Brunswick: Transaction Publishers.

Holman, R. (1980) 'Growth without roots', *Community Care*, 3rd January.

Holmes, A. and Maizels, J. (1976) *Social Workers and Volunteers*, London: George Allen and Unwin and BASW.

Home Office (1978) *The Government and the Voluntary Sector: A Consultative Document*, London: HMSO.

——(1987) *Report of the Charity Commissioners for England and Wales for the Year 1986*, London: HMSO.

Hood, C. (1991) 'A public management for all seasons?', *Public Administration*, 69, 1.

Illich, I. (1976) *Limits to Medicine*, London: Marion Boyars.

Independent Sector (1988) *Formal Education of Non-Profit Organization Leaders/Managers*, Report of the Academic Study Group, Washington, 12th May.

Ingleby, Viscount (1960) *Report of the Committee on Children and Young Persons*, Cmnd 1191, London: HMSO.

Jaques, E. (1951) *The Changing Culture of a Factory*, London: Tavistock.

——(1961) *Equitable Payment*, London: Heinemann.

——(1965a) 'Preliminary sketch of a general structure of executive strata' in W. Brown and E. Jaques, *Glacier Project Papers*, London: Heinemann.

——(1965b) 'Speculations concerning level of capacity', in W. Brown and E. Jaques, *Glacier Project Papers*, London: Heinemann.

——(1967) *Equitable payment* (2nd edition), Harmondsworth: Penguin.

——(1976) *A General Theory of Bureaucracy*, London: Heinemann.

Jones, G.W. (1973) 'The functions and organisation of councillors', *Public Administration*, 51, Summer.

——(1977) *Responsibility and Government*, London: The London School of Economics and Political Science.

Judge, K.P. (1982) 'The public purchase of social care: British confirmation of the American experience', *Policy and Politics*, 10, 4.

Kilbrandon, Lord (1964) *Children and Young Persons in Scotland*, Scottish Home and Health Department and Scottish Education Department, Cmnd 2306, London: HMSO.

King's Fund Centre (1979) *The Organisation of Hospital Clinical Work*, London: King's Fund Centre.

Kinston, W. (1987) *Stronger Nursing Organization Working Paper*, BIOSS, Brunel University.

Knapp, M., Robertson, E. and Thomason, C. (1987) *Public Money, Voluntary Action: Whose Welfare?* PSSRU Discussion Paper 514, University of Kent.

Kogan, M. and Terry, J. (1971) *The Organization of a Social Services Department: A Blueprint*, London: Bookstall Publications.

Kooiman, J. and Eliassen, A.K. (1987) *Managing Public Organizations*, London: Sage.

Kramer, R. (1965) 'Ideology, status and power in board executive relationships', *Social Work*, October.

——(1981) *Voluntary Agencies in the Welfare State*, University of California Press.

——(1985) 'Towards a contingency model of board-executive relationships', *Administration in Social Work*, 9, 3.

——(1988) 'Governmental funding of nonprofit social service organizations', mimeo, University of California.

——(1990) 'Change and continuity in British voluntary organisations', *Voluntas*, 1, 2.

Kramer, R. and Grossman, B. (1987) 'Contracting for social services: process management and resource dependencies', *Social Service Review*, 61, March.

Kramer, R. and Terrell, P. (1984) *Social Services Contracting in the Bay Area*, Institute of Governmental Studies, University of California Press.

Laffin, M. (1980) 'Professsionalism in central local relations' in G.W. Jones (ed.) *New Approaches to the Study of Central Local Government Relationships*, Gower.

Land, H. (1975) 'Detention centres: the experiment which could not fail' in P. Hall, H. Land, R. Parker and A. Webb, *Change, Choice and Conflict in Social Policy*, London: Heinemann.

Leach, E. (1976) *Culture and Communication*, Cambridge University Press.

Leat, D., Smolka, G. and Unell, J. (1981) *Voluntary and Statutory Collaboration: Rhetoric or Reality?*, Bedford Square Press.

Leat, D., Tester, S. and Unell, J. (1986) *A Price Worth Paying?: A Study of the Effects of Government Grant Aid to Voluntary Organisation*, Policy Studies Institute.

Le Grand, J. and Robinson, R. (1984) *Privatisation and the Welfare State*, Allen and Unwin.

Leonard, P. (1971) 'The challenge of primary prevention', *Social Work Today*, 3, 6.

Levine, S. and White, P.E. (1961) 'Exchange as a conceptual framework for the study of interorganizational relationships', *Administrative Science Quarterly*, 6.

Lipsky, M. (1980) *Street-level Bureaucracy*, New York: Russell Sage.

Local Government Training Board (1988) *The Development of Senior Managers within Social Service Departments*, Luton: Local Government Training Board.

Lohmann, P. (1989) 'And Lettuce is Nonanimal: Towards a Positive Economics of Voluntary Action', *Nonprofit and Voluntary Sector Quarterly*, Vol. 18, No. 4.

Longford, Lord (1964) *Crime: A Challenge to Us All*, Report of a Labour Party Study Group, June.

Lonsdale, S., Webb, A. and Briggs, T.L. (eds) (1980) *Teamwork in the Personal Social Services and Health Care*, Croom Helm and Syracuse University School of Social Work.

McBoyle, J. (1963) *Prevention of Neglect in Children*, Report of the Scottish Advisory Council on Child Care, Cmnd 1966, London: HMSO.

McCarthy, J.D. and Zald, M.N. (1977) 'Resource mobilization and social movements: a partial theory', *American Journal of Sociology*, 82, May.

McGregor, D. (1960) *The Human Side of Enterprise*, New York: McGraw-Hill.

Marris, P. and Rein, M. (1974) *Dilemmas of Social Reform*, 1974 2nd edn, Penguin Books, Harmondsworth.

Marshall, T. (1981) 'A study of the care of infants under two years of age at a local authority nursery', unpublished M.A. dissertation, Brunel University.

Martin, J. and Meyerson, D. (1988) 'Organizational cultures and the denial, channeling and acknowledgement of ambiguity, in L.R. Pondy, R.J. Boland and H. Thomas (eds) *Managing Ambiguity and Change*, New York: John Wiley and Sons.

Maslow, A.H. (1943) 'A theory of human motivation', *Psychological Review*, 50. Reprinted in E.V.H. Vroom and E.L. Deci, *Management and Motivation*, Harmondsworth: Penguin, 1970.

Mason, D.E. (1984) *Voluntary Nonprofit Enterprise Management*, New York, Plenum Press.

Mellor, H.W. (1985) *The Role of Voluntary Organisations in Social Welfare*, Croom Helm.

Metcalfe, L. and Richards, S. (1990) *Improving Public Management*, London: Sage.

Michels, R. (1915 in 1962) *Political Parties*, New York: The Free Press.

Middleton, M. (1987) 'Nonprofit boards of directors: beyond the governance function', in W.W. Powell (ed.) *The Nonprofit Sector: a Research Handbook*, Yale University Press.

Miller, E.J. and Rice, A.K. (1967) *Systems of Organisation*, London: Tavistock.

Milofsky, C. (1979) 'Not for Profit organisations and community; a review of the sociological literature', PONPO Working Paper 6, Yale: Yale University Press.

——(1987) *Community Organization*, Oxford University Press.

Moyer, M.S. (1981) *Bridging the Gap Between Voluntary Organizations and Business Schools*, Toronto.

NAHA/NCVO (1987) *Partnerships for Health*, National Association of Health Authorities.

National Marriage Guidance Council (1987) *Annual Review*, Rugby, UK: National Marriage Guidance Council.

NCVO (1984) *The Management and Effectiveness of Voluntary Organisations*, London: NCVO.

——(1986) *A Stake in Planning: Joint Planning and the Voluntary Sector*, Community Care Project, London: NCVO.

NCVO/RIPA (1988) *Into the 1990s: Voluntary Organisations and the Public Sector*, London: Royal Institute of Public Administration.

O'Neill, M. and Young, D.R. (1988) *Educating Managers of Nonprofit Organizations*, Praeger.

O'Shaughnessy, J. (1972) *Inquiry and Decision*, Allen and Unwin.

Olsen, M. (1971) *The Logic of Collective Action: Public Goods and the Theory of Groups*, Harvard University Press.

OPCS (1988) *General Household Survey 1985, Informal Carers*, London: HMSO.

Owens, P. and Glennerster, H. (1990) *Nursing in Conflict*, London: Macmillan.

Oxfordshire County Council (1980) *Delegation of Powers to Chief Officers*, mimeo.

Parker, R.A. (1970) 'The future of the personal social services' in W.A. Robson and B. Crick (eds) *The Future of the Social Services*, Penguin.

Patten, J. (1988) 'Active citizens who make a stand against life's grim realities', *The Sunday Times*, 11th December.

Perrow, C. (1969) 'The analysis of goals in complex organizations', in A. Etzioni (ed.) *Readings on Modern Organization*, Englewood Cliffs, New Jersey: Prentice-Hall.

Peters, T.J. and Waterman, R.H. (1982) *In Search of Excellence*, New York: Harper and Row.

Pfeffer, J. and Salancik, G.R. (1978) *The External Control of Organizations*, New York: Harper and Row.

Pfeffer, N. and Coote, A. (1991) *Is Quality Good for You? Critical Review of Quality Assurance in Welfare Services*, London: Institute for Public Policy Research.

Piachaud, D. (1991) 'Revitalising Social Policy', *The Political Quarterly*, 62, 2.

Pinker, R. (1971) *Social Theory and Social Policy*, London: Heinemann.

——(1979a) *The Idea of Welfare*, London: Heinemann.

——(1979b) 'Slimline social work', *New Society*, December 13.

Pollitt, C. (1990) *Managerialism and the Public Sector*, Oxford: Blackwell.

Popper, K.R. (1972) *Objective Knowledge*, London: Oxford University Press.

——(1974a) *Conjectures and Refutations: The Growth of Scientific Knowledge*, 5th edition, London: Routledge and Kegan Paul.

——(1974b) *Objective Knowledge*, London: Oxford University Press.

Posnett, J. (1988) 'An analysis of the distribution of charitable donations from the 1984 Family Expenditure Survey' in *Charity Trends*, 11th edition, Charities Aid Foundation.

Powell, W.W. and Friedkin, R. (1986) 'Organizational change in nonprofit organizations', in W.W. Powell (ed.) *The Nonprofit Sector*, Yale: Yale University Press.

Public Administration Review (1989) 'Changing Epochs of Public Administration', 49, 2.

Quinn, R.E. and Cameron, K. (1983) 'Organizational life cycles and shifting criteria of effectiveness: some preliminary evidence', *Management Science* 29, 1.

Rees, J. (1971) *Equality*, Macmillan.

Regan, D.E. (1980a) *The Headless State: The Unaccountable Executive in British Local Government*, Inaugural Lecture, University of Nottingham, May.

——(1980b) 'The pathology of British land use planning', in G. W. Jones, *New Approaches to the Study of Central Local Relationships*, Gower.

Rein, M. (1983) *From Policy to Practice*, London: Macmillan.

Residential Services Advisory Group (1973) *Staff Support and Development: The Homes Adviser – First Report*, January.

Rhodes, R. (1985) 'Corporatism, Pay Negotiations and Local Government', *Public Administration* 63, 3.

Richardson, A. and Goodman, M. (1983) *Self-help and Social Care*, Policy Studies Institute, May.

Righton, P. (1971) 'The objectives and methods of residential social work' in *Child in Care*, Residential Child Care Association.

Rose, G. (1976) 'Approaches to the organisation of social service organisations', *Journal of Social Policy*, July.

Rowbottom, R.W. (1973) 'Organising social services: hierarchy or . . . ?' *Public Administration*, 51, Autumn.

——(1977) *Social Analysis*, London: Heinemann.

Rowbottom, R.W. and Billis, D. (1975) 'The stratification of work and organisational design', unpublished paper, Brunel University, February.

——(1987) *Organisational Design*, Gower.

Rowbottom, R. and Hey, A.M. (1970) 'Towards an organisation of social services departments', *Local Government Chronicle*.

Rowbottom, R.W., Hey, A.M. and Billis, D. (1974) *Social Services Departments: Developing Patterns of Work and Organisation*, London: Heinemann.

Rowbottom, R.W., Balle, J., Cang, S., Dixon, M., Jaques, E., Packwood, T. and Tolliday, H. (1973) *Hospital Organisation*, London: Heinemann.

Rutter, M.L. (1978) 'Research into prevention of psychological disorders in childhood' in J. Barnes and N. Connelly (eds), *Social Care Research*, London: Bedford Square Press.

Salamon, L.M. (1987a) 'Of market failure, voluntary failure, and third-party government: towards a theory of government–nonprofit relations in the modern welfare state', *Journal of Voluntary Action Research*, 16, 1 and 2.

——(1987b) 'Partners in public service: the scope and theory of government–nonprofit relations' in W.W. Powell, *The Nonprofit Sector: A Research Handbook*, Yale University Press.

Savas, E.S. (1987) *Privatization: The Key to a Better Government*, Chatham House.

Schmidt, S.M. and Kochan, T.A. (1977) 'Interorganizational Relationships: Patterns and Motivations', *Administrative Science Quarterly*, 22, June.

Schon, D.A. (1971) *Beyond the Stable State*, London: Temple Smith.

Scott, W.R. (1987) *Organizations: Rational, Natural, and Open Systems*, (2nd edition) New York: Prentice Hall.

Seebohm, F. (1968) *Report of the Committee on Local Authority and Allied Personal Social Services*, Cmnd 3703, London: HMSO.

Self, P. (1971) 'Representatives and management in the local government: an alternative analysis', *Public Admininistration*, 49, Autumn.

——(1974) *Administrative Theories and Politics*, London: Allen and Unwin.

——(1976) 'Rational decentralisation', in J.A.G. Griffiths (ed.), *From Policy to Administration*, London: Allen and Unwin.

Sharkansky, I. (1980) 'Policy making and service delivery on the margins of government: the case of contractors', *Public Administration Review*, March/April.

Shumpeter, J.A. (1947) 'The creative response in industry', *Journal of Economic History*, 7, November.

Sills, D.L. (1957) *The Volunteers: Means and Ends in a National Organization*, Glencoe, Illinois: Free Press.

——(1966) 'Goal succession in four voluntary associations' in W.A. Glaser and D.L. Sills (eds) *The Government of Associations*, Totawa, New Jersey: Bedminster Press.

——(1968) *Voluntary Associations*, International Encyclopedia of the Social Sciences, New York: Free Press.

Silverman, D. (1970) *The Theory of Organisations*, London: Heinemann.

Simon, H.A. (1967) *Administrative Behaviour*, Free Press.

Slavin, S. (1978) *Social Administration – The Management of the Social Services*, New York: Haworth Press.

Smith, D.E. (1965) 'Front line organization of the state mental hospital', *Administrative Science Quarterly*, 10.

Smith, G. (1979) *Social Work and the Sociology of Organizations*, revised edition, London: Routledge and Kegan Paul.

——(1980) *Social Need: Policy, Practice and Research*, London: Routledge and Kegan Paul.

Smith, J.H. (1979) 'The human factor in social administration', *Journal of Social Policy*, 8, 4.

Smith, B.L.R. and Hague, D.C. (1971) *The Dilemmas of Accountability in Modern Government*, New York: St Martin's Press.

Smith, C. and Freedman, A. (1972) *Voluntary Associations: Perspectives on the Literature*, Harvard University Press.

Smith, G. and Ames, J. (1979) 'Area teams in social work practice: a programme for research', *British Journal of Social Work*, 6, 1.

Social Services Year Book (1975), Councils and Education Press.

Social Services Yearbook (1980), Councils and Education Press.

Stevenson, O. and Parsloe, P. (1978) *Social Service Teams: the Practitioners' View*, London: HMSO.

Stewart, J. and Ranson, S. (1988) 'Management in the Public Domain', *Public Money and Management*, 8, 1 and 2.

Stinchcombe, A.L. (1965) 'Social structure and organizations' in J.G. March (ed.) *Handbook of Organizations*, Chicago: Rand McNally.

Stoesz, D. and Karger, H. (1991) 'The corporatisation of the US welfare state', *Journal of Social Policy*, 20, April.

Stone, M. (1989) 'Planning as Strategy in Nonprofit Organizations: An Exploratory Study', *Nonprofit and Voluntary Sector Quarterly*, 18, 4.

Sugden, R. (1984) 'Voluntary organisations and the welfare state', in J. Le Grand and R. Robinson (eds) *Privatisation and the Welfare State*, London: Allen and Unwin.

Thomason, G.F. (1977) 'The organisation of professional work in the social services' in H. Heisler, *Foundations of Social Administration*, Macmillan.

Thorpe, D., Paley, J. and Green, C. (1979) 'Ensuring the right result', *Community Care*, 25, 10th May.

Titmuss, R.M. (1974) *Social Policy*, London: Allen and Unwin.

Travis, T. (1989) 'Offer they like to refuse', *Guardian*, 25th January.

Tucker, D.J. (1983) 'Environmental change and organizational policy-making', in M.S. Moyer (ed.) *Managing Voluntary Organizations*, Toronto: York University Press.

Van der Eyken, W. (1982) *Home-Start: A Four Year Evaluation Project*, Leicester: Home-Start Consultancy.

Van Til, J. (1988) *Mapping the Third Sector: Voluntarism in a Changing Social Economy*, New York: The Foundation Center.

Ware, A. (1989) *Charities and Government*, Manchester: Manchester University Press.

Ware, A. (1990) 'Meeting needs through voluntary action: Does market society corrode altruism?' in A. Ware and E. Goodwin (eds) *Needs and Welfare*, London: Sage.

Webb, A. (1971) 'Social service administration: a typology for research', *Public Administration*, 49, Autumn.

Webb, A.C. and Hobdell, M. (1980) 'Co-ordination and teamwork in the health and personal social services' in S. Lonsdale, A. Webb and T.L. Briggs (eds), *Teamwork in the Personal Social Services and Health Care*, London: Croom Helm and Syracuse University School of Social Work.

Webb, A. and Wistow, G. (1986) *Planning, Need and Scarcity*, Allen and Unwin.

——(1987) *Social Work, Social Care, and Social Planning: The Personal Social Services since Seebohm*, London: Longman.

Weisbrod, B.A. (1988) *The Nonprofit Economy*, Harvard: Harvard University Press.

Weitzel, W. and Jonsson, E. (1989) 'Decline in organizations: a literature integration and extension', *Administrative Science Quarterly*, 34.

Wertheim, E.G. (1976) 'Evolution of structure and process in voluntary organizations: a study of thirty-five consumer food cooperatives', *Journal of Voluntary Action Research*, 5, 1.

Westland, P. (1974) reviewing a book in *British Journal of Social Work*, 4, 4.

Wilensky, H.L. (1978) *The Welfare State and Equality*, Berkeley: University of California Press.

——(1968) *Caring for People*, George Allen and Unwin.

Williams, G. (Chair) (1967) *Caring for People – Staffing Residential Homes*, Report of a Committee of Enquiry set up by the National Council of Social Service, London: Allen and Unwin.

Williams, G. (1983) *Inner City Policy: A Partnership with the Voluntary Sector?*, London: Bedford Square Press.

Williamson, P.J. (1989) *Corporatism in Perspective: an Introductory Guide to Corporatist Theory*, London: Sage.

Wilson, D.C. and Butler, B.J. (1984) 'Corporatism in the British voluntary sector', unpublished paper, Organizational Analysis Research Unit, University of Bradford Management Centre.

——(1985a) 'Corporatism in the British voluntary sector' in W. Streck and P.C. Schmitter (eds) *Private Interest Government*, London: Sage.

——(1985b) 'Strategy, influence and control in British voluntary organizations', University of Bradford Management Centre.

Wolfenden, Lord (1978) *The Future of Voluntary Organisations*, London: Croom Helm.

Woodfield, P. (1987) *Efficiency Scrutiny of the Supervision of Charities*, London: HMSO.

Young, D.R. (1983) *If not for Profit, for What?*, Lexington: Lexington Books.

——(1987) 'Executive leadership in nonprofit organizations' in W.W. Powell (ed.) *The Nonprofit Sector: A Research Handbook*, Yale University Press.

——(1989) 'Local autonomy in a franchise age: structural change in national voluntary associations', *Nonprofit and Voluntary Sector Quarterly*, 18, 2.

Younghusband, E.L. (1959) *Report of the Committee on Social Workers in the Local Authority Health and Welfare Services*, Report of the Ministry of Health and Department of Health for Scotland, London: HMSO.

Yuchtman, E. and Seashore, S.E. (1967) 'A system resource approach to organizational effectiveness', *American Sociological Review*, 32.

Zald, M.N. (1970) *Organizational Change: the Political Economy of the YMCA*, Chicago: University of Chicago Press.

Index